Programming the ESP32 In C
Using the Arduino Library

Harry Fairhead

I/O Press
I Programmer Library

Harry Fairhead
Programming The ESP32 In C Using the Arduino Library
First Edition
ISBN Paperback: 9781871962925
ISBN Hardback: 9781871962291
First Printing, 2024
Revision 2

Published by IO Press   www.iopress.info
In association with I Programmer   www.i-programmer.info
and with I o T Programmer   www.iot-programmer.com

The publisher recognizes and respects all marks used by companies and manufacturers as a means to distinguish their products. All brand names and product names mentioned in this book are trade marks or service marks of their respective companies and our omission of trade marks is not an attempt to infringe on the property of others.

For updates, errata, links to resources and the source code for the programs in this book, visit its dedicated page on the IO Press website: iopress.info.

Preface

The Espressif ESP32 is a remarkable device. It is low in cost, but has many different subsystems that make it more powerful than you might at first think. You can use it for simple applications because it is cheap, but you can also use it for more sophisticated applications because it is capable.

For this book, the programming environment of choice is C using the Arduino library and its associated IDE. The use of C/C++ ensures that your programs are fast and efficient and the Arduino library makes it as easy to use as possible. It is true that the ESP32 IoT Development Framework (IDF), the official Espressif development system can do more, but it is hard to get started with and has a steep learning curve. In most cases you probably won't need to go beyond the Arduino library and the good news is that when you do you can simply use the parts of the ESP32 IDF that you need. The Arduino library runs on top of the ESP32 IDF as a simplifying layer and you can always drop down a level and make use of it when required.

The Arduino library uses C++ to implement access to the hardware as a set of classes and their related objects. This is what makes it easier to use despite the fact that C++ is a very large and potentially confusing language. Most of the time you don't need to make use of its features to make use of the predefined classes. In this book the language used is as simple as possible in an effort to make the examples clear.

The Arduino IDE is available as a cloud or a desktop implementation. The cloud offering is useful if you need to collaborate with others, otherwise the desktop implementation is faster and doesn't require a network connection. The desktop editor is used throughout this book, but there should be little difference if you want to use the online editor.

The purpose of the book is to reveal what you can do with the ESP32's GPIO lines together with widely used sensors, servos and motors and ADCs. After covering the GPIO, outputs and inputs, events and interrupts, it gives you hands-on experience of PWM (Pulse Width Modulation), the SPI bus, the I2C bus and the 1-Wire bus, using the UARTs and of course WiFi. To round out, it covers direct access to the hardware, adding an SD Card reader, sleep states to save power, the RTC and touch sensors. The final chapter is devoted to FreeRTOS which takes us into the realm of asynchronous processing.

The ESP32 has so many resources that a comprehensive account would fill a book twice this size. In order to make things fit in the space available it concentrates on things that are basic to getting started, avoiding "advanced" topics which generally lead the beginner into deep water far too quickly. Look elsewhere if you want to know about DMA, high-speed signal processing, ultra low-power and video interfacing.

This book doesn't teach you C or C++ in the sense of basic programming, but a knowledge of how to program in almost any language is all you really need. All examples are written in a very simple style that avoids the use of idioms that are very "neat" but tend to obscure the meaning of the code. Most of the code is very nearly pure C but C++ is used to create classes to wrap some peripherals.

This is not a projects book, although there isn't much left for you to do to round out the embryonic projects that are used as examples. Instead it is about understanding concepts and the acquisition of skills. The hope is that by the end of the book you will know how to tackle your own projects and get them safely to completion without wasting time in trial and error.

My thanks are again due to Sue Gee and Kay Ewbank for their editorial input. Programming is the art of great precision, but English doesn't come with a built-in linter. If errors remain please let me know.

For the source code for the programs in this book, together with any updates or errata, links to resources including recommendations for obtaining electronic components, visit its dedicated page on the IO Press website: www.iopress.info.

You can also contact me at harry.fairhead@i-programmer.info.

Harry Fairhead
December, 2024

Table of Contents

Chapter 5

Some Electronics   **59**

Chapter 6

Simple Input   **79**

Chapter 7
Advanced Input – Interrupts   **95**

Chapter 8
Pulse Width Modulation   **109**

Chapter 12
Using The I2C Bus   **195**

Chapter 13
One-Wire Protocols   **217**

Chapter 14
The Serial Port 249

Chapter 15
Using WiFi 273

Chapter 16
Flash Files 303

Chapter 17
Direct To The Hardware   **315**

Chapter 18   **335**
FreeRTOS For Task Management   **335**

Chapter 1

The ESP32 - Before We Begin

The ESP32 is a remarkable device. It is cheap enough to be used for tasks that were marginal for a microcontroller yet powerful enough to tackle tasks that until recently were too much for such a low-cost device. It has two cores, WiFi, Bluetooth and low-power consumption modes, together with a fast processor with enough memory to get most jobs done. It also has a great many built-in peripherals and interfaces such as the PWM, I2C, SPI, UART and ADC. It also has some novel peripherals such a motor controller PWM device, a remote control subsystem, touch input, a sine wave generating DAC and an ultra low-power processor that can run while the main processors are in sleep mode.

All of this makes the ESP32 suitable for very simple tasks such as a door or window open sensor or something much more sophisticated like a motor controller.

The ESP32 Family

The ESP32 is designed by Espressif Systems, a Chinese company that gained reputation by its first processor, the ESP8266, which incorporated a WiFi subsystem in a very small, low-cost, package. The ESP8266 gained a loyal following from enthusiasts, but in the early days it was difficult to find out about the device because of the lack of English documentation. With the release of the ESP32 family these difficulties are behind us. Not only is there a lot of good documentation, there is an official SDK, the Espressif IOT Development Framework (ESP-IDF), which runs on Windows, Linux, and macOS and supports C and C++. Designed for building Internet of Things (IoT) applications, it provides Wi-Fi, Bluetooth, power management, and other system features.

The ESP does suffer from the fact that there is no single reference implementation. With devices like those in the Arduino family and from Raspberry Pi there is a single source of product and information and this makes things simpler. However, most of the variation in the currently available ESP32 devices are minor and they are very compatible with one another.

The first thing to be clear about is that the ESP32 family is not based on the very common ARM processors. Currently ESP32 devices use either an Xtensa LX6 or LX7 processor or, less commonly, an open source RISC-V processor. As the ESP-IDF supports all of these processors, there is no difficulty in using any of them. However, most ESP32 development devices use the LX6.

At the time of writing there are five commonly encountered ESP32 devices; the S series based on the LX6/7 processor and the C series using the RISC-V processor:

The S Series:

- ◆ ESP32   (2014) LX6 using dual core WiFi 4 and Bluetooth
- ◆ ESP32-S2 (2019) LX7 single core WiFi 4 only
- ◆ ESP32-S3 (2020) LX7 dual core WiFi 4 and Bluetooth

The C series:

- ◆ ESP32-C3 (2020) RISC-V WiFi 4
- ◆ ESP32-C6 (2021) RISC-V WiFi 6

The devices also differ in terms of memory configuration, GPIO lines and other features. Newer devices seem to be using the RISC processor in preference to the LX6/7. At the time of writing the ESP32 is the cheapest and most commonly encountered. However, the upgraded ES32-S3, which is considerably faster, is also readily available. The ESP32 and the ESP32-S3 are both used as examples in this book.

Development Boards

In most cases the development boards that you are likely to use are constructed using surface mount modules that contain the basic device. These take the form of the small silver box mounted on the development board.

It is this "silver box" which determines the characteristics of a development system. Manufacturers select a module and add some components to create a development board. It is also worth pointing out that you can buy the modules not mounted on a PCB and design them into your own electronics for a 100% custom ESP32.

The main task of the development board is to convert the TTL serial port to a USB connector that provides power and a serial connection to the development machine. You can see a typical circuit diagram below:

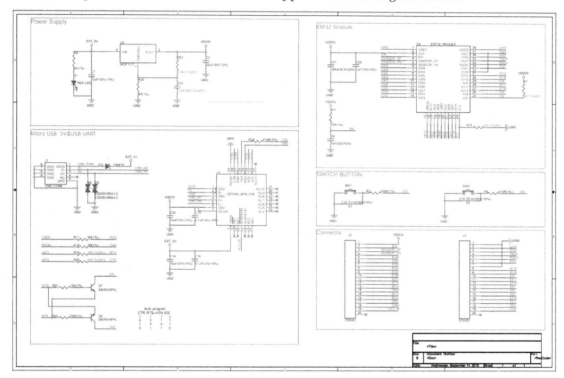

This is for the ESP32 DevKitC produced by Espressif and it is taken as the starting point for most other development boards. There is also an S3-based DevKitC.

The key thing is that the development board generally adds very little to the ESP32 module used. That is, the main characteristics of the board are determined by the ESP32 module in use, but they can still differ in what GPIO lines are brought out to external pins and what additional hardware is provided – some provide an LED connected to GPIO 2.

When you buy a development board the first consideration is which module it uses. At the time of writing there are two main module families – WROOM and WROVER. The main difference between them is that the WROVER family has a serial RAM device that is needed to support video devices. Other than this the two are identical. Nearly all development boards feature a WROOM or a WROOM S3 module and these come in a range with mostly minor differences. The most commonly encountered are:

Name	Flash Memory
ESP-WROOM-32	4 MB
ESP32-S3-WROOM-1	8 MB
ESP-WROOM-32-8M	8 MB
ESP-WROOM-32-16M	16 MB

While the ESP32 uses an LX6 dual-core processor, the S3 uses an LX7. There are other configurations that offer features for specific use cases. The 32U series, ESP-WROOM-32U etc, has an external U.FL (IPEX) connector for an external antenna rather than the internal PCB antenna and the HT series can withstand higher temperatures. Some very small development boards also make use of the ESP-Pico module which comes in a range of flash memory sizes.

Development boards also differ in which GPIO lines are brought out to external connectors.

A typical ESP32 is shown below:

The S3 usually has two connectors, a UART and a USB, and usually has an addressable RGB LED connected to GPIO38:

Smaller development boards generally bring out fewer GPIO lines to the outside world. For example:

There are usually two switches, boot loader and reset, and a power LED that can be a nuisance as you can't turn it off without a soldering iron. A serial UART to USB chip is also usually included and this is often a CP2120 or a CH340. Some users claim that one is better than the other, but in practice they both work well. Most development boards use the same pinouts as the Espressif designed boards, but you will encounter minor variations and smaller form factors which expose fewer GPIO lines to the outside world.

As already mentioned, you can also find development boards that don't have a USB connector. These are generally powered directly via the power pins and are programmed using the UART serial interface without the help of the USB conversion. Working with this sort of board is slightly more difficult as you have to find a way to connect to the UART, but it works in exactly the same way once you have sorted out supplying power and making the serial connection.

What all this means is that, despite there being a confusing number of ESP32 development boards, they are all highly compatible and programmable in the same way.

Apart from potential problems of differing amounts of memory and speed, a program written for one should run on another. The only exception to this rule is if the development board doesn't make the GPIO line available for external use, but all of the standard size boards have the same set of external connections.

The key points about the ESP32/S3 hardware that you are most likely to encounter in a development board:

- Dual-core LX6/LX7 processor, flexible clock running up to 240 MHz
- 520KB of SRAM, and 4/8MB of on-board Flash memory
- USB 1.1 with device and host support
- Low-power sleep and dormant modes
- 34/48 × multi-function GPIO pins 10/14 touch (capacitive) sensors
- 4 × SPI, 2 × I2C, 3 × UART, 2 x I2S, CAN bus, 1/2 × 12-bit ADC, 2 x 8-bit DAC and 16 PWM outputs
- Accelerated cryptographic hardware on-chip
- Separate low-power processor

Although it is early to be going into details, a diagram of the ESP32 pinouts will give you a good idea how versatile the device is:

ESP32-DevKitC

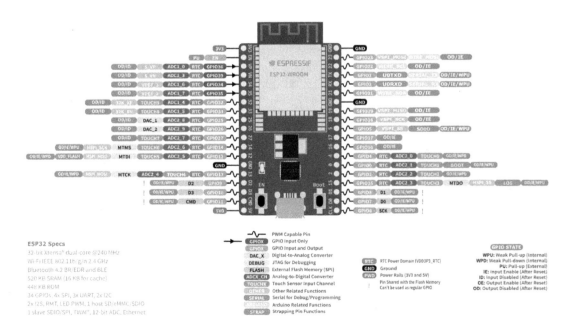

Notice that the lines that have in-pointing arrows are input only and the lines that are wavy are PWM compatible. Also notice the exclamation marks against GPIO6 to 11 indicating that these are not to be used as they form the interface to the flash memory.

The ES32-S3 has a similar but different arrangement of pins and no input only pins:

ESP32-S3-DevKitC-1

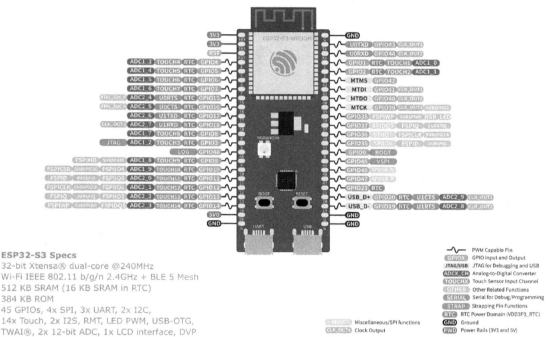

ESP32-S3 Specs
32-bit Xtensa® dual-core @240MHz
Wi-Fi IEEE 802.11 b/g/n 2.4GHz + BLE 5 Mesh
512 KB SRAM (16 KB SRAM in RTC)
384 KB ROM
45 GPIOs, 4x SPI, 3x UART, 2x I2C,
14x Touch, 2x I2S, RMT, LED PWM, USB-OTG,
TWAI®, 2x 12-bit ADC, 1x LCD interface, DVP

There is also an Arduino board, the Nano ESP32, based on the ESP32-S3. This is a perfectly normal ESP32-S3 board with some slight differences on what GPIO lines are made available. It is slightly better supported by the IDE in terms of debugging however it is presented as first an Arduino device. Notice also that the Nano ESP32 doesn't support all of the features available to the ESP32 S3 in software. In this respect it is a slightly worse choice than a generic ESP32 development board. The emphasis seems to be more on making the Nano ESP32 look as much as possible like a member of the Arduino family and this seems to imply supporting the core Arduino library and not making ESP32 extensions a priority. A standard ESP32 development board has more specific ESP32 support than the Nano ESP32.

Any specific differences in the Nano ESP32's behavior are documented on the book's website for each example program.

The pinouts can be seen below:

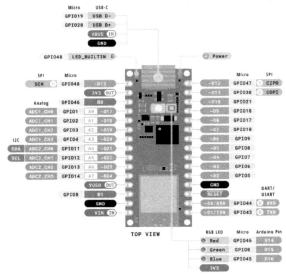

Notice that the Arduino diagram uses two different ways to indicate GPIO pins, GPIO numbers and Arduino Pin names. For example, GPIO02 is also labeled A1, standing for Analog 1. This is because the Arduino family of devices had an Analog 1 input and this has been mapped to GPIO02, which can be used as an analog input in the case of the ESP32. In practice, it is less ambiguous to use GPIO numbers. To do this use the menu command `Tools,Pin Numbering` and select `By GPIO number (legacy)`:

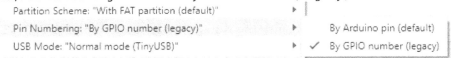

After this all pin numbers will be GPIO numbers as used in all of the programs and diagrams in this book.

Reset and Boot

It is worth knowing what the two buttons that are part of almost every development board actually do and why you generally don't need to make use of them. As its name suggests, the reset/enable button resets the system and reboots it. If you press the boot button nothing happens until you press the reset/enable button when the system will enter "firmware download mode" and run the loader to allow new code to be downloaded via the serial port.

Once in download mode you have to use a utility such as esptool to download the code but an IDE like the Arduino will also do the job, see the next chapter. The actual protocol used is documented, but usually you can ignore the details.

The reset enable button is connected to the EN line on the module and reset/enable button is connected to GPIO0. This means that you cannot use GPIO0 for other purposes:

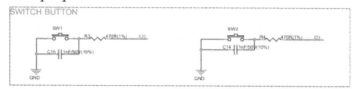

In practice, you rarely need to use the boot button to download code because most development boards use the standard configuration and connect the serial port's DTR and RTS control lines to EN and GPIO0:

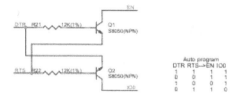

You can see that by toggling the serial control lines you can reset the system or set it into firmware upload mode. What this means is that you usually don't have to press the buttons because the software you are using to upload or run code does the job for you. It is important to know this because if you use the serial port for other purposes you need to be careful about how the RTS and DTR lines are used, see Chapter 14 on the serial port for more.

What To Expect

There are no complete projects in this book – although some examples come very close and it is clear that some of them could be used together to create finished projects. The reason for this is that the focus is on learning how things work so that you can move on and do things that are non-standard.

What matters is that you can reason about what the processor is doing and how it interacts with the real world in real time. This is the big difference between desktop and embedded programming. In the desktop world you don't really care much about when something happens, but when you are programming a physical system you care very much.

This is a book about understanding general principles and making things work at the lowest possible level. When you are working directly with the hardware knowing what is happening matters.

All of the examples are as basic as possible and the code is designed to be as easy to understand as possible. In most cases this means avoiding the use of constants that appear to come from nowhere and functions that make it difficult to see the basic steps. Also error handling is reduced to a bare minimum – simple programs look complicated if you add error handling code. Of course, there is no reason not to refactor these examples into something that looks more like production code and the effort in doing this is much less than getting the basic programs working in the first place.

The development environment used for this book is the Arduino desktop editor. It is easy to install and easy to use, but it occasionally lacks the ability to configure some infrequently-used parameters. An alternative is to use VS Code and the full ESP32 IDE with the Arduino component, but this is much more involved and best avoided until you have a reasonable amount of experience working with the ESP32 and the Arduino library.

What Do You Need?

Well – an ESP32 or an ESP32-S3 at least! In fact you probably are well advised to buy more than one just in case something goes wrong. The price that you have to pay for an ESP32 board varies according to the quantities you require. If buying single boards, the cheapest source is China with a single ESP32 board costing around $3 and an ESP32-S3 around $5, plus postage, of course.

You also need a machine to run the software you need to create programs on, which can be downloaded into the ESP32 – the development machine. The good news is that you can use almost any desktop machine – PC, Mac or Linux system.

As to additional hardware over and above the ESP32, you will need a solderless prototype board and some hookup wires, also known as Dupont wires. You will also need some LEDs, a selection of resistors, some 2N2222 or other general purpose transistors and any of the sensors used in later chapters. See the Resources page for this book on the I/O Press website for links.

A solderless prototype board and some Dupont wires

The ESP32 development board presents a particular problem for prototyping as it is too wide to fit on a standard board. There are some "slim" development boards that make a virtue out of being able to fit on a standard prototype board but a simple solution is to use two prototyping boards and plug one side into one board and the other into the other:

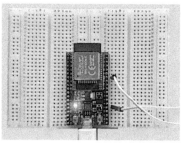

There is also an art to inserting and removing a large device such as the ESP32 from a prototype board. The trick is to use a plastic lever to slowly move each end of the device up from the board working evenly and slowly.

While you don't need to know how to solder, you will need to be able to hook up a circuit on a prototyping board. A multimeter (less than $10) is useful, but if you are serious about electronic projects, investing in a logic analyzer (less than $100) will repay itself in no time at all. You can get small analyzers that plug in via a USB port and use an application to show you what is happening. It is only with a multichannel logic analyzer that you have any hope of understanding what is happening. Without one and the slight skill involved in using it, you are essentially flying blind and left to just guess what might be wrong.

A Low Cost Logic Analyzer

Finally, if you are even more serious, then a small oscilloscope is also worth investing in to check out the analog nature of the supposedly digital signals that microcontrollers put out. However, if you have to choose between these two instruments, the logic analyzer should be your first acquisition.

It is worth noting that the ESP32 can generate signals that are too fast to be reliably detected by low-cost oscilloscopes and logic analyzers, which work at between 1MHz and 25MHz. This can mean that working with pulses much faster than $1\mu s$ can be difficult as you cannot rely on your instruments. There are reasonably priced 200MHz and 500MHz logic analyzers and one of these is certainly worthwhile if you are serious about hardware. It is worth knowing that both instruments can mislead you if you try to work with signals outside of the range that they can work with.

It is also assumed that you are able to program in a C-like language – Java, C#, Python are all similar to C and, of course, so is C++. There isn't space in this book to teach C programming, but the programs are easy enough to follow and any out-of-the-ordinary coding is explained. If you want to learn C in detail, see *Fundamental C: Getting Closer To The Machine*, ISBN: 9781871962604.

Community

Because so many companies produce ESP32 boards there isn't a single ESP32 community as there is for the Arduino or the Raspberry Pi. Espressif runs a lively forum at `https://www.esp32.com/index.php` and this is a good place to ask questions and to see if there are already answers although it isn't specifically about the ESP32 used with the Arduino library.

The Arduino community has a lively forum at `https://forum.arduino.cc/`, but there is no specifically ESP32 subforum which can make it difficult to know where to ask a question. There is also Stack Overflow, of course.

On any forum, the quality of answers varies from misleading to excellent. Always make sure you evaluate what you are being advised in the light of what you know. Be kind and supportive of anyone offering an answer that indicates that they misunderstand your question.

You also need to keep in mind that the advice is also usually offered from a biased point of view. Programmers experienced in C++ will often tell you a way to do something that isn't as simple as a direct C solution. Electronics beginners will offer you solutions that are based on "off-the-shelf" modules, when a simple alternative solution is available, based on a few cheap components. On the other hand, electronics experts will often suggest developing custom hardware that could take months to get right when an off-the-shelf solution is cheap. Even when the advice you get is 100% correct, it still isn't necessarily the right advice for you.

As a rule, never follow any advice that you don't understand.

Summary

- The ESP32 from Chinese manufacturer Espressif is a remarkably powerful device given its low cost and is ideal for building prototypes, one-offs and production devices.

- C/C++ is an excellent choice for programming the ESP32 as it is simple and fast.

- The ESP-IDF, Espressif IoT Development Framework, is very complete and dedicated to creating programs for the ESP32 family of devices, but it is very extensive and isn't easy to use.

- The Arduino library isn't specific to the ESP32, but it is very easy to use and compatible with other devices in the Arduino family. It is also built on top of the ESP-IDF which means you can always drop down and use it if necessary.

- There appear to be so many different ESP32 development boards that it can be difficult to know where to start. However, there are only a small number of ESP32 modules which are used to create development boards and these differ only in small ways.

- The original ESP32 is still available at a lower cost than its replacement ESP32-S3.

- Start with a WROOM-32 EPS32 or ESP32-S3 development board with a full set of pins exposed.

- You will need a pair of prototyping boards and some prototyping wires.

- You also need a multimeter and preferably a logic analyzer. After these basic instruments you can add what you can afford.

- If there is one piece of lab equipment you really should acquire it is a logic analyzer. Without it you are simply guessing at what is happening.

- There is an active ESP32 community forum hosted by Espressif and also an Arduino forum. If you get stuck these are the places to ask for advice. However, always evaluate any advice proffered and, generally, don't accept it unless you understand it.

Chapter 2
Getting Started

The C/C++ language isn't difficult but it is low-level and you need to adapt to using it to work with hardware. The software might be easy, but getting used to the ideas involved in working with hardware is another matter – you have to think a little differently. To put it simply, time matters. What this means will become clear in the rest of the book, but exactly when and in what order things happen are fundamental concerns to this sort of hardware programming, and this usually means needing the most efficient programming language possible – hence C/C++ is a perfect match.

The Arduino IDE and Library

The Arduino IDE is designed to make it easy to work with a device without having to worry about the quirks of the particular device or its dedicated development environment. Of course, there are times when you want to take notice of a device's quirks and then we have no choice but to either use the ESP32-specific features of the library or use the underlying ESP32-IDF SDK. It is also true that the Arduino IDE sometimes lacks the ability to configure the device and its system software to exactly what we want – this is the price of simplicity.

Starting to work with a new processor and its associated SDK is usually a time consuming and frustrating business. You generally have to set up a toolchain and make it work with the editor of your choice. This involves finding and installing a compiler and a build system. The fact that the compiler is usually one of the GCC family and the build system is usually based on CMake doesn't mean that it will go smoothly just because you have experience with them. Each SDK generally has tweaked the compiler and the build system and this is something you have to learn and perhaps modify. It can be a steep learning curve, but the Arduino IDE, which is a customized version of VS Code, is easy to install and even easier to use.

Install Arduino IDE

There are no prerequisites for getting started, all you need is a machine that will run the Arduino IDE. Simply download the version for the operating system you want to install it under. The download can be found at:

https://www.arduino.cc/en/software

Downloads

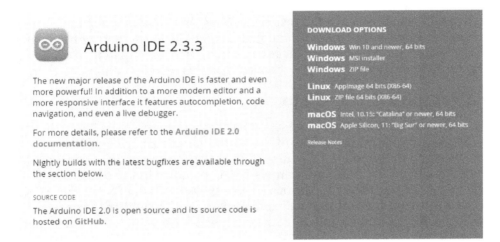

Installation is straightforward and, unusually there are no options to select and you can run the IDE as soon as installation finishes. There is no SDK or other system software to install as this is performed when you start using the IDE and tell it that you want to work with an ESP32.

A First Project

To get started you need an ESP32 or ESP32-S3 (or any other model if you are happy about making any small modifications to the procedure). The simplest thing to do in the first case is to connect the development board to the development machine via a USB cable. If you are using an ESP32-S3 development board it doesn't matter which USB connector you use, but the direct USB port is faster.

The only problem is that the desktop machine that you are using may not have the correct driver for the ESP32 USB port. This can be a tricky problem and it is covered in detail in the section on JTAG debugging.

Before you can sensibly start a new project you have to define what device you are targeting. To do this select the Select Board drop down:

and then select Select Other Board and Port:

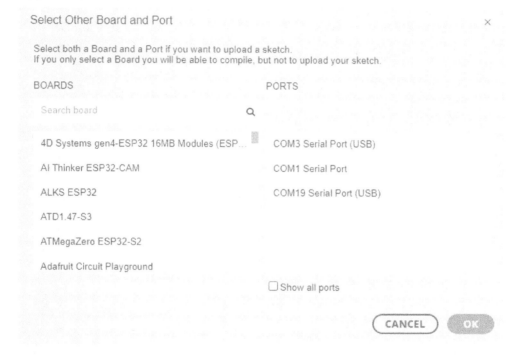

There are now two problems you need to solve. The first is selecting the correct board type as there are so many. You can use the search box to narrow down the selection to ESP32 devices, but even then there are a lot of possible choices. If you are using the standard ESP32 or ESP32-S3 C type development boards the correct choices are: ESP32 Dev Module and ESP32-S3 Dev Module. If you are using another board you may well find something that fits better. What is really important is that you select an ESP32 or an ESP32-S2 or ESP32-S3 or whatever device you are using rather than the particular development board.

You also have to select the USB Serial port that the device is connected to. If you don't know, trial and error usually works. If no USB port works then the chances are you don't have the correct USB driver installed.

Once you select the ESP32 device you are using the IDE will ask if you want to download the libraries needed to compile code for it:

Unless you know better, select YES and allow the IDE to install the SDK.

To get started with your first program enter the following into the editor:

```
void setup() {
  Serial.begin(9600);
  delay(2000);
  Serial.println();
  Serial.println("Hello World");
}

void loop() {
}
```

Now we need to build and run the program. To do this click the Upload button at the top of the window:

Despite this being called "Upload" what it actually does is compile and link your program into a runnable file which it then uploads

The tick icon next to it is labeled Verify, but it simply compiles and links the program without uploading it. The Right arrow icon is Debug and it doesn't work unless you have configured it, see later.

The first time you compile the program it takes longer than subsequent compiles. You can watch the progress of the compile on the progress bar:

When the program is downloaded it is run at once, but we have no way to see the results as there is no terminal connected to the serial port. Rather than connect a serial terminal, the simplest thing to do is to run the Monitor program using the Tools Serial Monitor command. If you do this and rerun the program you should see something like:

The strange symbols before Hello World are due to noise when the system is starting to run a program. Make sure you have selected the correct baud rate for the program you are running – 9600 in this case.

If you know the ESP IDF it is worth saying that the Arduino Monitor is not the same as the IDF Monitor and you cannot use any of the standard menu commands with it.

You have now created and run your first program. If it doesn't work then you need to find out why before moving on. The most common problem is that the USB driver is missing or incorrect. Other problems that occur more often than you might expect include bad USB cables, selecting the wrong ESP device e.g. an ESP32-S3 when you have an ESP32 and entering the code incorrectly.

Tools

The tools menu contains most of the options you can set.

The most useful to know about is the Core Debug Level. If you select Verbose or Debug you will see lots of additional messages in the Serial Monitor which can help you debug your program. Most of the other options you can leave at their defaults unless something goes wrong.

You can get more information about the compiler's actions in the File,Preferences menu:

Preferences

| | Settings | Network |

Sketchbook location:
c:\Users\Documents\Arduino   **BROWSE**
☐ Show files inside Sketches

Editor font size: 14

Interface scale: ☑ Automatic   100   %

Theme: Light   ⌄

Language: English   ⌄   (Reload required)

Show verbose output during   ☑ compile ☑ upload

Compiler warnings   All   ⌄

☐ Verify code after upload
☑ Auto save
☐ Editor Quick Suggestions

Additional boards manager URLs:

CANCEL

If you select Compiler warnings ALL and Show verbose output during compile and upload you will very likely be overwhelmed by data that isn't particularly useful. Of course, when things aren't working, the data suddenly becomes very useful indeed.

The Structure of an Arduino Program

The first thing to say is that Arduino programs are usually called Sketches and saved using an .ino extension. Even so the files still contain standard C/C++ code. Another difference from other C/C++ development systems that you may have used is that the system attempts to identify what libraries you are using and will add the necessary includes and library references behind the scenes. This makes your code look much simpler, but it can go wrong. When it does you have to add explicit #include statements.

In an effort to simplify IoT programs, which usually take the form of an infinite loop, the Arduino system hides the main program from you. Instead you write two functions – `setup` and `loop`. The former is called just once when your application starts and its role is, as its name suggests, where you put the code that sets things up. The latter is called repeatedly and it is generally where you put the code that does the work. That is, behind the scenes the system uses your functions in the following way:

```
setup();
for(;;){
  loop();
}
```

This is simple, but it has some interesting consequences. In particular, if `setup` and `loop` are to share variables they have to be declared in what looks like file level or global but of course they are local to the function that calls setup and loop.

So far everything has been standard for all Arduino programs, but the ESP32 has some additional features. In particular, the program runs under a simple operating system called FreeRTOS. This is a simple multitasking system that schedules tasks to share the power of the processor. What this means in practice is that you can expect any code you write to be interrupted and resumed at any time. You can mostly ignore this, but it does have an impact on actions that need precise timing relative to other actions. FreeRTOS is described in more detail in Chapter 18.

Debugging Using JTAG

Setting up debugging for the ESP32 can be tricky as it involves using a JTAG (Joint Test Action Group) adapter. Some ESP32 development boards, including the ESP32-S3, have an inbuilt JTAG adapter which avoids having to use an adapter. This is a significant advantage as it avoids having to buy an external JTAG adapter and also frees up the four GPIO pins the external adapter requires. The ESP32 doesn't have a JTAG adapter built in and this makes it more difficult to use in debug mode. In addition, at the time of writing, only a small number of JTAG adapters actually work. If you want debugging with the Arduino IDE then the simplest and most cost-effective solution is to use an ESP32-S3 or similar which has a built-in JTAG adapter.

You don't need to set up debugging to work with the examples in the following chapters and indeed many programmers rely on the use of the Monitor and log messages to debug their programs. You can leave tackling debugging until later, but it is well worth doing at some point as it will save you a lot of time in the long run. There are so many things that can go wrong that there is a specific ESP32 FAQ on the topic:

`https://github.com/espressif/openocd-esp32/wiki/Troubleshooting-FAQ`

ESP32-S3 JTAG

As already mentioned, the ESP32-S3 has a built-in JTAG adapter. It connects using the USB C socket. In general, all you have to do is connect both USB C sockets to the development machine:

The big problem with using the built-in JTAG is, once again, finding drivers for the USB ports. At the time of writing, the SDK doesn't install the correct drivers for Windows. You need to make use of Zadig again to install drivers. The important one is JTAG/serial debug unit (Interface 2) which needs WinUSB installed. Interface 1 is just a standard serial USB port.

You also need to use the Boards Manager, Tools,Board,Board Manager to install the Arduino ESP32 Boards package. This overlaps with the Espressif ESP32 Boards package, but it has some drivers that are needed for debugging.

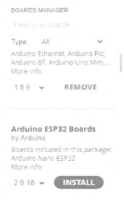

Under Linux, adding OpenOCD <u>udev</u> rules is required and is done by copying the udev rules file at:

```
https://github.com/espressif/openocd-esp32/blob/master/
                              contrib/60-openocd.rules
```

into the `/etc/udev/rules.d` directory.

With this change and a reboot you should be able to get JTAG debugging working.

First make sure that you have selected Integrated USB JTAG, Hardware CDC
and JTAG and Programmer Esptool:

You can now use the debug command to set breakpoints and single-step
through a program.

Notice that sometimes you have to press the step-over icon twice to move
the program on. All of the debug features work and you can examine values
stored in variables and you can see the tasks running under FreeRTOS in the
Threads window – see Chapter 18.

Notice that you have to build or run the program before you can debug it. If
anything goes wrong then simply close the debug windows and shut
everything down and start again. You cannot start another debug session
while one is in action.

Summary

- The Arduino IDE makes working with the ESP32 very easy, but it does this by covering up many of the details. When things go wrong, or you need to do something unsupported, then it can be difficult or impossible.

- Before you can create a program you need to select the board you are using.

- The Arduino library is installed on top of the full ESP IDF SDK and makes use of it to create programs.

- Arduino programs don't have a main function. Instead they have setup which is run once at the start of the program and loop which is called repeatedly.

- You can see the output of an application using the Monitor.

- Often the Monitor is sufficient for simple debugging, but sooner or later you are going to need JTAG-based debugging.

- For the ESP32 you need a JTAG adapter and this is complicated and not well supported.

- The ESP32-S3 has an adapter built in and you only need to make a second USB connection and it is reasonably well supported.

- The main problem with getting JTAG working is installing the correct drivers for the adapter.

Chapter 3

Getting Started With GPIO

In this chapter we take a look at the basic operations involved in using the ESP32's General-Purpose Input/Output (GPIO) lines with an emphasis on output. We'll consider questions such as how fast can you change a GPIO line, how do you generate pulses of a given duration and how can you change multiple lines in sync with each other?

ESP Pins

The first thing to make ourselves familiar with is the layout and range of GPIO pins available on a typical development board – some development boards have fewer or differently arranged pins. Most development boards are based on the ESP32-DevKitC or the ESP32-S3-DevKitC but they sometimes have additional onboard LEDs or reduced GPIO pins. The pins are usually described on the PCB and you can use this to confirm that the development board you are using has a particular pin configuration.

All of the pins have multiple uses, most of which we will explore in later chapters, but here we concentrate on their simplest use as GPIO lines. A GPIO line can be configured as an input or an output, but what is important even at this early stage is that you know that the ESP32 is a 3.3V device. This means that a GPIO line works with two voltages, 0V and 3.3V. If you try to use a GPIO line at a higher voltage then you risk damaging the ESP32.

You can power the ESP32 via the USB port, which is the easiest way while you are developing software. You can also supply 5V via the 5V pin and it will be regulated down to 3.3V or you can connect a 3.3V supply to the 3.3V pin. You can only use a single method of powering the ESP32.

The ESP32 usually has 34 physically accessible GPIO lines in four groups: GPIO0 to GPIO19, GPIO21 to GPIO23, GPIO25 to GPIO27 and GPIO32 to GPIO39.

Pins GPIO34 to GPIO39 are input only.

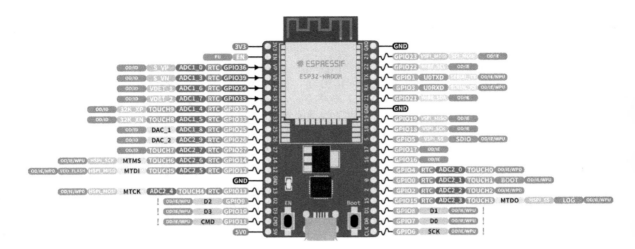

(A full-color version of this diagram that is easier to read can be found on the book's web page.)

Notice that GPIO37 and GPIO38 are not available on most development boards. The following GPIO lines are used for other purposes and should be avoided:

GPIO0	Used at boot to signal Firmware upload
GPIO1	Used for USB serial Tx
GPIO2	Sometimes used to drive onboard LED
GPIO3	Used for USB serial Rx
GPIO6-11	Shared with Flash memory SPI
GPIO16-17	Not available on WROVER modules SPI

The ESP32-S3 has 45 GPIO lines, but also has 34 physically accessible GPIO lines in two groups:

GPIO0 to GPIO 21 and GPIO35 to GPIO48

All GPIO lines are input/output.

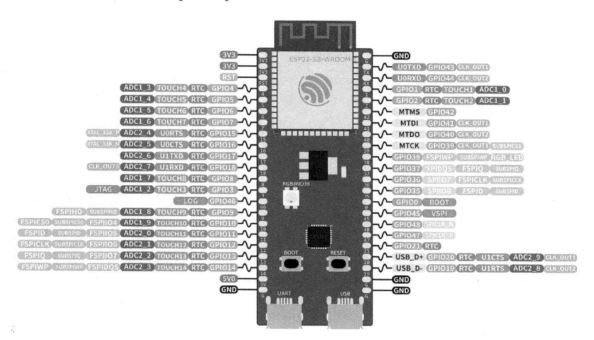

(A full-color version of this pinout diagram can be found on the book's web page.)

You can see that while there is a lot of overlap, GPIO assignments and use in the ESP32 and ESP32-S3 are not the same. The following GPIO lines are used by the ESP32-S3 for other purposes and should be avoided:

GPIO0	Used at boot to signal Firmware upload
GPIO19-20	Used for USB connection
GPIO38-42	Not available on WROVER modules SPI

As is the case with most microprocessors, each GPIO line has multiple uses as you can see in the diagrams. You can select what mode a pin is used in and in this chapter we concentrate on using pins in the simplest GPIO mode. Even so, which pins you select for general-purpose use should take into account what other uses you might put pins to.

Another complication is that some pins are used when the device boots to set its state. Pins GPIO0, 2, 5, 12, 15 on the ESP32 and pins GPIO0, 3, 45, 46 on the ESP32-S3 are "strapping pins" and if you use pull-up or pull-down resistors to set their initial state you will change the behavior at boot time. Each of the strapping pins has an internal resistor that will pull it either high or low and hence supplies the default behavior. If the strapping pins are connected to anything then these weak resistors are overcome and you can set the pins to any initial state. Strapping pins are useful in that you can use them to set up the device but they are often a nuisance when you forget that they exist and accidentally set them. Notice that the state of the pins is sampled and saved when the system boots – after this you can use them as general GPIO lines without worry.

Pins GPIO1, 3, 5, 14-15 are also used by the system at start up to send boot status data. This means that on booting up these pins change state rapidly and could trigger any devices connected to them, leading to difficult-to-find bugs.

Another consideration is that if you plan to use JTAG debugging you need to avoid pins GPIO12-15 in the ESP32 which implement the JTAG protocol. You can disable the JTAG protocol by programming an eFuse, but this isn't generally a good idea. The EPS32-S3 uses GPIO39-42 for JTAG, but this is normally disabled and you have to program an eFuse to turn it on. In most cases, you are better using the built-in JTAG adapter via the USB connector.

In general, with the ESP32 you can use pins GPIO4, 5, 13-33 for general I/O without restrictions and pins GPIO34-39 for input only. GPIO2 can also be used for general I/O if it isn't connected to an onboard LED.

For an ESP32-S3 you can usually use pins GPIO1, 2, 4-21, 38-44, 47-48 without worrying about strapping or other uses.

Notice that the two pin layouts only overlap in GPIO13-33 range.

It is also worth knowing at this early stage that there is a second set of GPIO lines referred to as RTC GPIO which use the same pins as the standard GPIO lines, but are only active in deep-sleep or ultra low-power mode. Their purpose is to allow the processor to control things while in low-power mode. You can ignore these additional lines for the moment and concentrate on using the standard GPIO lines.

Each GPIO line can be used for a range of different things depending on what hardware it is connected to internally. Rather than providing a function which sets the connection directly, the API provides components which automatically set the GPIO up correctly to be used with these connections. For example, when you set up a PWM, Pulse Width Modulation, component you specify the GPIO line to use and the software sets up the internal connection, i.e. the GPIO mode, for you.

The Nano ESP32 has fewer GPIO lines exposed to the outside world and, as already mentioned by default it uses a different naming convention which is standard for the Arduino family. These are automatically mapped to physical GPIO lines. As all of the programs in this book use ESP32 physical GPIO numbering make sure to select this option using the menu command `Tools,Pin Numbering` and select `By GPIO number (legacy)`.

The mapping between the two sets of names can be seen below:

ESP32	Nano	ESP32	Nano
GPIO0	BOOT1	GPIO12	A5
GPIO1	A0	GPIO13	A6
GPIO2	A1	GPIO14	A7
GPIO3	A2	GPIO17	D8
GPIO4	A3	GPIO18	D9
GPIO5	D2	GPIO21	D10
GPIO6	D3	GPIO38	D11
GPIO7	D4	GPIO44	D0
GPIO8	D5	GPIO43	D1
GPIO9	D6	GPIO46	BOOT0
GPIO10	D7	GPIO47	D12
GPIO11	A4	GPIO48	D13

Basic GPIO Functions

To use a GPIO line as a simple GPIO line, recall that they have many other more sophisticated uses, you can call the:

```
pinMode(id,state);
```

This sets the GPIO line specified by *id* to either input or output depending on the setting of *state* usually either `OUTPUT` or `INPUT`. There are other options and these are discussed later.

Notice that *id* is the GPIO number and not the hardware pin number. For example, **16** means GPIO16 and not "connector pin 16" but connector J3 pin 12 on an ESP32 and J1 pin 9 on an ESP32-S3.

Once you have the GPIO line set to output mode you can set the output level using:

```
gpio_set_level(id, level)
```

where *level* is 0 or 1 corresponding to a 0V or 3.3V output – you can also use HIGH and LOW.

Blinky

By tradition, the first IoT program you write is Blinky, which flashes an LED. A program to flash an LED uses a general I/O line and an external LED. Some development boards have an LED already connected to GPIO2. With this in mind, let's flash an LED connected to GPIO2 which will either use the onboard LED or an external LED you have connected.

Start a new project using the New Sketch menu command and enter the program:

Enter the program:

```
void setup() {
  pinMode(2, OUTPUT);
}

void loop() {
  digitalWrite(2, HIGH);
  delay(1000);
  digitalWrite(2, LOW);
  delay(1000);
}
```

The program doesn't use any constants in order to make what is happening clearer. It first initializes GPIO2 to a simple GPIO output line and sets it repeatedly high and low with a pause of one second in between.

If the board you are using has an LED connected to GPIO2 you will see it flashing. If not and you want to connect an LED to see the "blinking" for real then this is easy enough, but you do need a current-limiting resistor to avoid the LED drawing more current than the GPIO line can supply and possibly damaging the chip. A 200Ω resistor is a good choice, see Chapter 5, where a better way to drive an LED is also discussed.

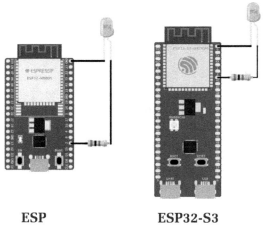

ESP   **ESP32-S3**

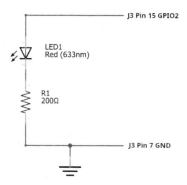

How you build the circuit is up to you. You can use a prototyping board or just a pair of jumper wires. The short pin and/or the flat on the side of the case marks the negative connection on the LED – the one that goes to ground.

If you can't be bothered to go through the ritual of testing Blinky with a real LED, then just connect a logic analyzer to J3 Pin 15 and you will see pulses at 1-second intervals.

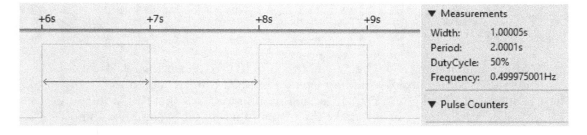

Adding A Toggle Function

As an example of something slightly more advanced, we can implement a toggle function which sets the line high if it is low and low if it is high. To do this we need to know the current state of the pin. One way of doing this is to create a static variable which stores the current state, but it is easier and more reliable to simply read the state from the GPIO line. The function:

```
gpio_get_level(id)
```

returns the level of the specified pin with 1 for high and 0 for low.. If you set the pin's mode to output then this function always returns 0. To read the current state it has to be configured to input/output mode.

The function:

```
void gpio_toggle(int gpio_num) {
  int state = !digitalRead(gpio_num);
  digitalWrite(gpio_num, state);
}
```

sets a line high if it is low and low if it is high. This form of the function
shows how it works, but in practice you would probably write it in a more
compact form:

```
void gpio_toggle(int gpio_num) {
  digitalWrite(gpio_num, !digitalRead(gpio_num));
}
```

With `toggle` it is even easier to implement Blinky:

```
void setup() {
  pinMode(2, OUTPUT);
}

void gpio_toggle(int gpio_num) {
  digitalWrite(gpio_num, !digitalRead(gpio_num));
}

void loop() {
  gpio_toggle(2);
  delay(1000);
  gpio_toggle(2);
  delay(1000);
}
```

Notice that creating a "higher" level function like `toggle` brings its own
problems. For example, what happens if the GPIO pin isn't set to
input/output mode? You can write the function to check that the GPIO mode
is set correctly but this will make the toggle function more complex. In no
time at all a small compact function grows to be a source of slowness.
Writing real time software that interacts with hardware always has this
balance of abstraction and robustness v simple speed of operation. Put
simply you can do it fast or safe but usually not both.

Summary

- The ESP32 has 34 GPIO lines and the ESP32-S3 has 45 in total, but some are already used by the development board.

- The Arduino library allows the use of GPIO pin labels but these are best avoided as they make working out which GPIO lines are in use difficult.

- The pin numbering used isn't standardized, but using the GPIO numbers that the ESP32 module uses is a safe option.

- The ESP32 GPIO lines are organized in four groups, GPIO0 to GPIO19, GPIO21 to GPIO23, GPIO25 to GPIO27 and GPIO32 to GPIO39. Pins GPIO34 to GPIO39 are input only.

- The ESP32-S3 GPIO lines are organized in two groups, GPIO0 to GPIO 21 and GPIO35 to GPIO48

- The ESP32 is a 3.3V device and the GPIO lines should not be used at a higher voltage.

- The SDK provides the function to control a single GPIO line and its basic methods let you set the line high or low and to discover what it is currently set to.

- A Blinky program is usually the first IoT program you write on a new machine. For either the ESP32 or ESP32-S3 you can easily arrange to make an externally connected LED blink on and off.

- An externally connected LED needs a current-limiting resistor.

- The ESP32-S3 has an RGB LED, but it is complicated to use and not suitable for a first program.

- It is easy to extend GPIO support to more complex functions. For example, the toggle function, but these are always compromises between speed and robustness.

Chapter 4

Simple Output

A GPIO line is either configured to be an input or an output. The electronics of working with inputs and outputs are discussed in the next chapter, but first we focus on the software side of the task of using GPIO lines in output mode. While it isn't possible to ignore electronics entirely, keep in mind that more details are provided in Chapter 5.

It is worth noting at this stage that output is easy. Your program chooses the time to change a line's state and you can use the system timer to work out exactly when things should happen. The real problems only start to become apparent when you are trying to change the state of lines very fast or when they need to be changed synchronously. This raises the question of how fast the ESP32 can change a GPIO line and this is something we consider at this early stage because it puts constraints on what we can easily do.

Basic GPIO Functions

We have already met the basic functions that let you work with a single GPIO line:

Method	Description
pinMode(*pin, mode*)	Sets the I/O direction
digitalWrite(*pin, value*)	Sets the line to *value*, 1 or 0,

Using these methods is very straightforward, but notice that there is no way to set multiple lines in one operation. This can be a problem, something we'll come to later.

You can get a long way using just these functions. There are a few more that are useful, but they mainly relate to the configuration of the electronic properties of the GPIO line and are discussed in the next chapter.

How Fast?

A fundamental question that you have to answer for any processor intended for use in embedded or IoT projects is, how fast can the GPIO lines work?

Sometimes the answer isn't of too much concern because what you want to do only works relatively slowly. Any application that is happy with response times in the tens of millisecond region will generally work with almost any processor. However, if you want to implement custom protocols or anything that needs microsecond (μs), or even nanosecond (ns), responses, the question is much more important.

It is fairly easy to find out how fast a single GPIO line can be used if you have a logic analyzer or oscilloscope. All you have to do is run the program:

```
void setup() {
  pinMode(2, OUTPUT);
}

void loop() {
  digitalWrite(2, HIGH);
  digitalWrite(2, LOW);
}
```

If you run this program you will discover that the pulses are not evenly spaced. The up time for the ESP32-S3 is 524ns, but the down time is 1µs. This is significantly slower than using the Espressif IDF SDK where a similar program produces a pulse train with an up time of 300ns and a down time of 324ns:

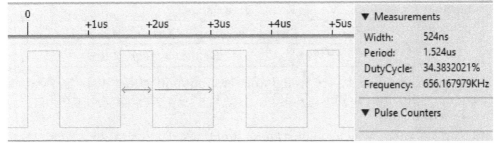

The ESP32 is slightly slower with an up time of 524ns and a down time of 1.12 µs. The unevenness is due to the internal workings of the loop. The line is set to high and then the loop has to jump back to the start and this takes longer than the time to execute the body of the loop. If you change the way that the code is specified, you are likely to see changes in timing.

For example, if you swap the order that the GPIO line is set:

```
void loop() {
  digitalWrite(2, LOW);
  digitalWrite(2, HIGH);
}
```

you will discover that the high time and the low time have swapped roles and now the output is low for longer than it is high. When you are working at this level of speed, small differences in code matter.

What if you want more equal pulses? The answer is that you have to include no-op instructions to increase the time in the part of the program that is running too fast. There is no no-op instruction in C, but the delay that we need is so long that we can use a time-wasting loop. For example:

```
void setup() {
  pinMode(2, OUTPUT);
}
volatile int waste;
void loop() {
  digitalWrite(2, HIGH);
  for(waste=0;waste<6;waste++);
  digitalWrite(2, LOW);
}
```

This evens up the pulse widths to about 1μs high and low on an EPS32-S3. The `volatile` modifier is needed to stop the compiler from optimizing out an instruction that obviously does nothing. There are many times when the compiler optimizes programs under the assumption that running time is irrelevant other than to make it as small as possible – this is sometimes not what you want in the case of an IoT program.

The speed is very good but, as already mentioned, not as good as can be achieved using the Espressif IDF SDK. Compare the 524ns pulse width to the 5.7μs pulse width that is typically achievable using MicroPython. The C program is around ten times faster.

Including Pauses

To generate pulses of a known duration, we need to pause the program between state changes. In the Blinky programs we used `delay()` to slow things down, but without properly introducing it. The function:

```
delay(t);
```

introduces a t-millisecond delay.

This leaves us with the problem of what to use to create delays in microseconds.

The solution is:

```
delayMicroseconds(t)
```

which pauses for t microseconds. It is accurate from about $3\mu s$ to $16383\mu s$, but of course other parts of the program will take microseconds to complete and so make timing more difficult.

As well as the two delay functions there are also:

```
micros()
millis()
```

which return the time since the processor was started in microseconds and milliseconds respectively. You can use them to time intervals.

You can easily use delayMicroseconds, but getting the timing right for short time intervals is very difficult. For example:

```
void setup() {
  pinMode(2, OUTPUT);
}
void loop() {
  digitalWrite(2, HIGH);
  delayMicroseconds(1);
  digitalWrite(2, LOW);
  delayMicroseconds(1);
}
```

The actual delay produced is usually longer than specified, For example, specifying $1\mu s$ produces pulses of around $2.2\mu s$. However, if you specify a delay of $10\mu s$, the pulses are around $10.7\mu s$. Longer times are easier to produce accurately.

The traditional way of introducing a busy wait (also known as a spin wait) is to simply use a time-wasting for loop which produces short wait times:

```
void setup() {
  pinMode(2, OUTPUT);
}
volatile int i = 0;
int n;
void loop() {
  for (n = 1; n < 11; n++) {
    digitalWrite(2, HIGH);
    for (i = 0; i < n; i++) {}
    digitalWrite(2, LOW);
    for (i = 0; i < n; i++) {}
  }
}
```

This generates pulses according to the setting of n:

n	Time in μs ESP32	Time in μs ESP32-S3
1	0.68	0.65
2	0.75	0.71
3	0.85	0.77
4	0.92	0.85
5	1.00	0.91
6	1.10	0.97
7	1.17	1.05
8	1.25	1.11
9	1.35	1.17
10	1.42	1.25

These figures are for the high time of the pulse and provide a ballpark figure of what you can expect. In any given application, you should repeat the measurement with the device you plan to use.

Fixed Time Delay

A common problem is making sure that something happens after a fixed time delay when you have a variable amount of work to do during that time interval. Consider the program snippet:

```
digitalWrite(2, HIGH);
for(int i=0;i<10;i++){}
delay(1)
digitalWrite(2, LOW);
```

where the for loop is intended to stand in for doing some other work. The intention is that the GPIO line should be set high for 1ms, but clearly how long the line is actually set high depends on how long the loop takes. It is clear that it is going to be longer than 1ms.

What is needed is a pause that takes into account the time that the loop uses up and simply delays the program for the remaining amount of time to make it up to 1ms.

It is simple to create some functions that can be reused, even if they are slower than using the timer directly:

```
unsigned long tick_us(unsigned long offset) {
  return micros() + offset;
}
void delay_until(unsigned long t) {
  do {
  } while (t > micros());
}
```

51

The `tick_us` function now has an offset which can be added to the current time to move it on by the given amount. The `delay_until` function simply blocks until the specified time, in microseconds, arrives.

Using these two functions we can now write a delay that waits for the specified time to be up:

```
unsigned long tick_us(unsigned long offset) {
    return micros() + offset;
}

void delay_until(unsigned long t) {
    do {
    } while (t > micros());
}

void setup() {
    pinMode(2, OUTPUT);
}

volatile int i = 0;
int n = 2;
unsigned long width = 1000;
unsigned long t;

void loop() {
    t = tick_us(width);
    digitalWrite(2, HIGH);
    for (i = 0; i < n; i++) {}
    delay_until(t);
    t = tick_us(width);
    digitalWrite(2, LOW);
    for (i = 0; i < n; i++) {}
    delay_until(t);
}
```

You can modify the value of n to simulate longer or shorter periods of work in the loop without altering the timing of the pulses. The times aren't particularly accurate because of the overheads in calling the functions and getting the time.

This is a very general technique and one that can often make difficult timing problems very simple.

The Interrupt Problem

The fact that we are using the ESP32 with a real-time operating system can cause problems if you are unaware of what is happening. Every `portTICK_PERIOD_MS`, usually around 10 ms but for the Arduino ESP32 set at 1ms, the operating system will interrupt the running task and possibly choose another to run. At the moment we are only running one task, but the OS still has to handle the fact that the second core is running the WiFi and other system requirements and so at the very least your task will be interrupted for typically 5μs every 1ms:

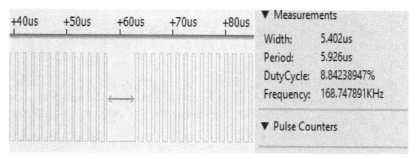

What this means is that any pulse train you attempt to generate will be stopped for around 5μs every 1ms. How important this is depends on the pulse width. For example, if you generate 10μs pulses using simple busy waits then every 1ms one of the pulses will be extended to 15μs:

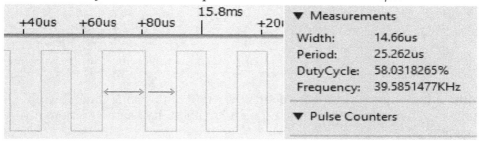

You can't solve this problem by turning off interrupts because this would mean that other parts of the system, WiFi for example, would stop working. The only easy solution is to use the system timer to correct the pulse width after the interrupt. That is, if you use `delay_until`, introduced in the previous section, to time the pulses there will be no longer pulses included in the pulse train. Notice that this is only important when you cannot allow a pulse to be around 5μs longer every 1ms, i.e. it is only an issue for short pulses.

Phased Pulses

As a simple example of using the output functions, let's try to write a short program that pulses two lines high and then low, out of phase.

The simplest program to do this job is:

```
void setup() {
  pinMode(2, OUTPUT);
  pinMode(4, OUTPUT);
}

void loop() {
  digitalWrite(2, HIGH);
  digitalWrite(4, LOW);
  digitalWrite(2, LOW);
  digitalWrite(4, HIGH);
}
```

There is no delay in the loop so the pulses are produced at the fastest possible speed and when GPIO2 goes high GPIO4 goes low and vice versa. Using a logic analyzer reveals that the result isn't what you might expect:

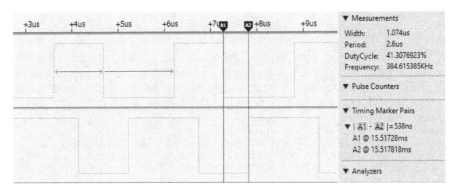

Although the intent is for both actions to occur at the same time, the top train switches on and the bottom train takes about half a pulse before it switches off.

The point is that it does take quite a long time to access and change the state of an output line. If we include a delay to increase the pulse width then the delay caused by accessing the GPIO lines in two separate actions isn't so obvious, but it is still there. There are applications where the switching speed is so low that the delay between switching doesn't matter – flashing LEDs for instance.

With a delay of around $0.5\mu s$ you could flash a line of around 40,000 LEDs before the lag between the first and the last became apparent. On the other hand, if you use out-of-phase pulses to control a motor or a DC to AC converter using a bridge, then the overlap when both GPIO lines were on would burn out the drivers quite quickly. Of course, any sensible, cautious, engineer wouldn't feed a bridge from two independently generated pulse trains unless they were guaranteed not to switch both sides of the bridge on at the same time.

Setting Multiple GPIO Lines

There is no way of using supplied functions to change multiple GPIO lines at the same time, even though the hardware makes it possible. To do the job you need to write some code that accesses the hardware directly, see Chapter 19 for more details. In this chapter we simply present and make use of the function explained there:

```
void gpio_set(int32_t value,int32_t mask){
    int32_t *OutAdd=(int32_t*) GPIO_OUT_REG;
    *OutAdd= (*OutAdd & ~mask) | (value & mask);
}
```

This works by directly accessing the GPIO registers. The function gpio_set uses a mask to determine which lines will be set and a value that gives the states to set them to. Any bits not set in the mask leave the corresponding GPIO line unchanged. Of course this makes the program specific to the ESP32 and isn't generic Arduino code any more.

It is easy to create a mask for any GPIO lines. For example, if you want to modify only lines GPIOn and GPIOm then the mask is:

```
mask = 1<<n | 1<<m
```

and so on if you have more lines to modify.

The value can be constructed in the same way. If you want to set the lines to a and b then value is:

```
value = a<<n | b<<m
```

Notice that if the corresponding bit isn't set in mask then the bit in value has no effect. That is, mask determines which bits you are going to modify and value determines what those bits are set to.

Making use of this we can write the previous program without lags as when value and mask are used to update the GPIO register all of the lines change at once:

```
void gpio_set(int32_t value, int32_t mask) {
  int32_t *OutAdd = (int32_t *)GPIO_OUT_REG;
  *OutAdd = (*OutAdd & ~mask) | (value & mask);
}

void setup() {
  pinMode(2, OUTPUT);
  pinMode(4, OUTPUT);
}
volatile int i = 0;
int32_t mask = 1 << 2 | 1 << 4;
int32_t value1 = 0 << 2 | 1 << 4;
int32_t value2 = 1 << 2 | 0 << 4;
void loop() {
  gpio_set(value1, mask);
  for (i = 0; i < 5; i++) {}
  gpio_set(value2, mask);
}
```

As we are changing the same pins each time, we only need a single mask. The value, however, changes each time. If you run this program you will see an almost perfect pair of out-of-phase 0.6μs pulses:

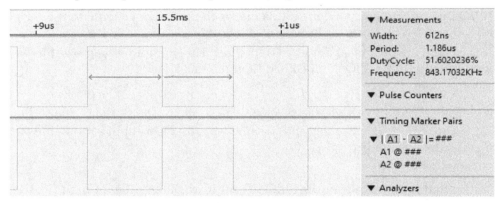

56

Summary

- Output is easy because the program decides when to change the state of a line. Input is hard because you never know when an input line will change state.

- GPIO lines can be set to act as inputs or outputs:
      pinMode(*pin*, *mode*)

- If a line is set to output it can be set high or low using the digitalWrite(*pin*, *value*) function.

- You can generate pulses as short as 524ns.

- A delay can be introduced into a program using delay(t) but this only works for times longer a few milliseconds or delayMicroseconds(t) which is accurate after about $3\mu s$

- An alternative is to use a busy wait loop which is simply a loop that keeps the CPU busy for an amount of time. It is easy to obtain an equation that gives the delay-per-loop repetition.

- By using micros() or millis() you can get the number of microseconds or milliseconds since the machine was switched on.

- Pulses with a fixed period can be produced using delay_until.

- The running task is interrupted every 1ms for a minimum of $5\mu s$You can compensate for this using delay_until.

- Producing pulses which are in accurately in phase is not possible using digitalWrite(*pin*, *value*) as it only changes one GPIO line at a time.

- If you access the hardware directly, you can change multiple lines in a single operation.

Chapter 5

Some Electronics

Now that we have looked at some simple I/O, it is worth spending a little time on the electronics of output and input. We cover the electronics of input before looking at how the software handles input because we need to understand some of the problems that the software has to deal with.

First some basic electronics – how transistors can be used as switches. The approach is very simple, but it is enough for the simple circuits that digital electronics makes use of. It isn't enough to design a high-quality audio amplifier or similar analog device, but it might be all you need.

How to Think About Circuits

For a beginner electronics can seem very abstract, but that's not how old hands think about it. Most understand what is going on in terms of a hydraulic model, even if they don't admit it. The basic idea is that an electric current running in a wire is very much like a flow of water in a pipe. The source of the electricity plays the role of a pump and the wires, the pipe. The flow of electricity is measured in Amps and this is just the amount of electricity that flows per second. The flow is governed by how hard the pump is pumping, which is measured by voltage and how restrictive the pipe is, the resistance which is measured in Ohms.

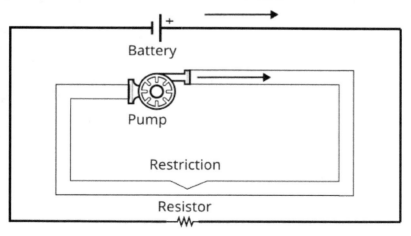

It is true that when you are doing electronics you are basically doing plumbing with a fluid that you generally can't see that flows in pipes called wires.

The only difficult one of these three ideas is the idea of pumping force. We tend to think of a pump providing a flow at the location of the pump but there is something, "a pumping force" that keeps the water flowing around every part of the circuit. In your imagination you have to think of the water being forced ever onward at every point in the pipe. In particular when there is constriction in the pipe then you might need more pumping force to get the water through. In a sense the pump provides the total pressure available and this distributes itself around the circuit as needed to push the flow through each restriction.

In electric circuits the pumping force is called EMF or ElectroMotive Force or just voltage. We also assume that the force needed to push electricity through wires is negligible and resistors are the only place that a voltage is needed to make the current flow.

The relationship between these quantities is characterized by Ohm's law:

$V = IR$ or $I = V/R$ or $R = V/I$

where V is the voltage in Volts, I is the current in Amps and R is the resistance in Ohms.

It is worth pointing out that we generally work in Volts (V) and milliamps (mA), one thousandth of an amp, in Ohm's law and this automatically gives resistance in kilo-ohms ($k\Omega$).

You can see that if you increase the voltage, the flow, then the current increases. If you increase the resistance then the current decreases. Slightly more difficult is the idea that for a given resistance you need particular pumping force to achieve a given flow. If you know the actual flow and the resistance then you can work out the pumping force needed to get that flow.

The following points should be obvious. The flow through a pipe has to be the same at each point in the pipe – otherwise water would backup or need to be introduced. The total pressure that the pump provides has to be distributed across each of the resistances in the pipe to ensure the same flow. These pressures have to add up to the total pressure that the pump provides.

Slightly less obvious, but you can still understand them in terms of water flow, pressures add, currents add and resistances to flow in the same pipe add.

One of the main reasons for understanding electrical flow is that you can use Ohm's law to avoid damaging things. As a current flows through a resistor it gets hot. The rule here is that the energy produced is proportional to VI. If you double the current, you double the heating effect. Most electronic devices have current limits beyond which they are liable to fail. One of the basic tasks in designing any electronic circuit is to work out what the current is and, if it is too high, add a resistor or lower the voltage to reduce it. To do this you need a good understanding of the hydraulic model and be able to use Ohm's law. There are examples later in this chapter.

It is also worth pointing out that there are devices which do not obey Ohm's law – so-called non-Ohmic devices. These are the interesting elements in a circuit – LEDs, diodes, transistors and so on, but even these devices can be understood in terms of the flow of a fluid.

This is a lightning introduction to electronics, pun intended, and there is much to learn and many mistakes to make, most of which result in blue smoke.

Electrical Drive Characteristics

If you are not familiar with electronics, the important thing to understand is the relationship between voltage, current and resistance. Voltage is like pressure and it makes the electrons flow. The current is the size of the flow and the resistance is what it sounds like – a resistance to the flow. For a fixed resistor the current flowing increases in proportion to the voltage. As already stated the relationship between voltage current and resistance is summarized by Ohm's law, $V = IR$ where V is the voltage in volts, I is the current in amps and R is the resistance in ohms.

So we need to know what voltages are being worked with and how much current can flow. The most important thing to know about the ESP32 is that it works with two voltage levels – 0V and 3.3V. Even though you can power most development boards from 5V there is a DC to DC chip that converts whatever you supply it with to 3.3V. It is theoretically possible to run the ESP32 digital portion at 1.8V and use 3.3V to run the analog portion of the chip, but the majority of development boards don't make this available.

If you have worked with other logic devices you might be more familiar with 0V and 5V as being the low and high levels. The ESP32 uses a lower output voltage to reduce its power consumption, which is good, but you need to keep in mind that you may have to use some electronics to change the 3.3V to other values. The same is true of inputs, which must not exceed 3.3V or you risk damaging the ESP32.

An important question is how much current the GPIO lines can handle without damaging the chip. This isn't an easy question and at the time of writing the documentation isn't clear on the matter. According to the documentation, each GPIO line can be set to "drive" up to 40mA. However, this doesn't quite mean what you might think. This is not an upper limit on the supplied current, but a configuration that is needed to ensure that the output voltages of the GPIO line are within specification, even if you connect something that requires a lot of current – see later.

According to the datasheet, while GPIO16 and GPIO17 are limited to 20mA the other GPIO lines can provide up to 40mA. This doesn't mean, however, that you can use every GPIO line to supply the maximum current at the same time. The datasheet is very vague on what the actual maximum is, but it refers to reducing the current to half the maximum as the number of GPIO lines using that current increases. You also need to be aware of the fact the development board's power supply is limited to 1200mA and the WiFi components can draw 200mA while transmitting. Clearly, if all 34 GPIO lines were drawing the maximum 40mA the total would be 1360mA which is well beyond what the power supply can source. This is an extreme and unlikely example, but it indicates that it is the total current draw subject to each line being less than 40mA is the important consideration.

In practice, you need to work out the total current draw from all of the GPIO lines in a worst case and then consider if this is reasonable in terms of total power consumption.

For reliable operation you need to stay away from the maximums.

Driving an LED

One of the first things you need to know how to do is compute the value of a current-limiting resistor. For example, if you just connect an LED between a GPIO line and ground then no current will flow when the line is low and the LED is off, but when the line is high, at 3.3V, it is highly likely that the current will exceed the safe limit. In most cases nothing terrible will happen as the ESP32's GPIO lines are rated very conservatively, but if you keep doing it eventually something will fail. The correct thing to do is to use a current-limiting resistor. Although this is an essential part of using an LED, it is also something you need to keep in mind when connecting any output device. You need to discover the voltage that the device needs and the current it uses and calculate a current-limiting resistor to make sure that is indeed the current it draws from the GPIO line.

An LED is a non-linear electronic component – the voltage across it stays more or less the same irrespective of the current passing through the device. Compare this to a more normal linear, or "ohmic", device where the current and voltage vary together according to Ohm's law, V =IR, which means that if the current doubles, so does the voltage and vice versa.

This is not how an LED behaves. It has a fairly constant voltage drop, irrespective of the current. (If you are curious about it, the relationship between current and voltage for an LED is exponential, meaning that big changes in the current hardly change the voltage across the LED.) When you use an LED you need to look up its forward voltage drop, about 1.7V to 2V for a red LED and about 3V for a blue LED, and the maximum current, usually 20mA for small LEDs. You don't have to use the current specified, this is the maximum current and maximum brightness. To work out the current-limiting resistor you simply calculate the voltage across the resistor and then use Ohm's law to give you the resistor you need for the current required. The LED determines the voltage and the resistor sets the current.

A GPIO line supplies 3.3V and if you assume 1.6V as the forward voltage across the LED, that leaves 1.7V across the current-limiting resistor since voltage distributes itself across components connected in series. If we restrict the current to 8mA, which is very conservative, then the resistor we need is given by:

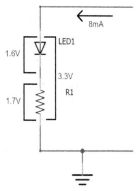

$R = V/I = 1.7/8 = 0.212$

The result is in kilo-ohms, kΩ, because the current is in milli-amps, mA. So we need at least a 212Ω resistor. In practice, you can use a range of values as long as the resistor is around 200 ohms – the bigger the resistor the smaller the current, but the dimmer the LED. If you were using multiple GPIO lines then keeping the GPIO current down to 1 or 2mA would be better, but that would need a transistor.

You need to do this sort of calculation when driving other types of output device. The steps are always the same. The 3.3V distributes itself across the output device and the resistor in some proportion and we know the maximum current – from these values we can compute the resistor needed to keep the actual current below this value.

LED BJT Drive

Often you need to reduce the current drawn from a GPIO line. The Bipolar Junction Transistor (BJT) may be relatively old technology, but it is a current amplifier, low in cost and easy to use. A BJT is a three-terminal device - base, emitter and collector - in which the current that flows through the emitter/collector is controlled by the current in the base:

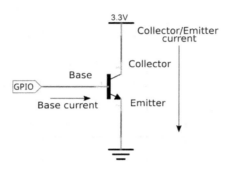

The diagram shows an NPN transistor, which is the most common. This diagram is a simplification in that, in reality, the current in the emitter is slightly larger than that in the collector because you have to add the current flowing in the base. In most cases you need just two additional facts. Firstly, the voltage on the base is approximately 0.6V, no matter how much current flows since the base is a diode, a non-linear device just like the LED in the previous section.

Secondly, you need to multiply the current in the collector/emitter by the current gain of the transistor, specified as hFE or ß (beta), a value you can look up for any transistor you want to use. While you are consulting the datasheets, you also need to check the maximum currents and voltages the device will tolerate. In most cases, the beta is between 50 and 200 and hence you can use a transistor to amplify the GPIO current by at least a factor of 50.

Notice that, for the emitter/collector current to be non-zero, the base has to have a current flowing into it. If the base is connected to ground then the transistor is "cut off", i.e. no current flows. What this means is that when the GPIO line is high the transistor is "on" and current is flowing and when the GPIO line is low the transistor is "off" and no current flows. This high-on/ low-off behavior is typical of an NPN transistor.

A PNP transistor works the other way round:

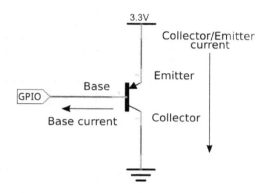

The 0.6V is between the base and the collector and the current flows out of the base. In this case to switch the transistor on you have to connect the base to ground. What this means is that the transistor is off when the GPIO line is high and on when it is low.

This complementary behavior of NPN and PNP BJTs is very useful and means that we can use such transistors in pairs. It is also worth knowing that the diagram given above is usually drawn with 0V at the top of the diagram, i.e. flipped vertically, to make it look the same as the NPN diagram. You always need to make sure you know where the +V line is.

A BJT Example

For a simple example we need to connect a standard LED to a GPIO line with a full 20mA drive. Given that all of the GPIO lines work at 3.3V and ideally only supply a few milliamps, we need a transistor to drive the LED which typically draws 20mA.

You could use a Field Effect Transistor (FET) of some sort, but for this sort of application an old-fashioned BJT (Bipolar Junction Transistor) works very well and is cheap and available in a thru-hole mount, i.e. it comes with wires. Almost any general purpose NPN transistor will work, but the 2N2222 is very common. From its datasheet you can discover that the max collector current is 800mA and its hFE is at least 50, which makes it suitable for driving a 20mA LED with a GPIO current of at most 20mA/50 = 0.4mA.

The circuit is simple but we need two current-limiting resistors:

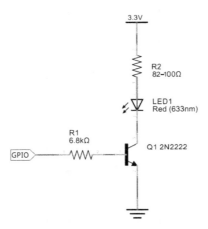

If you connected the base to the GPIO line directly then the current flowing in the base would be unrestricted – it would be similar to connecting the GPIO line to ground. R1 restricts the current to 0.39mA, which is very low and, assuming that the transistor has a minimum hFE of 50, this provides just short of 20mA to power it.

The calculation is that the GPIO supplies 3.3V and the base has 0.6V across it so the voltage across R1 is 3.3 - 0.6V = 2.7V. To limit the current to 0.4mA would need a resistor of 2.7V/0.4mA = 6.7kΩ. The closest preferred value is 6.8kΩ, which gives a slightly smaller current.

Without R2 the LED would draw a very large current and burn out. R2 limits the current to 20mA. Assuming a forward voltage drop of 1.6V and a current of 20mA the resistor is given by (3.3-1.6)V/20mA = 85Ω. In practice, we could use anything in the range 82Ω to 100Ω.

The calculation just given assumes that the voltage between the collector and emitter is zero, but of course in practice it isn't. Ignoring this results in a current less than 20mA, which is erring on the safe side. The datasheet indicates that the collector emitter voltage is less than 200mV.

The point is that you rarely make exact calculations for circuits such as this, you simply arrive at acceptable and safe operating conditions. Also notice that the transistor could be connected to a higher supply voltage than the 3.3V shown. Transistors are not just amplifiers, they are level shifters. You can also use the same design to drive something that needs a higher voltage. For example, to drive a 5V dip relay, which needs 10mA to activate it, you would use something like:

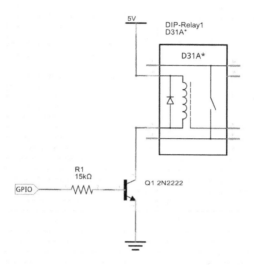

Notice that in this case the transistor isn't needed to increase the drive current – the GPIO line could provide the 10mA directly. Its purpose is to change the voltage from 3.3V to 5V. The same idea works with any larger voltage.

If you are using the 2N2222 then the pinouts are:

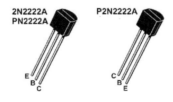

As always, the positive terminal on the LED is the long pin.

MOSFET Driver

There are many who think that the FET (Field Effect Transistor) or more precisely the MOSFET (Metal Oxide Semiconductor FET) is the perfect amplification device and we should ignore BJTs. They are simpler to understand and use, but it can be more difficult to find one with the characteristics you require.

Like the BJT, a MOSFET has three terminals called the gate, drain and source. The current that you want to control flows between the source and drain and it is controlled by the gate. This is analogous to the BJT's base, collector and emitter, but the difference is that it is the voltage on the gate that controls the current between the source and drain.

The gate is essentially a high resistance input and very little current flows in it. This makes it an ideal way to connect a GPIO line to a device that needs more current or a different voltage. When the gate voltage is low the source drain current is very small. When the gate voltage reaches the threshold voltage $V_{GS(th)}$, which is different for different MOSFETs, the source drain current starts to increase exponentially. Basically, when the gate is connected to 0V or below $V_{GS(th)}$ the MOSFET is off and when it is above $V_{GS(th)}$ the MOSFET starts to turn on. Don't think of $V_{GS(th)}$ as the gate voltage that the MOSFET turns on, but as the voltage below which it is turned off.

The problem is that the gate voltage to turn a typical MOSFET fully on is in the region of 10V. Special "logic" MOSFETs need a gate voltage around 5V to fully turn on and this makes the 3.3V at which the ESP32's GPIO lines work a problem. The datasheets usually give the fully on resistance and the minimum gate voltage that produces it, usually listed as Drain-Source On-State Resistance. For digital work this is a more important parameter than the gate threshold voltage.

You can deal with this problem in one of two ways – ignore it or find a MOSFET with a very small $V_{GS(th)}$. In practice MOSFETs with thresholds low enough to work at 3.3V are hard to find and when you do find them they are generally only available as surface-mount. Ignoring the problem sometimes works if you can tolerate the MOSFET not being fully on. If the current is kept low then, even though the MOSFET might have a resistance of a few ohms, the power loss and voltage drop may be acceptable.

What MOSFETs are useful for is in connecting higher voltages to a GPIO line used as an input – see later.

Also notice that this discussion has been in terms of an N-channel MOSFET. A P-channel works in the same way, but with all polarities reversed. It is cut off when the gate is at the positive voltage and on when the gate is grounded. This is exactly the same as the NPN versus PNP behavior for the BJT.

MOSFET LED

A BJT is the easiest way to drive an LED, but as an example of using a common MOSFET we can arrange to drive one using a 2N7000, a low-cost, N-channel device available in a standard TO92 form factor suitable for experimentation:

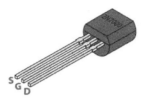

Its datasheet states that it has a $V_{GS(th)}$ typically 2V, but it could be as low as 0.8V or as high as 3V. Given we are trying to work with a gate voltage of 3.3V you can see that in the worst case this is hardly going to work – the device will only just turn on. The best you can do is to buy a batch of 2N7000 and measure their $V_{GS(th)}$ to weed out any that are too high. This said, in practice the circuit given below does generally work.

Assuming a $V_{GS(th)}$ of 2V and a current of 20mA for the LED the datasheet gives a rough value of 6Ω for the on resistance with a gate voltage of 3V. The calculation for the current-limiting resistor is the same as in the BJT case and the final circuit is:

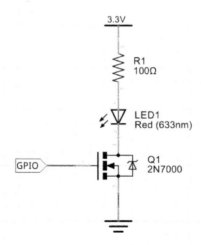

Notice that we don't need a current-limiting resistor for the GPIO line as the gate connection is high impedance and doesn't draw much current. In practice, it is usually a good idea to include a current-limiting resistor in the GPIO line if you plan to switch it on and off rapidly. The problem is that the gate looks like a capacitor and fast changes in voltage can produce high currents. Notice that there are likely to be devices labeled 2N7000 that will not work in this circuit due to the threshold gate voltage being too high, but encountering one is rare.

A logic-level MOSFET like the IRLZ44 has a resistance of 0.028Ω at 5V compared to the 2N2222's of 6Ω. It also has a $V_{GS(th)}$ guaranteed to be between 1V and 2V. It would therefore be a better candidate for this circuit.

Setting Drive Type

The GPIO output can be configured into one of a number of modes, but the most important is pull-up/down. Before we get to the code to do the job it is worth spending a moment explaining the three basic output modes, push-pull, pull-up and pull-down.

Push-Pull Mode

In push-pull mode two transistors of opposite polarity, one PNP and one NPN, are used:

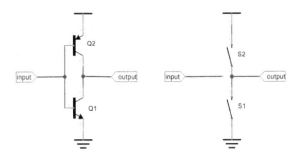

The circuit behaves like the two-switch equivalent shown on the right. Only one of the transistors, or switches, is "closed" at any time. If the input is high then Q1 is saturated and the output is connected to ground - exactly as if S1 was closed. If the input is low then Q2 is saturated and it is as if S2 was closed and the output is connected to 3.3V. You can see that this pushes the output line high with the same "force" as it pulls it low. This is the standard configuration for a GPIO output.

70

Pull-Up Mode

In pull-up mode one of the transistors is replaced by a resistor:

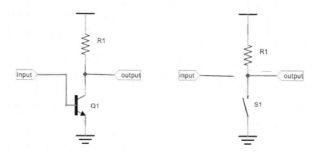

In this case the circuit is equivalent to having a single switch. When the switch is closed, the output line is connected to ground and hence driven low. When the switch is open, the output line is pulled high by the resistor. You can see that in this case the degree of pull-down is greater than the pull-up, where the current is limited by the resistor. The advantage of this mode is that it can be used in an AND configuration. If multiple GPIO or other lines are connected to the output, then any one of them being low will pull the output line low. Only when all of them are off does the resistor succeed in pulling the line high. This is used, for example, in a serial bus configuration like the I2C bus.

Pull-Down Mode

Finally the pull-down mode, which is the best mode for driving general loads, motors, LEDs, etc, is exactly the same as the pull-up, only now the resistor is used to pull the output line low.

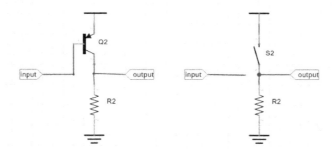

The line is held high by the transistor and pulled low by the resistor only when all the switches are open. Putting this the other way round, the line is high if any one switch is closed. This is the OR version of the shared bus idea.

71

Open Collector

There is one final output configuration – open collector or, when referring to a MOSFET, open drain. The idea is simple, you don't connect the collector or the drain to anything at all – you simply use it as the output:

There is no pull-up resistor, but you can supply one as an external pull-up if needed. You can also drive a device that needs a current flow through it rather than just a voltage – a coil is the standard example. However, a GPIO line usually cannot supply enough current for such devices.

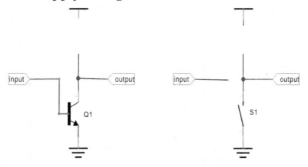

The real use of the open collector arrangement is to implement a shared data line:

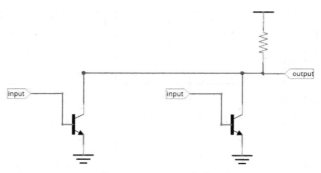

In this case two inputs control one output. If the first transistor is on then the output is low, irrespective of the state of the second transistor. The same is true if the second transistor is on. If you work through the possible combinations we have:

Input 1	Input 2	Output
Off	Off	High
Off	On	Low
On	Off	Low
On	On	Low

You might recognize this as the truth table for an OR gate. This is exactly what an open collector output used in this way implements. Early integrated circuits referred to as Resistor Transistor Logic or RTL implemented logic in this way. This was soon replaced by Transistor Transistor Logic or TTL because transistors are easier to implement in an integrated circuit.

In IoT applications, open collector connections are used to allow any number of devices to share a line. If all of the devices are configured to be open collectors then any one of them can pull the line low. In most cases only one device will be active and sending data at any one time.

Setting Pull Mode

The mode of a GPIO line is set by configuring the electronics which connects it to the outside world, the PAD. The Arduino library has very little support for configuring the way the PAD works. The reason is probably that making use of internal pull-up/pull-down resistors is very machine-specific and hence external resistors are a better idea. However, you can set an internal pull-up using:

```
pinMode(pin, INPUT_PULLUP)
```

Notice this only works for input. The pull-up resistor is 45kΩ.

If you want to make use of the ESP32's more sophisticated PAD configurations then you have to go beyond the core Arduino library. Specific to the ESP32 are the following driver modes:

- ◆ INPUT   Input with no internal pullups
- ◆ OUTPUT   ESP32 INPUT/OUTPUT mode, both read and write
- ◆ PULLUP   Enable internal pull up
- ◆ INPUT_PULLUP   Same as INPUT|PULLUP
- ◆ PULLDOWN   Enable internal pull down
- ◆ INPUT_PULLDOWN   Same as INPUT|PULLDOWN
- ◆ OPEN_DRAIN   Open drain configuration
- ◆ OUTPUT_OPEN_DRAIN   Same as OUTPUT|OPEN_DRAIN

Basic Input Circuit - The Switch

It is time to turn our attention to the electrical characteristics of GPIO lines as inputs. One of the most common input circuits is the switch or button. Many beginners make the mistake of wiring a GPIO line to a switch something like:

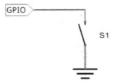

The problem with this is that, if the switch is pressed, the GPIO line is connected to ground and will read as zero. The question is, what does it read when the switch is open? A GPIO line configured as an input without pull-up or pull-down enabled has a very high resistance. The maximum current and input line will draw is 50nA. As it isn't connected to any particular voltage, the voltage on it varies due to the static it picks up. The jargon is that the unconnected line is "floating". When the switch is open the line is floating and if you read it the result, zero or one, depends on whatever noise it has picked up.

The correct way to do the job is to tie the input line either high or low when the switch is open using a resistor. A pull-up arrangement would be something like:

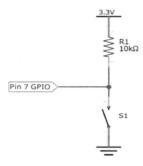

The value of the resistor used isn't critical. It simply pulls the GPIO line high when the switch isn't pressed. When it is pressed a current of a little more than 0.3mA flows in the resistor. If this is too much, increase the resistance to 100kΩ or even more - but notice that the higher the resistor value the noisier the input to the GPIO and the more it is susceptible to RF interference. This gives a zero when the switch is pressed.

If you want a switch that pulls the line high instead of low, reverse the logic by swapping the positions of the resistor and the switch in the diagram to create a pull-down:

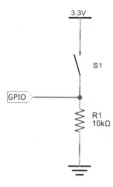

This gives a one when the switch is pressed.

Debounce

Although the switch is the simplest input device, it is very difficult to get right. When a user clicks a switch of any sort, the action isn't clean - the switch bounces. What this means is that the logic level on the GPIO line goes high then low and high again and bounces between the two until it settles down. There are electronic ways of debouncing switches, but software does the job much better. All you have to do is insert a delay of a millisecond or so after detecting a switch press and read the line again - if it is still low then record a switch press. Similarly, when the switch is released, read the state twice with a delay. You can vary the delay to modify the perceived characteristics of the switch.

A more sophisticated algorithm is based on the idea of integration to debounce a switch. All you have to do is read the state multiple times, every few milliseconds say, and keep a running sum of values. If you sum say ten values each time then a total of between 6 and 10 can be taken as an indication that the switch is high. A total less than this indicates that the switch is low. You can think of this as a majority vote in the time period for the switch being high or low.

The Potential Divider

If you have an input that is outside of the range of 0V to 3.3V then you can reduce it using a simple potential divider. In the diagram, V is the input from the external logic and V_{out} is the connection to the GPIO input line:

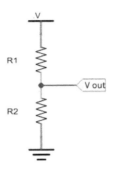

$$V_{out} = V*R2/(R1+R2)$$

You can spend a lot of time on working out good values of R1 and R2. For loads that take a lot of current you need R1+R2 to be small and divided in the same ratio as the voltages. For example, for a 5V device R1=18KΩ or 20KΩ and R2=33KΩ work well to drop the voltage to 3.3V.

A simpler approach that works for a 5V signal is to notice that the ratio R1:R2 has to be the same as (5-3.3):3.3, i.e. the voltage divides itself across the resistors in proportion to their value, which is roughly 1:2. What this means is that you can take any resistor and use it for R1 and use two of the same value in series for R2 and the V_{out} will be 3.3V.

The problem with a resistive divider is that it can round off fast pulses due to the small capacitive effects. This usually isn't a problem, but if it is then the solution is to use a FET or a BJT as an active buffer:

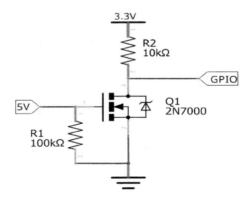

Notice that this is an inverting buffer, the output is low when the input is high, but you can usually ignore this and simply correct it in software, i.e. read a 1 as a low state and a 0 as a high state. The role of R1 is to make sure the FET is off when the 5V signal is absent and R2 limits the current in the FET to about 0.3mA. In most cases you should try the simple voltage divider and only move to an active buffer if it doesn't work.

This very basic look at electronics isn't all that you need to know, but it is enough for you to see some of the problems and find some answers. In general, this sort of electronics is all about making sure that voltages and currents are within limits. As switching speeds increase you have additional problems, which are mainly concerned with making sure that your circuits aren't slowing things down. This is where things get more subtle.

Summary

- You can get a long way with only a small understanding of electronics, but you do need to know enough to protect the ESP32 and things you connect to it.

- The maximum current from any GPIO line should be less than 40mA.

- All of the GPIO lines work at 3.3V and you should avoid directly connecting any other voltage.

- You can drive an LED directly from a GPIO line.

- Calculating a current-limiting resistor always follows the same steps: find the current in the device, find the voltage across the device and work out the resistor that supplies that current when the remainder of the voltage is applied to it.

- For any load you connect to a GPIO output, you generally need a current-limiting resistor.

- In many cases you need a transistor, a BJT, to increase the current supplied by the GPIO line.

- To use a BJT you need a current-limiting resistor in the base and generally one in the collector.

- MOSFETs are popular alternatives to BJTs, but it is difficult to find a MOSFET that works reliably at 3.3V.

- GPIO output lines can be set to active push-pull mode, where a transistor is used to pull the line high or low, or passive pull-up or pull-down mode, where one transistor is used and a resistor pulls the line high or low when the transistor is inactive.

- GPIO lines have built-in pull-up and pull-down resistors which can be selected or disabled under software control.

- When used as inputs, GPIO lines have a very high resistance and in most cases you need pull-up or pull-down resistors to stop the line floating.

- The Arduino library can only select the internal pull-up resistor for input and if you need to configure the PAD in more detail you need to use functions from the ESP IDF.

- Mechanical input devices have to be debounced to stop spurious input.

- If you need to connect an input to something bigger than 3.3V then you need a potential divider to reduce the voltage back to 3.3V. You can also use a transistor.

Chapter 6
Simple Input

There is no doubt that input is more difficult than output. When you need to drive a line high or low you are in command of when it happens, but input is in the hands of the outside world. If your program isn't ready to read the input, or if it reads it at the wrong time, then things just don't work. What is worse, you have no idea what your program is doing relative to the event you are trying to capture. Welcome to the world of input.

In this chapter we look at the simplest approach to input – the polling loop. This may be simple, but it is a good way to approach many tasks. In Chapter 7 we'll look at a sophisticated alternative – interrupts.

GPIO Input

GPIO input is a much more difficult problem than output from the point of view of measurement and verification. For output at least you can see the change in the signal on a logic analyzer and know the exact time that it occurred. This makes it possible to track down timing problems and fine tune things with good accuracy.

Input on the other hand is "silent" and unobservable. When did you read the status of the line? Usually the timing of the read is with respect to some other action that the device has taken. For example, you read the input line 20 μs after setting the output line high. But how do you know when the input line changed state during that 20 microseconds? The simple answer is in most cases you don't.

In some applications the times are long and/or unimportant, but in some they are critical and so we need some strategies for monitoring and controlling read events. The usual rule of thumb is to assume that it takes as long to read a GPIO line as it does to set it. This means we can use the delay mechanisms that we looked at with regard to output for input as well.

One common and very useful trick when you are trying to get the timing of input correct is to substitute an output command to a spare GPIO line and monitor it with a logic analyzer. Place the output instruction just before the input instruction and where you see the line change on the logic analyzer should be close to the time that the input would be read in the unmodified program. You can use this to debug and fine-tune and then remove the output statement.

Basic Input Functions

To read the current level of a GPIO line use:

```
digitalRead(pin)
```

which returns an `int` corresponding to the state of the line, `0` if it is low or `1` if it is high. You can also use `HIGH` and `LOW` as constants.

If the PAD is configured for output the function returns the current state of the line.

Once set to input, the GPIO line has high impedance so it won't take very much current, no matter what you connect it to. However, notice that the ESP32 uses 3.3V logic and you should not exceed this value on an input line. For a full discussion of how to work with input, see the previous chapter.

This is all there is to using a GPIO line as an input, apart from the details of the electronics and the small matter of interrupts.

As introduced in the previous chapter, you can also set the internal pull-up resistors with a value around 45kΩ.

The Simple Button

One of the most common input circuits is the switch or button. If you want an external button you can use any GPIO line and the circuit explained in the previous chapter. That is, the switch has to have either a pull-up or pull-down resistor provided by you or a built-in one enabled using software.

The simplest switch input program using an internal pull-up is:

```
void setup() {
  pinMode(2, OUTPUT);
  pinMode(4, INPUT_PULLUP);
}

void loop() {
  if (digitalRead(4)) {
    digitalWrite(2, 1);
  } else {
    digitalWrite(2, 0);
    delay(500);
  }
}
```

As the internal pull-up resistor is used, the switch can be connected to the line and ground without any external resistors:

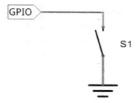

The program simply tests for the line to be pulled high by the switch not being closed and then sets GPIO2 high. If GPIO2 is connected, the on-board LED will light up while it is not pressed. Notice GPIO4 goes low when the switch is pressed.

If you add an external pull-down resistor the way the switch has to be connected becomes:

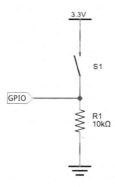

The program still works as long as you change the line

```
pinMode(4, INPUT_PULLUP);
```

to

```
pinMode(4, INPUT);
```

but now GPIO4 is high when the switch is pressed and hence the LED is on when the switch is pressed, which is the behavior that the user most likely expects.

Should you use an internal or external resistor? The answer is that it mostly doesn't matter as long as there is a resistor included in your circuit. So if you use None make sure there is an external resistor. The only problem with using an internal resistor is the possibility that the software fails to set the pull-up/down mode and leaves the input floating. Also notice that this switch input is not debounced. The simplest way to do this is include a time delay in the loop before the line is sampled again.

If you want to respond to a button press, that is a press event and a release event, then you have to test for a double transition:

```
void setup() {
  pinMode(2, OUTPUT);
  pinMode(4, INPUT_PULLUP);
}

void loop() {
  while (digitalRead(4) == 1) {};
  delay(10);
  while (digitalRead(4) == 0) {};
  digitalWrite(2, 1);
  delay(1000);
  digitalWrite(2, 0);
}
```

In this case you really do need the debounce delays if you want to avoid responding twice to what the user perceives as a single press. Notice that this is using a pull-up configuration so the LED comes on for one second if the button is pressed and released. The program works by waiting while the button reads 1, i.e. not pressed, then it waits while the button reads 0, i.e. held. This corresponds to a press and release. Notice that we need a delay between the two while loops to allow the button's signal to settle. Without it the program would turn the LED on when the button was pressed and not wait for the button to be released. The reason is that when you press the button the voltage level will go high, but there will be short duration transients that take the line low again and fool the program into thinking that you have released the button.

A 10-millisecond delay is probably the smallest delay that produces a button-press that feels as if it works. In practice, you would have to tune the delay to suit the button mechanism in use and the number of times you can allow the button to be pressed in one second.

Press or Hold

We can carry on elaborating on how to respond to a button. For example, most users have grown accustomed to the idea that holding a button down for a longer time than a press makes something different happen. To distinguish between a press and a hold all you need to do is time the difference between line down and line up:

```
unsigned long tick_ms(unsigned long offset) {
  return millis() + offset;
}

void setup() {
  pinMode(2, OUTPUT);
  pinMode(4, INPUT_PULLUP);
}

void loop() {
  while (digitalRead(4) == 1) {};
  int t = tick_ms(2000);
  delay(10);
  while (digitalRead(4) == 0) {};
  if (tick_ms(0) < t) {
    digitalWrite(2, 1);
    delay(1000);
    digitalWrite(2, 0);
  } else {
    for (int i = 0; i < 10; i++) {
      digitalWrite(2, 1);
      delay(1000);
      digitalWrite(2, 0);
      delay(1000);
    }
  }
}
```

In this case holding the button for 2 seconds registers a "hold", causing the LED to flash 10 times, and anything less is a "push" and the LED flashes just once. Notice the 10 ms debounce pause between the test for no-press and press. We also make use of a tick_ms function, which is a small modification to the tick_us function given earlier.

One of the problems with all of these sample programs is that they wait for the button to be pressed or held and this makes it difficult for them to do anything else. You have to include whatever else your program needs to do within the loop that waits for the button – the polling loop. You can do this in an ad hoc way, but the best approach is to implement a finite state machine, see later.

How Fast Can We Measure?

Buttons are one form of input, but often we want to read data from a GPIO line driven by an electronic device and decode the data. This usually means measuring the width of the pulses and this raises the question of how fast can we accept input?

The simplest way to find out how quickly we can take a measurement is to perform a pulse width measurement. Applying a square wave to GPIO4 we can measure the time that the pulse is high using:

```
unsigned long tick_us(unsigned long offset) {
    return micros() + offset;
}
void setup() {
    pinMode(4, INPUT);
    Serial.begin(9600);
}
void loop() {
    while (digitalRead(4) == 1) {};
    while (digitalRead(4) == 0) {};
    int t = tick_us(0);
    while (digitalRead(4) == 1) {};
    t = tick_us(0) - t;
    Serial.println(t);
    delay(1000);
}
```

This might look a little strange at first. The while loops are responsible for getting us to the right point in the waveform. First we loop until the line goes low, then we loop until it goes high again and finally measure how long before it goes low. You might think that we simply have to wait for it to go high and then measure how long till it goes low, but this misses the possibility that the signal might be part way through a high period when we first measure it.

If you run this program and apply a square wave of a known frequency to GPIO4 you will see values printed that correspond to the pulse width in microseconds. If you increase the frequency you should see the value change in step until the program cannot keep up with the input when the time suddenly jumps to values that are too large as pulses are missed.

This can be measured down to around 2 μs with poor accuracy after this simply because you are measuring in units of microseconds.

Notice that if you try measuring pulse widths much shorter than the lower limit that works, you will get results that look like longer pulses are being applied. The reason is simply that the ESP32 will miss the first transition to zero, but will detect a second or third or later transition. This is the digital equivalent of the aliasing effect found in the Fourier Transform of general signal processing.

The Finite State Machine

If your project requires a complex set of input and output lines then you need an organizing principle to save you from the complexity. When you first start writing IoT programs that respond to the outside world you quickly discover that all of your programs take a similar form:

```
while(True):
    wait for some input lines
    process the input data
    write some output lines
    wait for some input lines
    read some more input lines
    write some output lines
```

For most programmers this is a slightly disturbing discovery because programs are not supposed to consist of infinite loops, but IoT programs nearly always, in principle if not in practice, take the form of an apparently infinite polling loop. A second, and more important, aspect is that the way in which reading and writing GPIO lines is related can be so complex that it can be difficult to see exactly when any particular line is read and when it is written.

It is natural to try to find implementations that make this simpler. In most cases programmers discover or invent the idea of the event or, better, the interrupt. In this case when something happens in the outside world a function is automatically called to deal with it and the relation between the external state and the system's response is seemingly well-defined. Of course, in practice it isn't, as you have to deal with what happens when multiple events or interrupts occur at the same, or very nearly the same, time.

Often more sophisticated approaches are used to try and handle more external changes of state in a given time. Somehow the infinite polling loop is seen as wasteful. What is the CPU doing if it spends all its time looping round waiting for something to happen? Of course, if it has nothing better to do then it isn't a waste. In fact, IoT devices are often dedicated to just getting one job done so the "polling is wasteful" meme, so prevalent in the rest of computing, is completely unjustified.

What is more, the polling loop is usually the way to get the greatest throughput. If a processor can handle X external state changes per second and respond to these with Y external state changes per second, then moving to an event- or interrupt-based implementation reduces both X and Y. In short, if a processor cannot do the job using a polling loop then it cannot do the job. This is not to say that there aren't advantages to events and interrupts – there are, but they don't increase throughput.

So how should you organize a polling loop so that what it does is self-evident by looking at the code? There are many answers to this according to the system being implemented and there are no "pure" theoretical answers that solve all problems, but the finite state machine, or FSM, is a model that every IoT programmer should know.

A finite state machine is a very simple program. At any given time the machine/program has a record of the current state, S. At a regular interval the external world provides an input, I, which changes the state from S to S' and produces an output O. That's all there is to a finite state machine. There are variations on the definition of the FSM but this one, called a Mealy machine because its outputs depend on both its state and the input, is the most suitable for IoT programming.

You can design an FSM with the help of a diagram. In the FSM shown there are three states 1, 2 and 3 and, if you are in state 1, an input of A moves the system to state 2 and an input of B moves it into state 3.

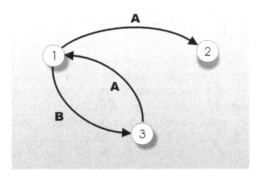

Your program simply needs to take the form of a polling loop that implements a finite state machine. It reads the input lines as I and uses this and the current state S to determine the new state S' and the output O. There is some overhead in using this organization, but it is usually worth it. Notice that this organization implies that you read input once, make changes once and set outputs once in the loop. If you fix the time that the polling loop takes then you know the characteristic time for any changes to the system.

FSM Button

As an example, let's implement the simple button given earlier in the chapter. The first version used multiple loops to wait for changes in the state of the input line.

The finite state version uses only a single polling loop:

```
unsigned long tick_us(unsigned long offset) {
  return micros() + offset;
}
void delay_until(unsigned long t) {
  do {
  } while (t > micros());
}

void setup() {
  pinMode(4, INPUT_PULLUP);
  Serial.begin(9600);
}

unsigned long t;
int s = 0;
int i;
int count = 0;
void loop() {
  i = digitalRead(4);
  t = tick_us(100 * 1000);
  switch (s) {
    case 0:  //button not pushed
      if (!i) {
        s = 1;
        count++;
        Serial.print("Button Push ");
        Serial.println(count);
      }
      break;
    case 1:  //Button pushed
      if (i) {
        s = 0;
      }
      break;
    default:
      s = 0;
  }
  delay_until(t);
}
```

This looks more complicated than the original, and there are more lines of code, but it is much easier to extend to more complex situations. In this case we have only two states, s = 0 for button not pushed and s = 1 for button pushed. Ideally, the states that we use shouldn't refer to inputs or outputs, but to the overall state of the system. For example, if you were using a ESP32 to control a nuclear reactor you might use a state "CoreMeltdown" in preference to "TempSensorOverLimit". States should be about the consequence of the inputs and the outputs should be the consequence of the current state. In the example above the inputs and output are too simple to give rise to an abstract concept of "state". Even if you were to change the state labels to "LEDOn" or "LEDOff" they are directly related to the state of a single output line.

The key idea, however, is that the states indicate the state of the system at the time of the input. That is, s = 0 (button not pushed) is the state when the system reads in a high on the GPIO line (recall the line is pulled high so pushing the button makes it go low). You can see at the start of the polling loop we read the input line and store its value in the variable i. Next, a case statement is used to process the input depending on the current state. You can see that if s = 0, i.e. button not pushed, then the state moves to s = 1, i.e. button pushed, and a message is printed giving the number of times the button has been pressed as a simple action. In general, the action could be setting a GPIO line high or doing anything that is appropriate for the new state. Notice that actions occur on state changes.

If the state is in s = 1, i.e. button pushed, then the input has to be 1 for anything to happen. In this case the state changes to s = 0 and any actions that are needed to take the system from state 1 to state 0 are performed, none in this case. Finally, if the state is anything other than 0 or 1, we set it to 0 as something is wrong.

Notice that the polling loop is set up so that the whole thing repeats every 100ms. The time is taken at the start of the loop and after everything has been processed we wait for 100ms to be up. What this means is that, no matter how long the processing in the loop takes, as long as it takes less than 100ms, the loop will repeat every 100ms.

This is a very simple finite state machine polling loop. In practice, there is usually a set of ifs that deals with each current state, but there is often another set of if statements within each state case to deal with what happens according to different inputs. An alternative way of designing a finite state machine loop is to use a lookup table, indexed by state and input, which gives you the new state and the actions.

FSM Hold Button

As a slightly more complicated example of using the FSM approach, let's implement a button with hold. You might think that a button with hold has three states – button not pushed, button pushed and button held. You can implement it in this way, but there is an argument that there are still only two states – not pushed and pushed. The held state is better implemented as extra input data to the state, i.e. the time the button has been in the pressed state. Remember, the output of a FSM depends on the state and the input and in this case the input is the line level and the time pressed:

```
unsigned long tick_us(unsigned long offset) {
  return micros() + offset;
}
void delay_until(unsigned long t) {
  do {
  } while (t > micros());
}
void setup() {
  pinMode(4, INPUT_PULLUP);
  Serial.begin(9600);
}
unsigned long t, tpush, twait;
int s = 0;
int i;
void loop() {
  i = digitalRead(4);
  t = tick_us(0);
  switch (s) {
    case 0:  //button not pushed
      if (!i) {
        s = 1;
        tpush = t;
      }
      break;
    case 1:  //Button pushed
      if (i) {
        s = 0;
        if ((t - tpush) > 2000000) {
          Serial.println("Button held");
        } else {
          Serial.println("Button pushed");
        }
      }
      break;
    default:
      s = 0;
  }
  delay_until(t + 100 * 1000);
}
```

It is clear that you can't know the time the button has been pressed until it is released, so the actions are now all in the button-pushed state. While the button is in the pushed state it can be released and we can compute the time it has been pressed and modify the action accordingly.

FSM Ring Counter

Another very common input configuration is the ring counter. A ring counter moves on to a new output each time it receives an input and repeats when it reaches the last output of the set. For example, if you have three output lines connected to three LEDs, then initially LED 0 is on, when the user presses the button, LED 1 is on and the rest off, the next user press moves on to LED 2 on and another press turns LED 0 on. You can see that as the user keeps pressing the button the LEDs go on and off in a repeating sequence.

A common implementation of a ring counter has a state for each button press and release for each LED being on. For three LEDs this means six states and this has a number of disadvantages. A better idea is to have just two states, button pressed and button released and use a press counter as an additional input value. This means that what happens when you enter the button-pressed state depends on the value in the counter.

We also change from using the measurement of the button as pressed or released and move to considering an "edge" signal. Generally we need inputs that indicate an event localized in time. Button "pressed" and button "released" are events that are extended in time but "press" and "release" are localized to small time intervals that can be thought of as single time measurements. In general we prefer "edge" signals because these indicate when something has changed.

Implementing this is fairly easy:

```
unsigned long tick_us(unsigned long offset) {
    return micros() + offset;
}
void delay_until(unsigned long t) {
    do {
    } while (t > micros());
}

unsigned long t;
int edge;
int buttonNow, buttonState;
int s = 0;
```

```
void setup() {
  pinMode(4, INPUT_PULLUP);
  buttonState = digitalRead(4);
  pinMode(1, OUTPUT);
  pinMode(2, OUTPUT);
  pinMode(3, OUTPUT);
  digitalWrite(1, 1);
  digitalWrite(2, 0);
  digitalWrite(3, 0);
  Serial.begin(9600);
}

void loop() {
  buttonNow = digitalRead(4);
  t = tick_us(0);
  edge = buttonNow-buttonState;
  buttonState = buttonNow;
  switch (s) {
    case 0:
      if (edge == 1) {
        s = 1;
        digitalWrite(1, 0);
        digitalWrite(2, 1);
        digitalWrite(3, 0);
      }
      break;
    case 1:
      if (edge == 1) {
        s = 2;
        digitalWrite(1, 0);
        digitalWrite(2, 0);
        digitalWrite(3, 1);
      }
      break;
    case 2:
      if (edge == 1) {
        s = 0;
        digitalWrite(1, 1);
        digitalWrite(2, 0);
        digitalWrite(3, 0);
      }
      break;
    default:
      s = 0;
  }
  delay_until(t + 100 * 1000);
}
```

First we set up the GPIO lines for input and output and set the outputs so that LED 0 is on, i.e. s = 0. Next we start the polling loop. Inside the loop there is a switch statement that manages three states. At the start of the loop the difference between the current button value and its previous value are used to calculate edge, which is 1 only when the button has changed from pressed, 0, to released, 1. That is, edge = 1 only on a up-going edge. If the button has just been pressed then the state is moved on to the next state, 0→1, 1→2 and 2→0, and the LEDs are set to the appropriate values.

You might wonder why all three LEDs are set and not just the two that are changing? There are a number of reasons including that it is easier to see what is happening from the code and it makes sure that all of the LEDs are in the state you intend. Notice that the polling loop is set up to repeat every 100ms so providing debouncing and a predictable service time. If you try this out you will find that the LEDs light up sequentially on each button press.

Like many more advanced methods, the FSM approach can make things seem more complicated in simple examples, but it repays the effort as soon as things get more complicated. A polling loop with tens of states and lots of input and outline lines to manage becomes impossible to maintain without some organizing principle.

Summary

- Input is hard because things happen at any time, irrespective of what your program might be doing.

- You can call the `digitalRead` function any time to discover the state of a GPIO line – the problem is when and how often to call it.

- You can choose between external or internal pull-up/down resistors.

- Mechanical input devices such as buttons have to be debounced.

- The power of software is that it can enhance a simple device. A simple button is either pushed or released, but you can use this to generate a third "held" state.

- Using a polling loop you can handle inputs as short as a few tens of microseconds.

- Most IoT programs are best written as a polling loop and the Arduino library makes this the default.

- The Finite State Machine (FSM) is one way of organizing a complex polling loop so that inputs are tested and outputs are set once for each time through the loop.

- Ideally the states of a FSM should not be simple statements of the inputs or outputs that determine the state, but for simple systems this can be difficult to achieve.

- It can be difficult to work out what constitutes the events of a FSM. Ideally they should be localized in time so that they indicate the moment that something happens.

Chapter 7

Advanced Input - Interrupts

When you start to work with multiple inputs that mean a range of different things, input really becomes a challenge. You can control much of the complexity using finite state machines and similar organizational principles, but sooner or later you are going to have to deal with the problem of input when your program isn't ready for it. Sudden urgent unexpected input is the most difficult to deal with and when in this situation it is natural to think of the interrupt because this is the essence of urgency. However, things are much more complicated than they seem at first and so we need to consider when and where it is appropriate to give up polling for an event and change to responding to an interrupt.

Interrupts Considered Harmful?

An interrupt is a hardware mechanism that stops the computer doing whatever it is currently doing and makes it transfer its attention to running an interrupt handler. You can think of an interrupt as an event flag that, when set, interrupts the current program to run the assigned interrupt handler. Using interrupts means the outside world decides when the computer should pay attention to input and there is no need for a polling loop. When the interrupt handler is finished the processor returns to what it was doing before the interrupt occurred. This means that the processor's state has to be saved when the interrupt happens and restored when the interrupt handler returns. The need to save and restore the state is the main overhead of using an interrupt.

Most hardware people think that interrupts are the solution to everything and polling is inelegant and only to be used when you can't use an interrupt. This is far from the reality. There is a general feeling that real-time programming and interrupts go together and if you are not using an interrupt you are probably doing something wrong. In fact, the truth is that if you are using an interrupt you are probably doing something wrong. So much so that some organizations are convinced that interrupts are so dangerous that they are banned from being used at all.

Interrupts are only really useful when you have a low-frequency condition that needs to be dealt with on a high-priority basis. The reason is that polling for an event that rarely occurs is a time waster and treating the rare event using an interrupt makes reasonable sense. Interrupts can simplify the logic of your program, but rarely does using an interrupt speed things up because the overhead involved in interrupt handling is usually quite high. If you have a polling loop that takes 100ms to poll all inputs and there is an input that demands attention in under 60ms,., then clearly the polling loop is not going to be good enough. Using an interrupt allows the high-priority event to interrupt the polling loop and be processed in less than 100ms. However, if this happens very often the polling loop will cease to work as intended. An alternative is to simply make the polling loop check the input twice per loop.

For a more real-world example, suppose you want to react to a doorbell push button. You could write a polling loop that simply checks the button status repeatedly and forever, or you could write an interrupt service routine (ISR) to respond to the doorbell. The processor would be free to get on with other things until the doorbell was pushed when it would stop what it was doing and transfer its attention to the ISR.

How good a design this is depends on how much the doorbell has to interact with the rest of the program and how many doorbell pushes you are expecting. It takes time to respond to the doorbell push and then the ISR has to run to completion - what is going to happen if another doorbell push happens while the first push is still being processed? Some processors have provision for forming a queue of interrupts, but that doesn't help with the fact that the process can only handle one interrupt at a time. Of course, the same is true of a polling loop, but if you can't handle the throughput of events with a polling loop, you can't handle it using an interrupt either, because interrupts add the time to transfer to the ISR and back again.

Finally, before you dismiss the idea of having a processor do nothing but ask repeatedly "is the doorbell pressed", consider what else it has to do. If the answer is "not much" then a polling loop might well be your simplest option. Also, if the processor has multiple cores, then the fastest way of dealing with any external event is to use one of the cores in a fast polling loop. This can be considered to be a software emulation of a hardware interrupt – not to be confused with a software interrupt or trap, which is a hardware interrupt triggered by software.

If you are going to use interrupts to service input then a good design is to use the interrupt handler to feed an event queue. This at least lowers the chance that input will be missed.

Despite their attraction, interrupts are usually a poor choice for anything other than low-frequency events that need to be dealt with quickly.

ESP32 Interrupts

The Arduino library makes the ESP32 interrupt handling much simpler, but this also means there are things you can do with the ESP IDF that you cannot do with the Arduino library. It is worth knowing a little about the underlying interrupt mechanisms.

The ESP32 supports 32 distinct interrupts, but only 26 can be associated with GPIO lines – the others are used internally or for timers. The ESP32 uses a flexible system where the interrupt hardware isn't enough to provide one interrupt per each possible interrupt source. This means that the 32 interrupts, each with a fixed priority, have to be shared among the sources and this in turn means you have to allocate an interrupt to a source.

In general, interrupts can be shared between multiple interrupt sources, but in this case interrupts can only be level-based. Edge-triggered interrupts cannot be shared. However, GPIO lines have software that makes it look as if they can. That is, GPIO lines use software to go beyond what you might expect from the raw hardware.

There is also the issue of dealing with more than two cores. By default, the interrupt functions register and work with the core that they are running on. This means we can more or less ignore the issue as long as we don't explicitly register an interrupt with a particular core. In this chapter all interrupts are set by tasks running on the App core and are serviced by tasks running on the App core.

Arduino Interrupts

The Arduino library hides all of this complication from you, but at the cost of only being able to use interrupts generated by GPIO lines. That is, you cannot handle a general interrupt using the Arduino library and you cannot do things like allocate shared interrupts or set which core the interrupt will be handled on. Notice that other parts of the library may provide interrupt handlers for specific peripherals as onEvent functions. For example, the I2C class has a:

```
Wire.onReceive(handler)
```

method which sets up an an interrupt handler called when data is received. These are described in later chapters.

To setup a GPIO interrupt you use:

```
attachInterrupt(digitalPinToInterrupt(pin), ISR, mode)
```

where `ISR` is the interrupt service routine, a function, that you want to use and `mode` is one of:

- ◆ `LOW` to trigger the interrupt whenever the pin is low,
- ◆ `CHANGE` to trigger the interrupt whenever the pin changes value
- ◆ `RISING` to trigger when the pin goes from low to high,
- ◆ `FALLING` for when the pin goes from high to low.

In most cases edge events are the most useful.

The `ISR` is a function with the signature:

```
void IRS(void)
```

If you want to stop handling an interrupt you can use:

```
detachInterrupt(digitalPinToInterrupt(pin))
```

You can also stop all interrupts and restart them using:

```
noInterrupts()
```

and

```
interrupts()
```

Stopping all interrupts is a good idea if you have a section of code that is time critical and should not be interrupted, but you need to turn them back on as quickly as possible to restore the normal working of the system. The WiFi uses interrupts to keep it running and so do the timing functions `delay()`, `micros()` and `millis()`. Long running ISRs stop the system from working. Notice that interrupts are on while the ISR is running unless you explicitly turn them off.

ISRs run in the same memory space as the rest of the program and therefore share all global variables with the rest of the program and these are used to transfer data. If you want to share a variable with an ISR then it should be marked as `volatile` to stop the compiler from optimizing access to it by loading its value into a register.

The simplest example of this is when you enable only one GPIO line as an interrupt source:

```
void ISR(void){
 digitalWrite(2, !digitalRead(2));
}
void setup() {
  pinMode(2, OUTPUT);
  pinMode(4, INPUT_PULLUP);
  attachInterrupt(digitalPinToInterrupt(4), ISR, CHANGE);
}

void loop() {}
```

This simple example sets up GPIO2 as an output and GPIO4 as an input with an edge-triggered interrupt. The ISR function simply toggles the state of GPIO2. If you run the program and apply a pulse train to GPIO4 you will see a copy of the pulse train output on GPIO2 with a phase that depends on the initial state of GPIO2.

IRAM

Another consideration is where the ISR is running. The ESP32 has flash memory which is used to hold the program code, but flash memory is slow and so there is a cache to speed things up. The problem is that ISRs need to be fast and there is always the possibility that the appropriate ISR isn't in the cache when an interrupt occurs and has to be loaded from flash. The ESP32 has typically 200Kbytes of fast instruction RAM (IRAM).

You can ask for any function to be stored in IRAM using the IRAM_ATTR macro:

```
void IRAM_ATTR ISR(void)
```

This not only speeds things up a little, it also means that there aren't problems with the function if the cache is disabled, due to a Flash write for example.

It is general advice that ISRs should be placed in IRAM, but this brings with it some complications. In principle, any function in IRAM should use Data RAM (DRAM) for its constant data and strings:

```
const static DRAM_ATTR uint8_t INDEX_DATA[] = { 45, 33, 12, 0 };
const static char *MSG = DRAM_STR("I am a string stored in RAM");
```

In practice, the increase in speed is negligible, undetectable even, unless there is something strange about the way the cache is used. It also means that your program is now ESP32 specific.

Multiple Interrupts

You can configure and enable interrupts on multiple GPIO lines – the problem is knowing which one caused the interrupt. For example, consider the following modification to the previous main program:

```
void IRAM_ATTR ISR(void) {
  digitalWrite(2, !digitalRead(2));
}
void setup() {
  pinMode(2, OUTPUT);
  pinMode(4, INPUT_PULLUP);
  attachInterrupt(digitalPinToInterrupt(4), ISR, CHANGE);
  pinMode(5, INPUT_PULLUP);
  attachInterrupt(digitalPinToInterrupt(5), ISR, CHANGE);
}
void loop() {}
```

If you try this out you will find that now GPIO 2 is toggled in response to rising or falling edges on GPIO 4 or GPIO 16. In this case we don't care which GPIO line caused the interrupt as the action of the ISR is the same.

The problem with using the same ISR for different interrupts is that you cannot find out which GPIO line caused the interrupt. The usual solution is to provide a separate ISR for each interrupt but sometimes this is inefficient as what is to happen is largely the same. The hardware records the source of the interrupt in the interrupt status register. Unfortunately you cannot use this with the Arduino interrupt handling because it is cleared before the ISR is called.

How Fast Is An Interrupt?

You can estimate the fastest repeat rate that an interrupt handler can deal with by simply measuring the delay between the interrupt occurring and the first response to it. For example, in our earlier program the ISR function simply toggled the state of GPIO 2. We can easily measure the time difference between the edge applied to GPIO 4 and how long it takes before GPIO changes state:

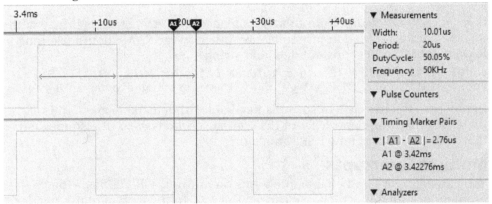

You can see that the response time, latency, is roughly 2.5μs for the ESP32-S3 and about 3μs for the ESP32. This isn't the raw interrupt response time because it includes the time to toggle the GPIO output, but the work involved is so minimal as to represent the smallest task an interrupt routine could carry out. Given the interrupt routine takes at least 3μs to complete, it clearly cannot respond again during this time and this makes the maximum repeat rate greater than 3μs. Experimentally the ISR misses pulses soon after 70kHz or 7μs which is roughly the largest repeat rate for ISRs that do very little work. In practice, the maximum repeat rate is likely to be much less. Note that if an interrupt occurs during an interrupt then it is simply lost – there is no default interrupt queue.

Measuring Pulse Width

In Chapter 6 we saw how to use polling to measure pulse widths. You can do the same job with interrupts – simply detect a rising and then a falling edge. In general, it is nearly always a good idea to get the ISR to set the value of a few state variables and then return as soon as possible. This approach reduces the ISR to a minimum and makes the program work faster and more reliably, for example:

```
volatile unsigned long t = 0;
volatile int state = 0;
unsigned long tick_us(unsigned long offset) {
  return micros() + offset;
}
void ISR(void) {
  t = tick_us(-t);
  state++;
  digitalWrite(2, !digitalRead(2));
}
void setup() {
  pinMode(2, OUTPUT);
  pinMode(4, INPUT);
  attachInterrupt(digitalPinToInterrupt(4), ISR, CHANGE);
  Serial.begin(9600);
}
void loop() {
  while (state != 2) {};
  detachInterrupt(digitalPinToInterrupt(4));
  Serial.print(t);
  Serial.print("   ");
  Serial.println(state);
  state = 0;
  t = 0;
  delay(1000);
  attachInterrupt(digitalPinToInterrupt(4), ISR, CHANGE);
}
```

The main program simply tests the state variable and waits for state to equal 2. This means that the interrupt routine has been called twice – the first time it records the time and the second time it records the time difference. Following this the interrupt is disabled, the result printed and then enabled after a one-second pause.

If you try this out, you will find that the pulse measurements are reasonably accurate down to $10\mu s$, after which the system locks up and nothing more is printed. Once the system locks up in this way reducing the pulse rate doesn't allow it to recover. That is if interrupts are happening too fast then the ISR might not complete before it has to service another interrupt and this puts the ESP32 into an unstable state. This might be fixed in future editions of the Arduino library as it doesn't happen using the ESP IDF.

Race Conditions and Starvation

Implementing an ISR is a step into the complex world of asynchronous programs and if this is something of interest see *Applying C for the IoT Under Linux and POSIX*, ISBN:978-1871962611. The biggest new problem that asynchronicity introduces is the possibility of race conditions. A race condition occurs when two sections of code modify a shared resource in such an uncontrolled way that the final outcome depends on the timing of the code execution. Race conditions are particularly difficult to debug because they look random and the tendency is to think that they are due to faulty hardware and, worse, an intermittent fault.

It is difficult to provide a clear and simple example of a race condition for the ESP32 because real time programming is inherently difficult to test. Consider the problem of setting a char array to either all ones or all zeros. In an ideal world this data structure would always be in either one of the two states – the setting would be atomic and not interruptible. The following program uses an interrupt on GPIO4 to set a byte array to all zeros and a while loop in the main program to set it to all ones:

```
volatile char data[3];
void ISR(void) {
   for (int i = 0; i < 3; i++) data[i] = 'A';
}
void setup() {
   pinMode(4, INPUT);
   attachInterrupt(digitalPinToInterrupt(4), ISR, CHANGE);
   Serial.begin(9600);
}
void loop() {
   for (int i = 0; i < 3; i++) data[i] = 'B';
   if (data[0] != data[1] || data[1] != data[2]
       || data[2] != data[0]) {
     Serial.print(data[0]);
     Serial.print(data[1]);
     Serial.println(data[2]);
   }
}
```

If you run this program you will discover that the byte array is often in a state that is a mix of the two states with values at A and B. This occurs frequently, even with interrupts occurring at ten per second. What happens is that the for loop starts to set the byte array to all As a byte at a time. If an interrupt occurs during this process then the bytes affected are set to Bs and when the loop restarts only the remaining bytes are set to ones. Small changes to the way that the program is organized can alter the rate of race conditions occurring.

For example, changing the `for` loop for a direct assignment:

`data[0] = 'A';data[1] = 'A';data[2] = 'A';`

virtually eliminates the errors because of the small time between each assignment – but they still happen.

The point is that while interrupt routines share the data that is in scope for other functions in the program, they access them asynchronously and as such things are more complicated than you might expect.

If you don't want the array to be in an inconsistent state then you need to disable the ISR while the loop is using it:

```
void loop() {
  detachInterrupt(digitalPinToInterrupt(4));
  for (int i = 0; i < 3; i++) data[i] = 'B';
  if (data[0] != data[1] || data[1] != data[2]
                         || data[2] != data[0]) {
    Serial.print(data[0]);
    Serial.print(data[1]);
    Serial.println(data[2]);
  }
  attachInterrupt(digitalPinToInterrupt(4), ISR, CHANGE);
}
```

This now works and you never see an inconsistent state for the byte array but now the ISR hardly ever gets to run.

This is an example of "starvation" where one process hogs the CPU for so much of the time that other processes fail to make much progress. In this case it is the ISR that is slowed down but a CPU-hogging ISR can slow the main program down in exactly the same way.

In practice you could also use a lock to stop asynchronous access to any shared resource, but in this case the problem is what the interrupt routine should do when it finds access to the shared resource blocked – it can't just wait because that would cause deadlock.

The solution to the problem is to arrange to use resources that can be safely used in a lock free way – but this is hard to achieve.

Timers

A very common use of interrupts is to run a function after a delay or run one regularly, every so often. The ESP32 typically has four hardware timers that can be used to do just this. The General Purpose Timer, GPTimer, is very flexible and easy to understand once you have seen a simple example. It can be used as a timer and generate events or interrupts on a one-shot or periodic basis. Depending on the ESP32 you are using you can have two or four timers, but their use is identical. Also note that, in general, the Arduino library does not support timers – this is ESP32-specific.

Each timer is controlled by a hw_timer_t struct which you create using:

```
hw_timer_t * timerBegin(uint32_t frequency)
```

where frequency in Hz sets the rate that the timer "ticks" at. If the initialization worked the function returns a pointer to a hw_timer_t struct. This also starts the timer counting. If there aren't any free timers then you will see the error message:

```
gptimer: gptimer_register_to_group(75): no free timer
```

Not all frequencies can be set using the hardware. You can find the actual resolution using:

```
uint16_t timerGetFrequency(hw_timer_t * timer)
```

There are two functions which start, stop and restart the timer:

```
void timerStart(hw_timer_t * timer)
void timerStop(hw_timer_t * timer)
void timerRestart(hw_timer_t * timer)
```

The start function clears the timer and starts it counting if it has been stopped. The restart function simply clears the count but doesn't restart the count if it has been stopped.

You can set or get the current count using:

```
void timerWrite(hw_timer_t * timer, uint64_t val)
uint64_t timerRead(hw_timer_t * timer)
```

You can also read the time in more convenient time units

When you have finished with a timer it should be deleted with:

```
void timerEnd(hw_timer_t * timer)
```

This is all you need to know to use a timer to perform a count:

```
hw_timer_t *timer;
uint64_t count;
void setup() {
  timer = timerBegin(1221);
  Serial.begin(9600);
}
void loop() {
  do {
    count = timerRead(timer);
  } while (count < 1000);
  timerStop(timer);
  Serial.println(count);
  timerStart(timer);
}
```

The timer is set up with the lowest resolution, 1221Hz, and after starting it, count is monitored until it reaches 1000 when the program stops the timer, prints it and then starts the timer again.

A Microsecond Timer

As an example of using the timers we can construct a replacement for the tick_us function given earlier using a timer:

```
hw_timer_t *timer;
hw_timer_t *tick_us_start(void) {
  return timerBegin(1000000);
}
int64_t tick_us(hw_timer_t *timer, int64_t offset) {
  return timerRead(timer) + offset;
}
void setup() {
  timer = tick_us_start();
  Serial.begin(9600);
}
void loop() {
  int64_t tick = tick_us(timer, 1000000);
  while (tick_us(timer, 0) < tick) {};
  Serial.println(tick_us(timer, 0));
}
```

The tick_us_start function sets the timer up and starts it running. It returns a pointer to the timer struct which has to be used in calls to the tick_us function. This simply returns the number of ticks adding in the offset. The main program uses both functions to create a one-second delay and then prints the current count.

The advantage of this method is that it is fast and simple. The disadvantage is that you have to remember to start the timer and there is the possibility that no timer will be available. A function to disable and delete the timer is also a good idea for a production program.

Alarms

The timer can also act as an alarm – triggering when the count limit is reached. The alarm can be set up as a one-shot or a periodic alarm. To turn a counting timer into an alarm you use:

```
void timerAlarm(hw_timer_t *timer, uint64_t alarm_value,
                bool autoreload, uint64_t reload_count);
```

where:

- ◆ alarm_value   Alarm target count value
- ◆ reload_count   Alarm reload count value
- ◆ freload_count   true or false

To register a callback when the alarm is raised use:

```
void timerAttachInterruptArg(hw_timer_t * timer,
            void (*userFunc)(void*), void * arg);
```

where userFunc is set to ISR to be used as the callback and arg is a pointer to an argument that is passed to the ISR.

The callback has the same general form of an ISR with some additional details:

```
void ISR(void* user_data)
```

You can remove a callback using:

```
void timerDetachInterrupt(hw_timer_t *timer);
```

As an example, this program toggles a GPIO line about once per second:

```
hw_timer_t* timer;

void ISR(void* user_data) {
  digitalWrite(2, !digitalRead(2));
}

void setup() {
  pinMode(2, OUTPUT);
  timer = timerBegin(1221);
  timerAlarm(timer, 1000, true, 0);
  timerAttachInterruptArg(timer, ISR, NULL);
}

void loop() {
}
```

It is important to remember that the timer callback is an interrupt service routine and it is subject to all of the same problems.

Responding to Input

This look at methods of dealing with the problems of input isn't exhaustive, there are always new ways of doing things, but it does cover the most general ways of implementing input. As already mentioned, the problem with input is that you don't know when it is going to happen. What generally matters is speed of response.

For low-frequency inputs, interrupts are worthwhile. They can leave your program free to get on with other tasks and simplify its overall structure. For high-frequency inputs that need to be serviced regularly, a polling loop is still the best option for maximum throughput. How quickly you can respond to an input depends on how long the polling loop is and how many times you test for it per loop.

Given the current problems that the Arduino library has dealing with interrupts that happen too quickly, keeping the repeat interrupt rate slow is even better advice. Notice that at best an interrupt approach to data handling can only make the program better able to handle bursts of data – the program is still limited to processing a maximum average throughput.

Summary

- The ESP32 supports 32 distinct interrupts, but only 26 can be associated with GPIO lines. The others are used internally or for timers.

- The Arduino library simplifies the way interrupts are presented to the programmer and you can only associate a GPIO line with a specific interrupt handler.

- The response time, latency, is roughly $3\mu s$ for GPIO interrupts

- Race conditions can occur if the update of shared resources isn't atomic. You can make an update atomic by disabling interrupts.

- The general-purpose timers are very flexible and can be used to time and generate events or interrupts on a one-shot or periodic basis.

- ISRs need to be carefully crafted to get the best out of the system and are subject to a number of restrictions.

- You can set alarms to run functions at set intervals.

Chapter 8

Pulse Width Modulation

One way around the problem of getting a fast response from a microcontroller is to move the problem away from the processor. In the case of the ESP32 there are some built-in devices that can use GPIO lines to implement protocols without the CPU being involved. In this chapter we take a close look at the use of Pulse Width Modulation (PWM) including generating sound, driving LEDs and servos.

When performing their most basic function, i.e. output, the GPIO lines can be set high or low by the processor. How fast they can be set high or low depends on the speed of the processor.

Using the GPIO line in its Pulse Width Modulation (PWM) mode you can generate pulse trains up to 40 MHz. The reason for the increase in speed is that the GPIO is connected to a pulse generator and, once set to generate pulses of a specific type, the pulse generator just gets on with it without needing any intervention from the GPIO line or the processor. In fact, the pulse output will continue after your program has ended. Of course, even though the PWM line can generate very fast pulses, usually what you want to do is change the nature of the pulses and this is a slower process involving the processor.

In this chapter we look at the LEDC hardware which is designed to provide PWM to specifically drive LEDs – however it is more generally useful as a PWM generator.

Some Basic PWM Facts

There are some facts worth getting clear right from the start, although their full significance will only become clear as we progress.

First, what is PWM? The simple answer is that a pulse width modulated signal has pulses that repeat at a fixed rate, say one pulse every millisecond, but the width of the pulse can be changed. There are two basic things to specify about the pulse train that is generated, its repetition rate and the width of each pulse. Usually the repetition rate is set as a simple repeat period and the width of each pulse is specified as a percentage of the repeat period, referred to as the duty cycle. So, for example, a 1ms repeat and a

109

50% duty cycle specifies a 1ms period, which is high for 50% of the time, i.e. a pulse width of 0.5ms. The two extremes are 100% duty cycle, i.e. the line is always high, and 0% duty cycle, i.e. the line is always low.

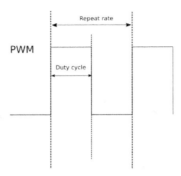

Notice it is the duty cycle that carries the information in PWM and not the frequency. What this means is that, in general, you select a repeat rate and stick to it and what you change as the program runs is the duty cycle.

In many cases PWM is implemented using special PWM-generator hardware that is either built into the processor chip or provided by an external chip. The processor simply sets the repeat rate by writing to a register and then changing the duty cycle by writing to another register. This provides the ideal sort of PWM with no load on the processor and glitch-free operation. You can even buy add-on boards that will provide additional channels of PWM without adding to the load on the processor.

The alternative to dedicated PWM hardware is to implement it in software. You can work out how to do this quite easily. All you need is a timing loop to set the line high at the desired repetition rate and then set it low again according to the duty cycle. You can implement this using either interrupts or a polling loop and in more advanced ways, such as using a DMA (Direct Memory Access) channel.

Arduino Simple DAC

The Arduino library provides a very simple way to generate a PWM signal. The only problem is that the frequency is fixed and all you can alter is the duty cycle:

```
analogWrite(pin, value)
```

where pin is the GPIO line to use and value is the duty cycle specified as a number between 0 and 255 corresponding to 0% and 100%. Obviously to set a duty cycle of d all you have to do is set value to 255*d/100.

For example, for a 50% duty cycle you would set value to 255*50/100=127.5 which is 127 or 128 depending on rounding.

The fixed frequency used depends on the processor, but for the ESP32 it is 1kHz. This is a high enough frequency not to be noticeable when driving an LED or a motor, but for other loads you might need a filter to smooth out the signal.

Controlling an LED

You can also use PWM to generate physical quantities such as the brightness of an LED or the rotation rate of a DC motor. The only differences required by these applications are to do with the voltage and current you need and the way the duty cycle relates to whatever the physical effect is. In other words, if you want to change some effect by 50%, how much do you need to change the duty cycle? For example, how do we "dim" an LED?

The simplest example is to drive the LED using a PWM signal:

```
void setup() {
}

void loop() {
  for (int d = 0; d < 256; d++) {
    analogWrite(2, d);
    delay(10);
  }
}
```

If you try this out you will see the LED slowly increase in brightness, but it seems to be a longer time at maximum brightness than at any other value. This is a consequence of the non-linear relationship between duty cycle and perceived brightness.

By changing the duty cycle of the PWM pulse train you can set the amount of power delivered to an LED, or any other device, and hence change its brightness. If you use a 50% duty cycle, the LED is on 50% of the time and this makes it look as if it is half as bright. However, this is not the end of the story as humans don't respond to physical brightness in a linear way. The Weber-Fechner law gives the general relationship between perceived intensity and physical stimulus as logarithmic.

In the case of an LED, the connection between duty cycle and brightness is a complicated matter, but the simplest approach uses the fact that the perceived brightness is roughly proportional to the cube root of the physical brightness.

The exact equations, published as CIE 1931, are:

$L = 903.3 \cdot (Y / Y_n)$ $\qquad$ $(Y / Y_n) \leq 0.008856$

$L = 116 \cdot (Y / Y_n)^{1/3} - 16$ $\qquad$ $(Y / Y_n) > 0.008856$

where L is the perceived brightness and Y / Y_n is a measure of physical brightness. While the exact relationship is complicated, in most cases a roughly cubic law, obtained by inverting the CIE relationship, can be used:

$d = kb^3$

where b is the perceived brightness and d is the duty cycle. The constant k depends on the LED.

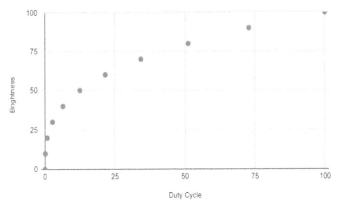

The graph above shows the general characteristic of the relationship for a duty cycle of 0 to 100% on the y-axis and arbitrary, 0 to 100, perceived brightness units on the x-axis.

As the LED, when powered by a PWM signal, is either full on or full off, there is no effect in the change in LED light output with current - the LED is always run at the same current. What all of this means is that if you want an LED to fade in a linear fashion you need to change the duty cycle in a non-linear fashion. Intuitively, it means that changes when the duty cycle is small produce bigger changes in brightness than when the duty cycle is large.

A program to implement cubic dimming can be created by simply changing one line in the previous program:

```
void setup() {
}
void loop() {
  for (int d = 0; d < 256; d++) {
    analogWrite(2, d * d * d / 255 / 255);
    delay(10);
  }
}
```

If you try this out you should notice that the LED changes brightness more evenly across its range.

In most cases it is irrelevant exactly how linear the response of the LED is, a rough approximation looks as smooth to the human eye. You can even get away with using a square law to dim the LED. The only exception is when you are trying to drive LEDs to create a gray-level or color display when color calibration is another level of accuracy.

There is also the question of what frequency we should use. Clearly it has to be fast enough not to be seen as flickering and this generally means it has to be greater than 80Hz, the upper limit for human flicker fusion, but, because of the strobe effect, flickering becomes more visible with moving objects. The faster the LED switches on and off, the less flicker should be visible, but before you select frequencies in the high kHz range it is worth knowing that an LED has a minimum time to turn on and so frequencies at low kHz work best.

If you want to dim something other than the on-board LED, you will often need a driver to increase the brightness. For a simple example, consider connecting a standard LED to the PWM line using the BJT driver circuit introduced in Chapter 5.

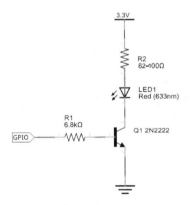

Uses of PWM – Digital to Analog

What sorts of things do you use PWM for? There are lots of very clever uses for PWM. However, there are two applications which account for most PWM applications - voltage or power modulation and signaling to servos.

The amount of power delivered to a device by a pulse train is proportional to the duty cycle. A pulse train that has a 50% duty cycle is delivering current to the load only 50% of the time and this is irrespective of the pulse repetition rate. So the duty cycle controls the power, but the period still matters in many situations because you want to avoid any flashing or other effects. A higher frequency smooths out the power flow at any duty cycle.

If you add a low-pass filter to the output of a PWM signal then what you get is a voltage that is proportional to the duty cycle. This can be looked at in many different ways, but again it is the result of the amount of power delivered by a PWM signal. You can also think of it as using the filter to remove the high-frequency components of the signal, leaving only the slower components due to the modulation of the duty cycle.

How fast you can work depends on the duty cycle resolution. If you work with 8-bit resolution your D-to-A conversion will have 256 steps, which at 3.3V gives a potential resolution of 3.3/256 or about 13mV. This is often good enough. The PWM output in this configuration mimics the workings of a, very slow, 8-bit D-to-A converter.

To demonstrate the sort of approach that you can take to D-to-A conversion, the following program creates a sine wave. To do this we need to compute the duty cycle for 256 points in a complete cycle. We could do this each time a value is needed, but to make the program fast enough we have to compute the entire 256 points and store them in an array. Notice that the ESP32-S2 doesn't have floating-point arithmetic implemented in hardware, but the original ESP32 and the ESP32-S3 do support hardware floating point although it isn't very fast.

The program is:

```
uint8_t wave[256];
void setup() {
  for (int i = 0; i < 256; i++) {
    wave[i] = (uint8_t)((128.0 + sinf((float)i * 2.0 *
                                3.14159 / 255.0) * 128.0));
  }
}

void loop() {
  for (int i = 0; i < 256; i++) {
    analogWrite(2, wave[i]);
    delayMicroseconds(1000);
  }
}
```

The 8-bit duty cycle values needed are computed and stored in the wave array. A for loop is used to set the duty cycle from the array. To make it work we need to perform an update roughly every timer overflow and this is done automatically using the delayMicroseconds. The waveform repeats after around 250ms, which makes the frequency around 4Hz.

To see the analog waveform, we need to put the digital output into a low-pass filter. A simple resistor and capacitor work reasonably well:

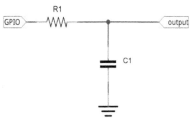

With R1 at 7.5kΩ and C1 at 0.22µF the filter's cutoff is around 100Hz and might be a little on the high side for this low-frequency, 4Hz, output, but it produces a reasonable waveform:

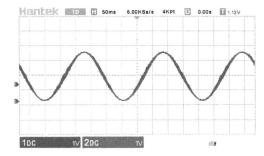

You can use this technique to create a sine wave, or any other waveform you need, but for high-quality audio you need a higher sampling rate. This is also the highest frequency 256 level sine wave that you can produce by this method. To do better we need to increase the PWM frequency so that it can be updated faster.

ESP32 PWM

If you want to modify the frequency of the PWM signal then there is no alternative but to use the ESP32 specific PWM library. To do this it helps to know about the ESP32 PWM hardware.

The ESP32 has two PWM hardware implementations. One, MCPWM, is intended for use in motor control and has extra features such as a dead zone and auto-braking. This is not supported by the Arduino library and if you want to use it then you need to move to the ESP IDF and refer to *Programming the ESP32 in C Using the Espressif IDF*, ISBN:978-1871962918.

The second, LEDC, is specifically designed to drive LEDs with facilities such as auto-dimming plus more exotic features. The Arduino library supports LEDC but not all of its facilities. At the time of writing the Nano ESP32 does not support the LEDC library.

A PWM generator can be assigned to any GPIO pin. The number of PWM generators an ESP32 has depends on its exact model. They come in two groups – fast and slow. The fast type has the auto-dimming features and is able to smoothly change frequency and duty cycle. The slow type lacks these features and it is up to software to change its frequency and duty cycle. Each group also has a set number of timers which determine how many different frequencies can be generated and a given number of channels.

The EP32 has two groups, one fast and one slow, of PWM with eight channels in each group. The ESP32-S2 only has one fast group, but is otherwise identical. The ESP32-C3, which is RISC based, is the same as the ESP32-S2, but with only six channels. All ESP32 devices have four timers in each group, meaning you can set four different frequencies.

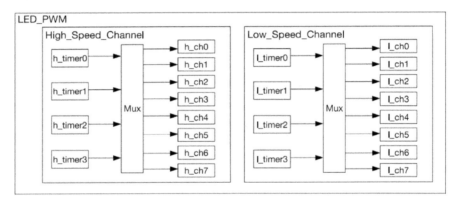

Notice that a single timer can be shared by more than one channel and any timer can be assigned to any channel.

The difference between the high-speed and low-speed channels isn't as important as you might think. Both can work with an 80MHz clock, but the low-speed channels can also work with an 8MHz clock:

APB_CLK	80 MHz	High / Low	
REF_TICK	1 MHz	High / Low	Dynamic Frequency Scaling compatible
RC_FAST_CLK	~ 8 MHz	Low	Dynamic Frequency Scaling compatible, Light sleep compatible

Another difference is that the high-speed channels will change the timer at the end of a count, so generating a glitch-free signal whereas a low-speed channel will change as soon as software instructs it to.

Another difference is that the high-speed channels will change the timer at the end of a count, so generating a glitch-free signal whereas a low-speed channel will change as soon as software instructs it to.

The structure of the hardware is very simple. The timer is simply a 20-bit counter driven from the clock signal reduced in frequency by a divider. The reference pulses from the timer are passed to the channel hardware which has a pair of comparators which trigger when the count reaches set values. The high-level comparator triggers when the count reaches a value and sets the output high and the low-level comparator triggers when the count reaches a second value and sets the output low:

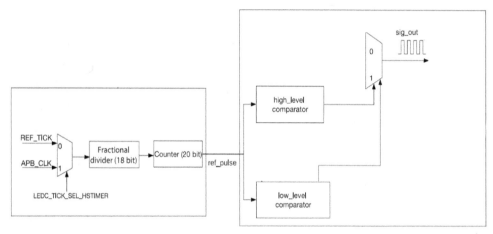

The different ESP32 version support different numbers of PWM channels:

ESP32 SoC	Number of LEDC channels
ESP32	16
ESP32-S2	8
ESP32-S3	8
ESP32-C3	6
ESP32-C6	6
ESP32-H2	6

In principle you can assign any of the four timers to any of the channels but the library makes fixed assignments. For example the ESP32-S3 has timer 0 assigned to channel 0 and 1, timer 1 is assigned to channel 2 and 3 and so on..

What happens is that the timer starts off at zero and counts up to the `hpoint` value when the output goes high. It then carries on counting until it reaches the `lpoint` value when the output is set low. The output remains low until the timer rolls over and the process repeats:

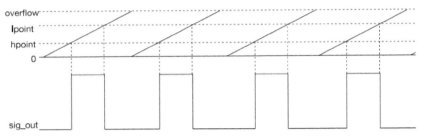

The frequency of the PWM signal is set by the rollover, which depends on the number of bits used in the counter, i.e. between 1 and 20, and the clock frequency. The number of bits used in the counter is related to the resolution with which the duty cycle can be set. For example, if the counter was set to 2 bits the count would be `00`, `01`, `10` and `11` with rollover at `11`. Clearly now you can only set the comparators to the four values which means in theory you could produce a 0%, 50%, 75% or 100% duty cycle.

For this reason the number of bits used in the counter is specified as `duty_resolution` and

$$\text{PWM frequency} = \frac{clock\ frequency}{divider \times 2^{duty\ resolution\ bits}}$$

For example, if the clock frequency is 80MHz and the divider is set to 2 the input pulses to the controller are 40MHz. If the duty resolution is set to 8 bits then 2^8 is 256 and hence the PWM frequency is 156.25kHz and the duty cycle can be set to any of 256 different ratios.

Notice that there is more than one way to obtain a given PWM frequency corresponding to different clock frequencies and duty resolutions. In general, you want to select the clock frequency that gives the highest duty resolution. There is a helper function:

```
duty_res = ledc_find_suitable_duty_resolution(
                              src_clk_freq, timer_freq)
```

which will find the maximum duty cycle resolution for any given clock and PWM frequency.

Duty Cycle and Phase

The software lets you set the duty cycle resolution in terms of the number of bits, the duty cycle as a `count` and hpoint as a `count`. This makes it slightly difficult to see what is going on and in particular why you might want to set `hpoint` at all. Suppose you select `duty_res` to be 8 bits, that makes the timer roll over at 2^8-1 = 255 and if you set `hpoint` to 0 then the output goes high as soon as the timer starts counting. If you set the duty cycle to `127`, then `lpoint`, computed as hpoint+duty cycle is 127. The result is the output goes high at when `count` is `0`, goes low when `count` is `127` and goes high at the rollover after `255`. This is an output with a 50% duty cycle.

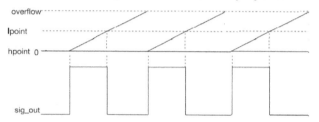

Now consider what happens if you set `hpoint` to `127`. Now when the count starts the output stays low until the count reaches `127`. The `lpoint`, again computed as hpoint+duty cycle is now `127+127`, i.e. `254`, which means the output goes low right at the end of the count, just before the rollover.

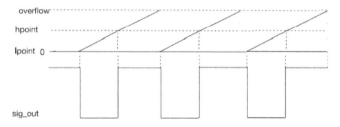

You can see that moving the hpoint has not affected the duty cycle, but has changed where the pulse starts going high. That is, hpoint sets the phase. If you set hpoint too close to the overflow, the `lpoint` that completes the pulse will be in the next clock cycle. That is, the position of `lpoint` is given by:

`lpoint = (duty cycle + hpoint) mod  overflow count`

This means you can change the phase from zero to 360 degrees. Notice that PWM channels always start from a low state and this means if `hpoint` isn't `0` the very first low may be longer than the following pulses. You can see an example of this later.

Setting up the PWM

The LED Control (LEDC) library provides functions to control the LEDC hardware. Setting up a PWM source is much simplified using this library.

First you need to either set the clock source used by all of the LEDC timers – usually you can ignore this and accept the default APB clock:

```
bool ledcSetClockSource(ledc_clk_cfg_t source)
ledc_clk_cfg_t ledcGetClockSource(void)
```

The source can be any of:

- ◆ LEDC_AUTO_CLK   Automatic selection
- ◆ LEDC_USE_APB_CLK   Use APB clock
- ◆ LEDC_USE_RC_FAST_CLK   Select RC_FAST
- ◆ LEDC_USE_XTAL_CLK   Select XTAL_CLK

To create a PWM channel you use:

```
bool ledcAttach(uint8_t pin, uint32_t freq, uint8_t resolution)
```

where

- ◆ pin   GPIO line to use
- ◆ freq   Frequency of the PWM signal
- ◆ resolution   Duty cycle resolution, 1-14 bits or 1-20 bits for ESP32

Not all frequency resolution combinations can be achieved and the function returns false if there is a problem.

The attach selects a timer and a channel for you and you can also associate more than one pin to a channel:

```
bool ledcAttachChannel(uint8_t pin, uint32_t freq,
                       uint8_t resolution, int8_t channel)
```

If you set pin to a channel that has already been configured then the freq and resolution parameters are ignored. Notice that all of the pins connected to the same channel run at the same frequency and have the same duty cycle. Usually it is easier to allow the system to allocate channels to pins, i.e. use ledcAttach rather than ledcAttachChannel.

You can set the frequency of an existing channel associated with a pin using:

```
uint32_t ledcChangeFrequency(uint8_t pin, uint32_t freq,
                                        uint8_t resolution)
```

which also returns the actual frequency set. Notice that frequency and resolution are set per channel and duty cycle is set per pin. A hardware invert can be set per pin using:

```
bool ledcOutputInvert(uint8_t pin, bool out_invert)
```

Removing a pin from a channel is easy:

```
bool ledcDetach(uint8_t pin);
```

Once you have setup a channel you can set the duty cycle by pin or by channel using:

```
bool ledcWrite(uint8_t pin, uint32_t duty)
bool ledcWriteChannel(uint8_t channel, uint32_t duty)
```

You can discover what the frequency or duty of a pin is using;

```
uint32_t ledcReadFreq(uint8_t pin)
uint32_t ledcRead(uint8_t pin)
```

For example the earlier dim an LED program can be written using LEDC as:

```
void setup() {
 ledcAttach(2, 1000, 8);
}
void loop() {
  for (int d = 0; d < 256; d++) {
    ledcWrite(2, d);
      delay(10);
  }
}
```

You can easily generate multiple PWM streams with different duty cycles and even different frequencies. If the frequencies are the same the system tries to use the same timer with the channel. For example:

```
void setup() {
 ledcAttach(2, 1000, 8);
 ledcAttach(4, 1000, 8);
}
void loop() {
  for (int d = 0; d < 256; d++) {
    ledcWrite(2, d);
    ledcWrite(4, 255-d);
    delay(10);
  }
}
```

This generates two same frequency in phase PWM signals with different duty cycles:

Notice that the pulses are in phase i.e. the count starts at the same time.

Things are a little more complicated than this simple example suggests. If you allocate pins to channels then you don't necessarily get pulses that are in phase. It all depends on whether or not the channels share a timer. For example, the ESP32-S3 has four timers, each allocated to consecutive pairs of channels. So, for example:

```
void setup() {
  ledcAttachChannel(2, 1000, 8, 0);
  ledcAttachChannel(4, 1000, 8, 1);
  ledcWrite(2, 200);
  ledcWrite(4, 100);
}
```

produces a pair of same frequency signals in phase with different duty cycles. However:

```
void setup() {
  ledcAttachChannel(2, 1000, 8, 0);
  ledcAttachChannel(4, 1000, 8, 2);
  ledcWrite(2, 200);
  ledcWrite(4, 100);
}
```

produces a pair of same frequency signals with different duty cycles with an arbitrary phase difference:

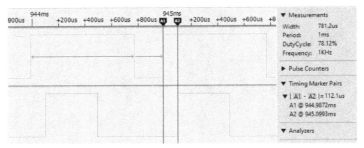

Of course, if you specify different frequencies then the system allocates the channel associated with a different timer.

Finally, you can use a versions of the Arduino PWM commands with some extensions:

- ◆ void analogWrite(uint8_t pin, int value)
  sets the duty cycle of a pin with value 0 to 255
- ◆ void analogWriteResolution(uint8_t pin, uint8_t resolution)
  sets the resolution of the channel associated with the pin
- ◆ void analogWriteFrequency(uint8_t pin, uint32_t freq)
  sets the frequency of the channel associated with the pin

For example, we can change the program to generate a sine wave given earlier to use a LEDC pin without changing any other part of the program. This allows us to set a higher frequency for the PWM output and so increase the frequency of the sine wave. The highest frequency that you can use that provides an eight bit duty cycle resolution is a little more than 156kHz and this makes the time between each pulse 6.4 μs.

```
uint8_t wave[256];

void setup() {
  ledcAttach(2, 150000, 8);
  for (int i = 0; i < 256; i++) {
    wave[i] = (uint8_t)((128.0 +
            sinf((float)i * 2.0 * 3.14159 / 255.0) * 128.0));
  }
}

void loop() {
  for (int i = 0; i < 256; i++) {
    analogWrite(2, wave[i]);
    delayMicroseconds(7);
  }
}
```

Notice that the only line that has changed is the `ledcAttach` which sets the frequency. If you try this out you will find that the sine wave frequency is around 320Hz. If it is passed through a low-pass filter with R1 changed to 110Ω, which gives a cutoff of around 1.5kHz, then the signal is reasonably acceptable:

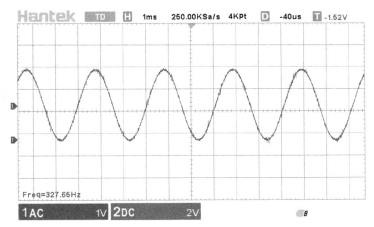

Frequency Modulation

Using PWM to create musical tones, and sound effects in general, is a well-explored area which is too wide to cover in this book. In most cases we choose to vary the duty cycle at a fixed sample rate, but an alternative is to leave the duty cycle fixed at, say, 50% and modulate the frequency. You can use this approach to create simple musical tones and scales.

The Arduino library provides two easy to use functions that generate tones:

- uint32_t ledcWriteTone(uint8_t pin, uint32_t freq)
- uint32_t ledcWriteNote(uint8_t pin, note_t note,
                                     uint8_t octave)

Both produce 50% duty cycle PWM waves with a given frequency. note can be any of:

NOTE_C	NOTE_Cs	NOTE_D	NOTE_Eb	NOTE_E	NOTE_F
NOTE_Fs	NOTE_G	NOTE_Gs	NOTE_A	NOTE_Bb	NOTE_B

Where the suffix s means sharp and b means flat.

As the frequency of middle C is 261.6Hz, to generate middle C you could use:

```
void setup() {
  ledcAttach(2, 10000, 8);
  ledcWriteTone(2, 262);
}

void loop() {
}
```

Notice that you have setup the PWM channel to an arbitrary frequency and resolution before using ledcWriteTone. The resulting output is a square wave with a measured frequency of 282Hz which isn't particularly nice to listen to. You can improve it by feeding it through a simple low-pass filter like the one used above for waveform synthesis. You can look up the frequencies for other notes and use a table to generate them. Alternatively you can use ledcWriteNote and work in terms of musical notation. For example, to generate middle C:

```
void setup() {
  ledcAttach(2, 10000, 8);
  ledcWriteNote(2,NOTE_C, 4);
}

void loop() {
}
```

This produces a tone at 261Hz and changing the octave doubles or halves the frequency as you add one or subtract one.

Hardware Fade

The PWM hardware has the ability to implement a fade in hardware. This is only useful if you can arrange for the program to do something else while the fade proceeds.

There are three hardware fade functions and the simplest is:

```
bool ledcFade(uint8_t pin, uint32_t start_duty,
                    uint32_t target_duty, int max_fade_time_ms);
```

- ◆ `pin`   GPIO to use
- ◆ `start_duty`   Starting duty of fade
- ◆ `target_duty`   Target duty of fade
- ◆ `max_fade_time_ms` Set maximum time for fade

The pin used has to be configured to a frequency and resolution before the fade is started and the start and target duty cycles are specified to the same resolution. The fade time is an upper limit as the fade times that can be achieved depends on the frequency and resolution. For example, if you set a frequency of 1000Hz and a resolution of 4 bits then a fade from 0 to 3 can only have four steps and hence can only approximate a given fade time.

For example to create a 1-second fade from off to full on:

```
void setup() {
  ledcAttach(2, 1000, 8);
  ledcFade(2, 0, 255, 1000);
}

void loop() {
}
```

In this case we have 256 steps from a duty cycle of 0 to 255 and hence at a frequency of 1000 Hz each step has to take $1000/256 = 3.9$ cycles. Rounding down gives 3 cycles per step which means that the total fade takes $3 \times 256 = 768$ms and this is indeed what the fade takes. Notice that as this is a hardware fade, the fade function returns as soon as it has started the fade and this means you program continues on while the fade is occurring.

Given that the fade occurs without holding up your program, the question is how to know when it is complete? The answer is

```
bool ledcFadeWithInterrupt(uint8_t pin, uint32_t start_duty,
    uint32_t target_duty, int max_fade_time_ms,
                                void (*userFunc)(void));
```

or

```
bool ledcFadeWithInterruptArg(uint8_t pin, uint32_t start_duty,
    uint32_t target_duty, int max_fade_time_ms,
              void (*userFunc)(void*), void * arg);
```

They work in the same way, but the first calls an ISR with the signature:

```
void ISR(void)
```

and the second calls one with the signature:

```
void ISR(void*)
```

and passes it *arg, i.e. a pointer to an argument.

For example, to start a fade over again when it ends you could use something like:

```
volatile int fading;

void ISR(void) {
  fading = false;
}

void setup() {
  ledcAttach(2, 1000, 8);
  ledcFadeWithInterrupt(2, 0, 255, 1000, ISR);
  fading = true;
}

void loop() {
  if (!fading) {
    delay(100);
    ledcFadeWithInterrupt(2, 0, 255, 1000, ISR);
    fading = true;
  }
}
```

In this case the ISR simply sets a flag, fading, to indicate if a fade is in progress or not. The main loop then tests fading to see if a new fade is needed.

Phase

Phase only becomes important when you are generating more than one PWM signal. Unfortunately the LEDC library doesn't support controlling phase but you can borrow a function from the ESP IDF SDK. It is worth explaining how to do this as controlling phase is a common requirement, but this approach is highly machine-dependent.

As explained earlier, in the section on PWM hardware, setting hpoint moves the position within the waveform of the rising edge. The ESP IDF function that controls hpoint is:

◆ ledc_set_duty_with_hpoint(speed_mode, channel, duty, hpoint)

As with setting duty, the problem is that hpoint has to be set in terms of the resolution.

To set a percentage phase shift you need to use:

$$\text{hpoint} = 2^{duty\,resolutionbits} \times percentage\ phase\ shift / 100$$

For example, working with 8-bit resolution, a 50% phase shift needs:
hpoint = 256 × 0.5 = 128.

For example:

```
#include "driver/ledc.h"
void setup() {
  ledcAttach(2, 1000, 8);
  ledcAttach(4, 1000, 8);
  ledcWrite(2, 128);
  ledcWrite(4, 128);

  ledc_set_duty_with_hpoint(LEDC_LOW_SPEED_MODE,
                        LEDC_CHANNEL_1, 128,64);
}

void loop() {
}
```

Notice that the two GPIO pins use the same timer, 0, but different controllers, 0 and 1 – these are the default assignments used by the system. It also uses the low-speed PWM hardware before using the high-speed. The phase and duty are set in the controller, not the timer, and so we can set different values of hpoint. If you run this program the result is two pulse trains out of phase by 25%:

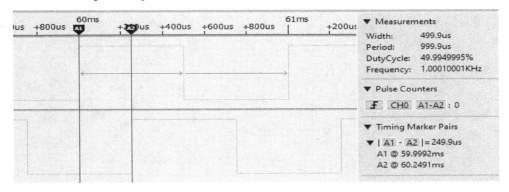

What Else Can You Use PWM For?

PWM lines are incredibly versatile and it is always worth asking the question "could I use PWM?" when you are considering almost any problem. The ESP32's PWM generator is particularly versatile.

The LED example suggests how you can use PWM as a power controller. You can extend this idea to a computer-controlled switch-mode power supply. All you need is a capacitor to smooth out the voltage and perhaps a transformer to change the voltage. You can also use PWM to control the speed of a DC motor and, by adding a simple bridge circuit, you can control its direction and speed.

Finally, you can use a PWM signal as a modulated carrier for data communications. For example, most infrared controllers make use of a 38kHz carrier, which is roughly a 26μs pulse. This is switched on and off for 1ms and this is well within the range that the PWM can manage. So all you have to do is replace the red LED in the previous circuit with an infrared LED and you have the start of a remote control, or data transmission, link. Of course the RMT hardware also does this job and it does it better.

One big area of use is in controlling motors, and servo motors in particular, and this is the subject of the next chapter.

Summary

- PWM, Pulse Width Modulation, has a fixed repetition rate but a variable duty cycle, i.e. the amount of time the signal is high or low changes.

- PWM can be generated by software simply by changing the state of a GPIO line correctly, but it can also be generated in hardware so relieving the processor of some work.

- As well as being a way of signaling, PWM can also be used to vary the amount of power or voltage transferred. The higher the duty cycle, the more power/voltage.

- The ESP32 has 16 hardware PWM generators and the ESP32-S3 has 8. These can be used with any of the GPIO lines capable of output.

- There are only four timers per 8 PWM generator group which determine the frequency that the PWM lines work at. A single timer can be connected to multiple controllers.

- The higher the frequency of the PWM, the lower the duty cycle resolution.

- You can modify the frequency and duty cycle of a running PWM generator.

- PWM can be used to implement digital-to-analog conversion simply by varying the duty cycle. You can dim an LED in the same way.

- The PWM controllers can be set to auto fade an LED by varying the duty cycle.

- By adjusting `hpoint` you can generate a signal with a fixed phase relationship to another signal.

Chapter 9

Controlling Motors And Servos

Controlling motors is an obvious use for the ESP32, but it is important to understand the different types of motor that you can use and exactly how to control them using PWM. In addition to PWM control, we also look at the very useful stepper motor, which doesn't make use of PWM.

The ESP32 has a PWM generator, MCPWM, which is specifically targeted at motor control. It includes the ability to set deadtime, synchronize PWM output with external events and detect faults, but as already mentioned it is not supported by the Arduino library. It also has a simpler PWM generator, LEDC, aimed at controlling LEDs. Despite its name, however, it can be used for motor control, the advanced features of the MCPWM. In this chapter the LEDC library, described in Chapter 8, is used to implement PWM for motor control. However, in many cases the basic Arduino `analogWrite` function is sufficient. When it comes to servos there is an Arduino Servo library but this cannot be used with the ESP32 so once again we have to fall back to the LEDC functions.

The simplest division among types of motor is AC and DC. AC motors are generally large and powerful and run from mains voltage. As they are more difficult to work with, and they work at mains voltage, these aren't used much in IoT applications. DC motors generally work on lower voltage and are much more suitable for the IoT. In this chapter we will only look at DC motors and how they work thanks to pulse width modulation. The parts used are listed in the Resources section of the book's webpage at www.iopress.info.

DC Motor

There are two big classes of DC motor – brushed and brushless. All motors work by using a set of fixed magnets, the stator, and a set of rotating magnets, the rotor. The important idea is that a motor generates a "push" that rotates the shaft by the forces between the magnet that makes up the stator and the magnet that makes up the rotor. The stronger these magnets are, the stronger the push and the more torque (turning force) the motor can produce. To keep the motor turning, one of the two magnetic fields has to change to keep the rotor being attracted to a new position.

DC motors differ in how they create the magnetism in each component, either using a permanent magnet or an electromagnet.

This means there are four possible arrangements:

	1	2	3	4
Stator	Permanent	Permanent	Electromagnet	Electromagnet
Rotor	Permanent	Electromagnet	Permanent	Electromagnet
Type	Can't work	Brushed DC	Brushless DC	Series or shunt

Arrangement 1 can't produce a motor because there is no easy way of changing the magnetic field. Arrangement 4 produces the biggest and most powerful DC motors used in trains, cars and so on. Arrangement 2, brushed DC, is the most commonly encountered form of "small" DC motor. However, arrangement 3, brushless DC, is becoming increasingly popular.

Different arrangements produce motors which have different torque characteristics, i.e. how hard they are to stop at any given speed. Some types of motor are typically low torque at any speed, i.e. they spin fast but are easy to stop.

Low torque motors are often used with gearboxes, which reduce the speed and increase the torque. The big problem with gearboxes, apart from extra cost, is backlash. The gears don't mesh perfectly and this looseness means that you can turn the input shaft and at first the output shaft won't move. Only when the slack in the gears has been taken up will the output shaft move. This makes a geared motor less useful for precise positioning, although there are ways to improve on this using feedback and clever programming.

Brushed Motors

To energize the electromagnets, a brushed motor supplies current to the armature via a split ring or commutator and brushes. As the rotor rotates, the current in the coil is reversed and it is always attracted to the other pole of the magnet.

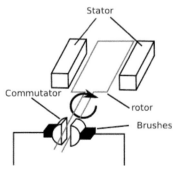

The only problem with this arrangement is that, as the brushes rub on the slip ring as the armature rotates, they wear out and cause sparks and hence RF interference. The quality of a brushed motor depends very much on the design of the brushes and the commutator.

Very small, cheap, brushed DC motors, of the sort in the picture below, tend to have brushes that cannot be changed and when they wear out the motor has to be replaced. They also tend to have very low torque and high speed. This usually means that they have to be used with a gearbox. If you overload a brushed motor then the tendency is to demagnetize the stator magnets. The cheapest devices are basically toys.

Higher quality brushed motors are available and they also come in a variety of form factors. For example, the 775 motor is 66.7 by 42mm with a 5mm shaft:

775 motor

12000/min

Even these motors tend not to have user-serviceable brushes, but they tend to last a long time due to better construction.

Unidirectional Brushed Motor

A brushed motor can be powered by simply connecting it to a DC supply. Reversing the DC supply reverses the direction of the motor. The speed is simply proportional to the applied voltage. If all you want is a unidirectional control then all you need is a PWM driver that can supply the necessary current and voltage.

A single transistor solution is workable as long as you include a diode to allow the energy stored in the windings to discharge when the motor is rotating, but not under power:

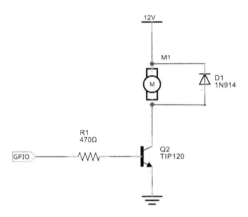

This circuit is simple and will work with motor voltages up to 40V and motor currents up to 5A continuous, 8A peak. The only small point to note is that the TIP120 is a Darlington pair, i.e. it is two transistors in the same case, and as such the base voltage drop is twice the usual 0.6V, i.e. 1.2V, and this has to be taken into account when calculating the current-limiting resistor.

It is sometimes said that the TIP120 and similar are inefficient power controllers because, comprising two transistors, they have twice the emitter-collector voltage you would expect, which means they dissipate more power than necessary.

If you are running a motor from a battery you might want to use a MOSFET, but, as described earlier, 3.3V is low to switch a MOSFET on and off. One solution is to use a BJT to increase the voltage applied to the gate:

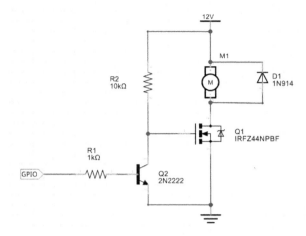

The BJT connects the gate to 12V. As the IRFZ44NPBF has a threshold voltage between 2V and 4V, devices should work at 5V and sometimes at 3.3V without the help of the BJT, but providing 12V ensures that the MOSFET is fully on. One problem with the circuit is that the use of the BJT inverts the signal. When the GPIO line is high the BJT is on and the MOSFET is off and vice versa. In other words, GPIO line high switches the motor off and low switches it on. This MOSFET can work with voltages up to 50V and currents of 40A. The 2N2222 can only work at 30V, or 40V in the case of the 2N2222A.

A third approach to controlling a unidirectional motor is to use half an H-bridge. Why this is so-called, and why you might want to do it, will become apparent in the next section on bidirectional motors. Half an H-bridge makes use of two complementary devices, either an NPN and a PNP BJT or an N- and P-type MOSFET.

For example:

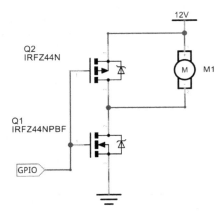

If the GPIO line is high then Q1 is on and Q2 off and the motor runs. If the GPIO line is low then Q1 is off and Q2 is on and the motor is braked – it has a resistance to rotating because of the back electromotive force (EMF) generated when the rotor turns. You probably need a BJT to feed the MOSFETs as selected.

Unidirectional PWM Motor Controller

A function to control the speed of a unidirectional motor is very simple. The speed is set by the duty cycle – the only parameter you have to choose in addition is the frequency. If you want an optimal controller then setting the frequency is a difficult task. Higher speeds make the motor run faster and quieter – but too high a frequency and the motor loses power and the driving transistor or MOSFET becomes hot and less efficient. The determining factor is the inductance of the motor's coil and any other components connected to it such as capacitors. In practice, PWM frequencies from 100Hz to 20kHz are commonly used, but in most cases 1kHz to 2kHz is a good choice. If you can use a frequency of 1kHz then the basic Arduino `analogWrite` function is sufficient.

Now that we have a PWM source, how should we implement code to make motor control easy? A good pattern, which has many of the advantages of object-oriented programming, is to create a class which has fields that represent the state of the entity and methods that modify the state of the motor.

For example, to implement a unidirectional motor we can create a UniMotor class:

```
class UniMotor {
private:
  int gpio;
  int duty;
public:
  UniMotor(int pin) {
    gpio = pin;
  }
  void setSpeed(float s) {
    duty = s * 255;
    analogWrite(gpio, duty);
  }
};
```

You can see that this has all of the information needed to define the current state of a motor and a method to set the speed. Turning the motor off is a matter of setting speed to zero.

A main program to run the motor is:

```
UniMotor *motor1;
void setup() {
  motor1 = new UniMotor(2);
  motor1->setSpeed(0.5);
}

void loop() {
}
```

The complete program listing can be found on the book's website at www.iopress.info.

You can create other instances of UniMotor that work on other GPIO lines.

Bidirectional Brushed Motor

If you want bidirectional control then you need to use an H-bridge:

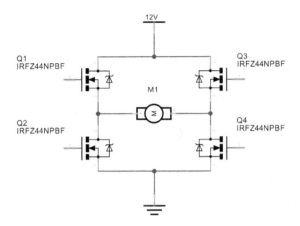

It is easy to see how this works. If Q1 and Q4 are the only MOSFETs on the motor, + is connected to 12V and − to ground. The motor runs in the forward direction. If Q2 and Q3 are the only MOSFETs on the motor, + is connected to ground and − is connected to 12V. The motor runs in the reverse direction. Of course, if none or any single one is on the motor is off. If Q1 and Q3, or Q2 and Q4, are on then the motor is braked as its windings are shorted out and the back EMF acts as a brake.

You can arrange to drive the four MOSFETs using four GPIO lines - just make sure that they switch on and off in the correct order. To make the bridge easier to drive, you can add a NOT gate to each pair so that you switch Q1/Q2 and Q3/Q4 to opposite states.

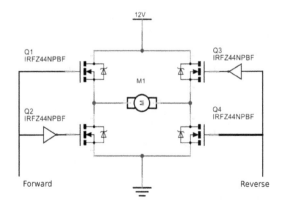

138

An alternative design is to use complementary MOSFETs:

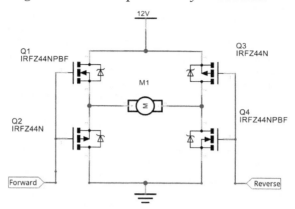

In this configuration, the first GPIO line drives the motor forward and the second drives it in reverse. The effect of setting the two lines is:

Forward	Reverse	Motor
Low	Low	Off
Low	High	Reverse
High	Low	Forward
High	High	Braked

You can also drive the GPIO lines for Forward/Reverse with a PWM signal and control the motor's speed as well as direction. If you use the MOSFETs shown in the diagram then you would also need a BJT to increase the drive voltage to each MOSFET, as in the unidirectional case. You also need to include diodes to deal with potential reverse voltage on each of the MOSFETs. The most important thing about an H-bridge is that Q1/Q2 and Q3/Q4 should never be on together – this would short circuit the power supply.

If working with four power BJTs or MOSFETs is more than you want to tackle, the good news is that there are chips that implement two H-bridges per device. You can also buy low-cost ready-made modules with one or more H-bridges. One of the most used devices is the L298 Dual H-bridge which works up to 46V and total DC current of 4A.

The block diagram of one of the two H-bridges shows exactly how it works:

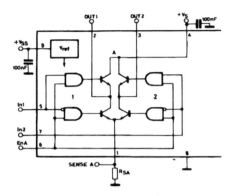

You can see that the bridge is made up of four BJTs and there are logic gates to allow IN1 and IN2 to select the appropriate pairs of devices. The only extras are AND gates and that the ENA (enable) line is used to switch all of the transistors off. The line shown as SENSE A can be used to detect the speed or load of the motor, but is rarely used.

A typical module based on the L298 can be seen below.

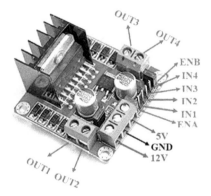

It is easier to describe how to use this sort of module with a single motor. The motor is connected to OUT1 and OUT2. Three GPIO lines are connected to ENA, IN1 and IN2. ENA is an enable line, which has to be high for the motor to run at all. IN1 and IN2 play the role of direction control lines – which one is forward and which is reverse depends on which way round you connect the motor. Putting a PWM signal onto ENA controls the speed of the motor and this allows IN1 and IN2 to be simple digital outputs.

Notice that the power connector shows 5V and 12V supplies, but most of these modules have a voltage regulator which will reduce the 12V to 5V. In this case you don't have to supply a 5V connection. If you want to use more than 12V then the regulator has to be disconnected and you need to arrange for a separate 5V supply – check with the module's documentation. Notice that the transistors in the H-bridge have around a 2V drop, so using 12V results in just 10V being applied to the motor.

Another very popular H-bridge device is the SN754410 driver. This is suitable for smaller, lower-powered, motors and has two complete H-bridges. It can supply up to 1A per driver and work from 4.5 to 36V. It has the same set of control lines as the L298, i.e. each motor has a forward/reverse control line and an enable line. You don't have to use the enable line - it can be connected to +5V to allow PWM to be applied on the forward/reverse lines.

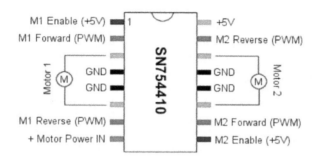

Bidirectional Motor Software

Depending on the way the bridge is implemented, software control uses either a single GPIO line for a PWM signal or one or two lines for direction. The most common way to do things is to provide two GPIO lines, each carrying the same PWM signal.

We can easily extend the idea in the UniMotor class and its methods to work with a bidirectional motor. The only real difference is that now we have to use two GPIO lines. For forward we activate the first GPIO line and for reverse we activate the second.

We could use inheritance but it is simpler and more robust to implement a new class:

```
class BiMotor {
private:
  int gpio1;
  int gpio2;
  int duty;
  bool forward;
public:
  BiMotor(int pin1, int pin2) {
    gpio1 = pin1;
    gpio2 = pin2;
  }
  void setSpeedDirection(float s, bool f) {
    duty = s * 255;
    forward = f;
    if (forward) {
      analogWrite(gpio1, 0);
      analogWrite(gpio1, duty);
    } else {
      analogWrite(gpio2, 0);
      analogWrite(gpio2, duty);
    }
  }
};
```

The method that sets the speed now also has to set the direction. Notice that we need to switch the currently on PWM signal off before we switch the alternative PWM on to avoid having both on at the same time.

A main program to create a bidirectional motor and set it going in reverse is:

```
BiMotor *motor1;
void setup() {
  motor1 = new BiMotor(2, 4);
  motor1->setSpeedDirection(0.5, false);
}

void loop() {}
```

The complete program listing can be found on the book's website at www.iopress.info.

This is a very basic set of functions, you can add others to improve motor control according to how sophisticated you want it to be. For example, a brake function would set both lines high for brake mode, or you could introduce limits on how fast the speed can be changed. There are also problems of how to change direction – if you simply put the motor into reverse it will generate a large back emf which could damage the drive electronics. A much better idea is to take the motor's speed down to zero before reversing its direction. Motor control is a big topic.

There are H-bridges that use two lines to control Phase and Enable (PWM). These map to the usual Forward, Reverse and Enable as shown below:

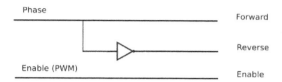

The disadvantage of this arrangement is that you cannot set Forward and Reverse to put the motor into brake mode. If you do have this sort of controller, anything based on the MAX14870/2 for example, then you can modify the functions to use a single PWM line and one standard GPIO line for speed and direction.

Using A Single Full H-Bridge As Two Half H-Bridges

It is easy to think of an H-bridge as being only for bidirectional control, but each full bridge is composed of two half bridges and this means a typical dual full H-bridge can control four unidirectional motors:

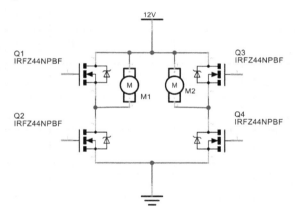

In this case Forward is now MotorM1 speed control and Reverse is now MotorM2 speed control. Any enable line has to be set high to allow the two motors to be controlled. You can make use of this arrangement with the unidirectional software given earlier.

143

Controlling a Servo

Hobby servos, of the sort used in radio control models, are very cheap and easy to use and they connect via a standard PWM protocol. Servos are not drive motors, but positioning motors. That is, they don't rotate at a set speed, they move to a specified angle or position.

A servo is a motor, usually a brushed DC motor, with a feedback sensor for position, usually a simple variable resistor (potentiometer) connected to the shaft. The output is usually via a set of gears which reduces the rotation rate and increases the torque. The motor turns the gears, and hence the shaft, until the potentiometer reaches the desired setting and hence the shaft has the required angle/position.

A basic servo has just three connections, ground, a power line and a signal line. The colors used vary, but the power line is usually red, ground is usually black or brown and the signal line is white, yellow or orange. If a standard J-connector is fitted then the wire nearest the notch, pin 3, is Signal, the middle wire, pin 2, is 5V and outer wire, pin 1, is Ground.

The power wire has to be connected to a 5V supply capable of providing enough current to run the motor - anything up to 500mA or more depending on the servo. The good news is that the servo's signal line generally needs very little current, although it does, in theory, need to be switched between 0V and 5V using a PWM signal.

You can assume that the signal line needs to be driven as a voltage load and so the appropriate way to drive the servo is:

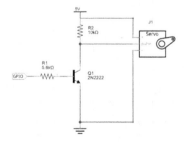

You can assume that the signal line needs to be driven as a voltage load and so the appropriate way to drive the servo is with the + line connected to an external 5V power supply. However, resistor R1 can be a lot larger than 10K for most servos - 47K often works. The 5.6K resistor limits the base current to slightly less than 0.5mA. Notice, however, that if you are using a single BJT driver, like the one shown above, the input is inverted.

While this is the correct way to drive a servo, in nearly all cases you can drive the servo signal line directly from the 3.3V GPIO line with a 1K resistor to limit the current if anything goes wrong with the servo. Some servos will even work with their motor connected to 3.3V, but at much reduced torque.

There is an Arduino Servo class in the library, but it doesn't work with the ESP32 and our best choice is to implement the signal using basic PWM functions. All we have to do is set the PWM line to produce 20ms pulses with pulse widths ranging from 0.5ms to 2.5ms – i.e. a duty cycle of 2.5 to 12.5%. If we use 8 bit resolution this corresponds to a count of 6 to 32 which gives just 26 positions. However if we use 8 bit resolution the default clock cannot be divided down to give 50Hz. If we use 10 bit resolution then it can. Alternatively we can change the clock to a slower source.

In this case we cannot use the analogWrite function to implement a servo driver because it doesn't work at 50Hz it is fixed at 1kHz. Instead we have to use LEDC which is ESP32-specific and not supported by the Nano ESP32.

A class to implement a servo is fairly easy:

```
class Servo {
private:
  int gpio;
  int max;
  int min;
public:
  Servo(int pin) {
    gpio = pin;
    max = (2 << 9) * 12.5 / 100;
    min = (2 << 9) * 2.5 / 100;
    ledcAttach(pin, 50, 10);
  }
  void setAngle(float a) {
    int duty = (float)(max - min) * a + min;
    ledcWrite(2, duty);
  }
};
void loop() {
  servo1->setAngle(1.0);
  delay(100);
  servo1->setAngle(0.5);
  delay(100);
  servo1->setAngle(0.0);
  delay(100);
}
```

Notice that we set the frequency to 50Hz and resolution to 10 bits. If you want to work with a non-standard servo you can change this or make either settable. The setAngle function sets the position in terms of percentages of rotation. That is, setAngle(.5) sets the servo to the middle of its range. This assumes that the servo has a standard positioning range and most don't. In practice to get the best out of a servo, you need to calibrate each servo and discover what range of movement is supported. The main program creates a Servo object on GPIO 2 and then moves the servo to its maximum, middle and minimum positions.

If you run the program using the transistor circuit given earlier, you will discover that the servo does nothing at all, apart perhaps from vibrating. The reason is that the transistor voltage driver is an inverter. When the PWM line is high, the transistor is fully on and the servo's pulse line is effectively grounded. When the PWM line is low, the transistor is fully off and the servo's pulse line is pulled high by the resistor. The solution is to invert the duty cycle from 2.5% to 12.5% to 100-2.5% to 100-12.5%:

```
Servo(int pin) {
  gpio = pin;
  max = (2 << 9) * (100-12.5) / 100;
  min = (2 << 9) * (100-2.5) / 100;
  ledcAttach(pin, 50, 10);
}
```

Alternatively you can simply invert the signal:

```
Servo(int pin) {
  gpio = pin;
  max = (2 << 9) * 12.5 / 100;
  min = (2 << 9) * 2.5 / 100;
  ledcAttach(pin, 50, 10);
  ledcOutputInvert(pin, true);
}
```

It is worth mentioning that servos make good low-cost DC motors, complete with gearboxes. All you have to do is open the servo, unsolder the motor from the control circuits and solder two wires to the motor. If you want to use the forward/reverse electronics you can remove the end stops on the gearbox, usually on the large gear wheel, and replace the potentiometer with a pair of equal value resistors, 2.2kΩ, say.

Brushless DC Motors

Brushless DC motors are more expensive than brushed DC motors, but they are superior in many ways. They don't fail because of commutator or brush wear and need no maintenance. They provide maximum rotational torque at all points of the rotation and generally provide more power for the same size and weight. They can also be controlled more precisely. The only negative points are their higher cost and slightly more complex operation. In practice, it is usually sufficient to use a brushed DC motor unless you really need something extra.

A brushless DC motor is basically a brushed motor turned inside out – the stator is a set of electromagnets and the rotor is a set of permanent magnets. In some designs the permanent magnets are inside the stator in the manner of a brushed motor, an inrunner, and sometimes the magnets are outside of the stator, an outrunner.

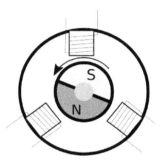

An inrunner – the permanent magnets form the rotor and the coils are switched to attract.

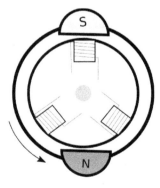

An outrunner – the permanent magnets are on the outside of the stator and the whole cover rotates.

A brushless motor works in exactly the same way as a brushed motor. As the coils are stationary there is no need for a mechanical commutator, but there is still need for commutation – the coils have to be switched on in sequence to create a rotating magnetic field which pulls the rotor around with it. This means that you have to implement an electronic commutator, which is another name for a brushless DC motor.

An electronic commutator has to sense the position of the rotor and change the magnetic field generated by the stator to keep the rotor moving. Brushless motors differ in the number of magnets they have and the number of phases. The most common is a three-phase motor as these are used in radio control modeling. Essentially you need at least a driver for each of the phases and a GPIO line to generate the signal. In practice, you need two drivers for each phase and they have to be driven from a dual supply so that the magnetic field can be positive, zero or negative.

This would be possible to do with software, but it isn't easy and a more reasonable alternative is to buy a ready-built controller. There are two types of brushless motor, with Hall effect sensors and without. The former are more expensive, but easier to control because the electronics always knows where the rotor is and can apply the correct drive. The ones without sensors are controlled by measuring the back EMF from the motor and this is much harder. Most of the lower-cost speed controllers need motors with Hall sensors.

The ESP32 MCPWM system has everything needed to implement a brushless motor controller using Hall sensors, including an example program in the documentation, which is worth reading if you want to know more. It is also worth saying that driving a brushless motor is very like driving a stepper motor, see the next section.

The radio control community has taken to using three-phase brushless motors and this has resulted in a range of motors and controllers at reasonable prices intended as high-power, high-speed, unidirectional motors for use in quadcopters and model planes. If you can live with their limitations they provide a good way to couple the ESP32 to a brushless motor. In this case all you need is a three-phase brushless motor of the sort used in RC modeling and an ESC (Electronic Speed Controller) of the sort shown below:

The three leads on the left go to the three phases of the motor and the red and black leads on the right go to a power supply, often a LiPo battery. The small three-wire connector in the middle is a standard servo connector and you can use it exactly as if the brushless motor was a servo, with a few exceptions. The first is that pin 2 supplies 5V rather than accepts it. Don't connect this to anything unless you want a 5V supply. The second problem is that ESCs are intelligent. When you first apply power they beep and can be programmed into different modes by changing the PWM signal from Max to Min. Also, to use an ESC you have to arm it. This is to avoid radio control modelers from being injured by motors that start unexpectedly when the power is applied. The most common arming sequence is for the ESC to beep when power is applied. You then have to set the PWM to Min, when the ESC will beep again. After a few moments you will have control of the motor.

The need for an arming procedure should alert you to the fact that these model motors are very powerful. Don't try working with one loose on the bench as it will move fast if switched on and at the very least make a twisted mess of your wires. Most importantly of all, don't run a motor with anything attached to it until you have everything under control.

Stepper Motors

There is one sort of brushless motor that is easy to use and low cost, the stepper motor. This differs from a standard brushless motor in that it isn't designed for continuous high-speed rotation. A stepper motor has an arrangement of magnets and coils such that powering some of the coils holds the rotor in a particular position. Changing which coils are activated makes the rotor turn until it is aligned with the coils and stops moving. Thus the stepper motor moves the rotor in discrete steps. This makes driving it much simpler, but note it doesn't use PWM for speed control.

Stepper motors have no brushes and so don't wear out as fast as brushed motors. They also have roughly the same torque at any speed and can be used at low speeds without a gearbox. They can remain in a fixed position for a long time without burning out, as DC motors would. Unlike a servo, however, if a stepper motor is mechanically forced to a new position, it will not return to its original position when released. The only disadvantage of a stepper motor is that the continuous rotation produced by repeated stepping can make the motor vibrate.

Stepper motors vary in the size of step they use – typically 1.8 degrees giving 200 steps per rotation, although gearing can be used to reduce the step size. Another big difference is that the rotor is made up either of permanent magnets or soft iron. The first type is called a Permanent Magnet or PM stepper and the second is called a Variable Reluctance or VR and they differ in how you drive them with PM steppers being easier to understand. There are also hybrid steppers which share the good characteristics of both PM and VR stepper motors. These are more expensive and are generally only used where accuracy of positioning is important. They also differ in the number of phases, i.e. independent banks of coils, they have.

The diagram below shows a two-phase PM motor with Phase 1 activated:

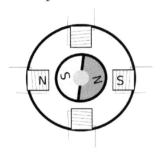

If Phase two is activated, the rotor turns through 90 degrees. This is the simplest stepper motor you can make.

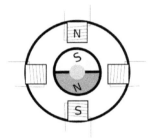

A typical stepper motor will have many more coils than four, but they are usually connected into two or three phases.

Another big difference is bipolar versus unipolar. A bipolar motor is like the one shown in the diagram. To generate a north pole the current has to flow in the opposite direction to when you want to create a south pole. This means you have to drive each bank of coils with a bidirectional driver, e.g. an H-bridge. A unipolar motor has two windings, one in each direction, and both windings can be driven by a unidirectional driver – one giving a north pole and the other a south pole. Notice that a unipolar motor has twice the number of coils to drive and the switching sequence is slightly different.

A two-phase bipolar motor with Phases A and B would switch on in the sequence:

A → B → A- → B- → A etc

where the minus sign means the current flows the other way. This is called single-phase stepping.

An alternative sequence, called full step drive is to activating both phases:

AB → A- B → A- B - → AB-

Full stepping works in the same way as single-phase stepping but it provides a higher torque.

A two-phase unipolar motor has two coils per phase, A1, A2 and B1, B2 with the 1 and 2 windings creating opposite magnetic fields for the same current flow. Now the sequence is:

A1 → B1 → A2 → B2 → A1 etc

and all the coils are driven in the same direction.

Switching single phases fully on and off in sequence makes the motor make repeated steps. You can also switch on more than one phase at a time to generate micro-steps or half-stepping. For example, in our two-phase example, switching on two phases makes the rotor settle between the two, so producing a half micro-step:

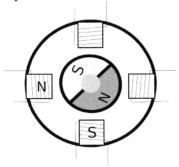

The driving sequence for a two-phase bipolar motor is:

A → AB →B → BA- → A- → A- B- → B- → AB- → A

with minus indicating that the coil is energized in the opposite direction, giving a total of eight, rather than four, steps.

You can even vary the current through the coils and move the rotor to intermediate positions. At the extreme limit you can vary the current sinusoidally and produce a smooth rotation. Micro-stepping is smoother and can eliminate buzzing. For high accuracy positioning, micro-stepping is a poor performer under load.

Stepper Motor Driver

How best to drive a stepper motor using an ESP32? There are some specialized chips that work with unipolar and bipolar stepper motors. However, you can easily control a bipolar stepper motor using one the H-bridges described in the section on directional motor control.

For example, using complementary MOSFETS:

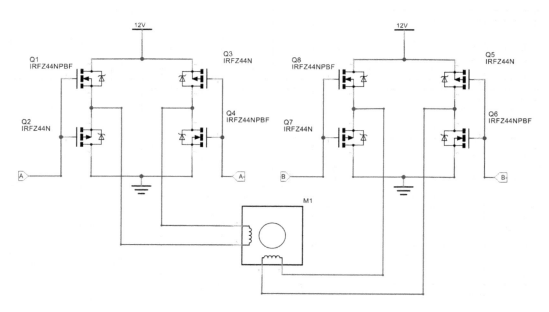

You can use a dual H-bridge module in the same way if you don't want to build it from scratch. The motor has to be a bipolar two-phase motor, often called a four-wire stepper motor. You can see that for this arrangement you need four GPIO lines, A, A-, B and B-.

What about driving the dual H-bridge using software? You need four GPIO lines and you need to pulse them in a specific phase to make the motor rotate. The first question to answer is how to specify the four GPIO lines to be used. As we will see, there is a big advantage and simplification in using a block of four consecutive lines:

GPIOn → A, GPIOn+1 → B, GPIOn+2 → A- , GPIOn+3 → B-

The Stepper Library

There is an Arduino library that will drive a unipolar or bipolar stepper motor, but it doesn't support half stepping. It is however very easy to use.

To use the Stepper library all you need is to include:

```
#include <Stepper.h>
```

and create a Stepper object:

```
Stepper(steps, pin1, pin2, pin3, pin4)
```

If you supply four pins you create a bipolar object and if you only supply two pins you create a unipolar driver. The steps parameter sets the number of steps for a full rotation.

The Stepper object has just two methods:

```
setSpeed(rpms)
```

which sets the step rate in revs per minute and:

```
step(s)
```

which turns the motor through s steps at the speed specified by the last setSpeed call. Negative values of s step in reverse.

For example:

```
#include <Stepper.h>

Stepper stepMot1 = Stepper(200, 16, 17, 18, 19);

void setup() {
  stepMot1.setSpeed(1);
  stepMot1.step(100);
}

void loop() {
}
```

This sets up GPIO16 to GPIO19 as outputs to the motor and then executes 100 steps at 1 rpm, i.e. half a turn of a 200-step motor.

If you are using the Arduino Nano ESP32 then use pins GPIO5 to GPIO8.

To try this you need an H-bridge connected so that GPIO 16 is A, GPIO 17 is A-, GPIO 18 is B and GPIO 19 is B-. If you are using one of the many dual H-bridge modules then the wiring is as shown below:

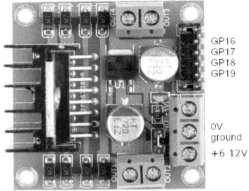

Notice that you have to connect the ground of the power supply and the ESP32's ground together. It is also a good idea to use a power supply with a current trip when first trying things out.

The signal produced is:

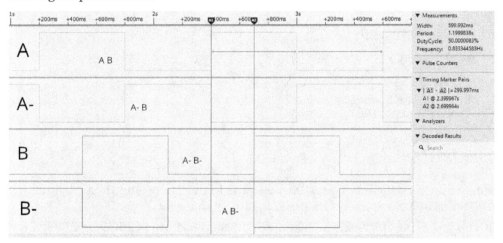

You can see that this is full-stepping as both A and B are active at the same time.

Half Stepping

You can fairly easily implement your own stepper class to implement half-stepping. Given that this involves nothing but switching GPIO lines at the correct time, this is machine-independent using the Arduino library.

The key to simplifying most problems that involve changing output lines in a sequence is the Finite State Machine (FSM), see Chapter 6. The switching sequence for half-stepping gives rise to eight states and for a forward step sn→sn+1 and for a reverse step sn→sn-1:

State	GPIO lines
s0	{1, 0, 0, 0}
s1	{1, 1, 0, 0}
s2	{0, 1, 0, 0}
s3	{0, 1, 1, 0}
s4	{0, 0, 1, 0}
s5	{0, 0, 1, 1}
s6	{0, 0, 0, 1}
s7	{1, 0, 0, 1}

You can see that each state change only involves a single GPIO line. If you annotate the table with the number of the GPIO line that changes you should see the pattern:

A → AB → B → BA- → A- → A-B- → B- → AB- → A

GPIO	GPIO lines				Change
	16	17	18	19	
	A	A-	B	B-	
	0	1	2	3	
s0	{1,	0,	0,	0}	+2
s1	{1,	0,	1,	0}	-0
s2	{0,	0,	1,	0}	+1
s3	{0,	1,	1,	0}	-2
s4	{0,	1,	0,	0}	+3
s5	{0,	1,	0,	1}	-1
s6	{0,	0,	0,	1}	+0
s7	{1,	0,	0,	1}	-3

where a change of +n means turn line GPIO16+n on and − means turn the line off. So to get from state s0 to state s1 you have to turn GPIO16+2 on. To move from state s1 to s2 you have to turn GPIO16+0 off. Of course the table wraps round and to move from state s7 to s0 you turn GPIO16+3 off. Notice that even states correspond to turning a GPIO line on and odd states turn a GPIO line off.

For the Arduino Nano ESP32 use pins GPIO5 to GPIO8.

155

There are a number of ways of implementing this state transition table including keeping a single counter, but the most direct and the one that is most easy to customize is to use an array:

```
int stepTable[8] = { 2, 0, 1, 2, 3, 1, 0, 3 };
```

and use the rule that even elements indicate which GPIO line to turn on and odd ones indicate which GPIO line to turn off. If we assume that the system is in state sn, a step forward, sn→sn+1, can be implemented as:

```
digitalWrite(gpio + stepTable[state], (state + 1) % 2);
state = (state + 1) % 8;
```

where gpio is the number of the first GPIO line used and (state + 1) % 2 is 1 if state is even and 0 if it is odd.

A reverse step, sn→sn-1, is only slightly harder to get right:

```
state = (state +7) % 8;
digitalWrite(gpio + stepTable[state], state % 2);
```

In this case we have to move back one place in the table and if the GPIO line indicated was turned on we have to now turn it off and vice versa. The only implementation detail is that we avoid the use of:

```
state = (state -1) % 8;
```

as this can go negative and the remainder operator doesn't do what you might expect with a negative value. The solution is to add 8 to the state before subtracting one to avoid it going negative – notice that adding any multiple of 8 makes no difference to the remainder.

Putting this together gives the complete step method:

```
  void step(int step) {
    if (step > 0) {
      digitalWrite(gpio + stepTable[state], (state + 1) % 2);
      state = (state + 1) % 8;
    } else {
      state = (state +7) % 8;
      digitalWrite(gpio + stepTable[state], state % 2);
    };
  }
```

where step is positive for a forward step and negative for a reverse step.

You can see that if GPIO 16 is A, GPIO 17 is A-, GPIO 18 is B and GPIO 19 is B- and stepping through the stepTable gives the sequence given earlier:

A → AB → B → BA- → A- → A-B- → B- → AB- → A

A complete stepper class is:

```
class Stepperbi {
private:
  int gpio;
  int stepTable[8] = { 1, 0, 2, 1, 3, 2, 0, 3 };
  int state = 0;
public:
  Stepperbi(int pin1) {
    gpio = pin1;
    for (int i = 0; i < 4; i++) {
      pinMode(gpio + i, OUTPUT);
      digitalWrite(gpio + i, 0);
    }
    digitalWrite(gpio, 1);
  }
  void step(int step) {
    if (step > 0) {
      digitalWrite(gpio + stepTable[state], (state + 1) % 2);
      state = (state + 1) % 8;
    } else {
      state = (state +7) % 8;
      digitalWrite(gpio + stepTable[state], state % 2);
    };
  }
};
Stepperbi stepper1=Stepperbi(16);
void loop() {
  stepper1.step(1);
  delay(10);
}
void setup(){};
```

The constructor initializes the GPIO lines to output and sets them to state s0, i.e all line off apart from the first. The main program simply steps the motor every 10 ms. If you are using an Arduino Nano ESP32 change the constructor call to:

```
Stepperbi stepper1=Stepperbi(5);
```

and use pins GPIO5 to GPIO8.

157

The outputs are as you would expect for a half-stepping motor:

| A | A | AB | B | BA- | A- | A-B- | B- | AB- |

| A- |

| B |

| B- |

You can use a single phase step table if you want to, as long as you remember to work in mod 4 rather than 8:

A → B → A- → B- → A

	GPIO lines				Change
GPIO	16	17	18	19	
	A	A-	B	B-	
	0	1	2	3	
s0	{1,	0,	0,	0}	-0 +2
s1	{0,	0,	1,	0}	-2 +1
s2	{0,	1,	0,	0}	-1 +3
s3	{0,	0,	0,	1}	-3 +0

Now we have two lines changing at each step, but we still only need to record one as the GPIO line to be turned off is always the one turned on at the last step. The step table is:

```
int stepTable[4] = { 0,2,1,3 };
```

and the step method is:

```
void step(int step) {
  if (step > 0) {
    digitalWrite(gpio + stepTable[state],0);
    state = (state + 1) % 4;
    digitalWrite(gpio + stepTable[state],1);
  } else {
    digitalWrite(gpio + stepTable[state],0);
    state = (state + 3) % 4;
    digitalWrite(gpio + stepTable[state], 1);
  };
}
```

158

We need to make more changes to implement full stepping:

```
AB → A- B → A- B - → AB-
        GPIO lines        Change
GPIO  16 17 18 19
       A  A- B  B-

       0  1  2  3
s0    {1, 0, 1, 0}    -0 +1
s1    {0, 1, 1, 0}    -2 +3
s2    {0, 1, 0, 1}    -1 +0
s3    {1, 0, 0, 1}    -3 +2
```

Notice that this is just the odd lines of the half-stepping table given earlier. In this case we need to turn on one line GPIOn at each step and turn off the line that we turned on two states earlier. The modified class is:

```
class Stepperbi {
private:
  int gpio;
  int stepTable[4] = { 0,2,1,3 };
  int state = 0;
public:
  Stepperbi(int pin1) {
    gpio = pin1;
    for (int i = 0; i < 8; i++) {
      pinMode(gpio + i, OUTPUT);
      digitalWrite(gpio + i, 0);
    }
    digitalWrite(gpio, 1);
    digitalWrite(gpio+2, 1);
  }
  void step(int step) {
    if (step > 0) {
      digitalWrite(gpio + stepTable[(state+2) % 4],0);
      digitalWrite(gpio + stepTable[state],1);
      state = (state + 1) % 4;
    } else {
      state = (state + 3) % 4;
      digitalWrite(gpio + stepTable[(state+2) % 4],1);
      digitalWrite(gpio + stepTable[state],0);

    };
  }
};
```

Summary

- There are a number of different types of electric motor, but DC brushed or brushless motors are the most widely used in the IoT.

- Brushed motors can be speed controlled using a single transistor driver and a PWM signal.

- For bidirectional control you need an H-bridge. In this case you need two PWM signals.

- You can also use an H-bridge to generate AC from DC. In this case you also need to add deadtime to the out-of-phase signals.

- Servo motors set their position in response to the duty cycle of a PWM signal.

- Brushless DC motors are very powerful and best controlled using off-the-shelf electronic modules. They are very powerful and thus dangerous if used incorrectly. They can be driven using a simple PWM signal.

- Stepper motors are a special case of a brushless DC motor. They move in discrete steps in response to energizing different coils.

- A unipolar motor has coils that can be driven in the same direction for every step. A bipolar motor has coils that need to be driven in reverse for some steps.

- Bipolar motors need two H-bridges to operate and four GPIO lines.

- You can easily create a stepper motor driver using four GPIO lines.

Chapter 10

Getting Started With The SPI Bus

The Serial Peripheral Interface (SPI) bus can be something of a problem because it doesn't have a well-defined standard that every device conforms to. Even so, if you only want to work with one specific device it is usually easy to find a configuration that works - as long as you understand what the possibilities are.

SPI Bus Basics

The SPI bus is commonly encountered as it is used to connect all sorts of devices from LCD displays, through realtime clocks to A-to-D converters (ADCs), but as different companies have implemented it in different ways, you have to work harder to implement it in any particular case. However, it does usually work, which is a surprise for a bus with no standard, or clear, specification.

The reason it can be made to work is that you can specify a range of different operating modes, frequencies and polarities. This makes the bus slightly more complicated to use, but generally it is a matter of looking up how the device you are trying to work with implements the SPI bus and then getting the ESP32 to work in the same way.

The SPI bus is odd in another way - it does not use bidirectional serial connections. There is a data line for the data to go from the master to the slave and a separate data line from the slave back to the master. That is, instead of a single data line that changes its transfer direction, there is one for data going out and one for data coming in. It is also worth knowing that the drive on the SPI bus is push-pull and not open-collector/drain. This provides higher speed and more noise protection as the bus is driven in both directions.

In the configuration most used for the ESP32, there is a single master and, at most, two slaves. The signal lines are:

- ◆ MOSI (Maste Output Slave Input) or COPI (Controller Output Peripheral Input), i.e. data to the slave
- ◆ MISO (Master Input Slave Output), or CIPO (Controller In Peripheral Out) i.e. data to the master
- ◆ SCLK (Serial Clock), which is always generated by the master

In general, there can also be any number of SS (Slave Select), CE (Chip Enable) or CS (Chip Select) lines, which are usually set low to select which slave is being addressed. Notice that unlike other buses, I2C for example, there are no SPI commands or addresses, only bytes of data. However, slave devices do interpret some of the data as commands to do something or send some particular data.

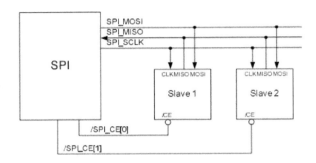

There are two other modes of operation of the SPI interface – bidirectional and LoSSI mode. The bidirectional mode simply uses a single data line, MIMO, for both input and output. The direction of the line is determined by writing a command to the slave. LoSSI mode is used to communicate with sophisticated peripherals such as LCD panels. Both of these are beyond the scope of this chapter as are the quad and octal modes that work with 4 and 8 data lines respectively. However, once you know how standard mode works, the others are simple variations. In this chapter we concentrate on the basic workings of SPI.

The data transfer on the SPI bus is slightly odd. What happens is that the master pulls one of the chip selects low, which activates a slave. Then the master toggles the clock SCLK and both the master and the slave send a single bit on their respective data lines. After eight clock pulses, a byte has been transferred from the master to the slave and from the slave to the master. You can think of this as being implemented as a circular buffer, although it doesn't have to be.

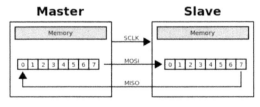

This full-duplex data transfer is often hidden by the software and the protocol used. For example, there is a read function that reads data from the slave and sends zeros or data that is ignored by the slave. Similarly, there is a write function that sends valid data, but ignores whatever the slave sends. The transfer is typically in groups of eight bits, usually most significant bit first, but this isn't always the case. In general, as long as the master supplies clock pulses, data is transferred. You can also opt for a half duplex approach where the master first transmits and then the slave sends data back.

Notice this circular buffer arrangement allows for slaves to be daisy-chained with the output of one going to the input of the next. This makes the entire chain one big circular shift register. This can make it possible to have multiple devices with only a single chip select, but it also means any commands sent to the slaves are received by each one in turn. For example, you could send a convert command to each ADC in turn and receive back results from each one.

The final odd thing about the SPI bus is that there are four modes which define the relationship between the data timing and the clock pulse. The clock can be either active high or low, which is referred to as clock polarity (CPOL), and data can be sampled on the rising or falling edge of the clock, which is clock phase (CPHA).

All combinations of these two possibilities gives the four modes:

SPI Mode*	Clock Polarity CPOL	Clock Phase CPHA	Characteristics
0	0	0	Clock active high data output on falling edge and sampled on rising
1	0	1	Clock active high data output on rising edge and sampled on falling
2	1	0	Clock active low data output on falling edge and sampled on rising
3	1	1	Clock active low data output on rising edge and sampled on falling

*The way that the SPI modes are labeled is common but not universal.

There is often a problem trying to work out what mode a slave device uses. The clock polarity is usually easy and the clock phase can sometimes be worked out from the data transfer timing diagrams bearing in mind that if the first clock transition at the start of a data bit CPHA is a 1 and if it is in the middle of a data bit CPHA is a 0.

So to configure the SPI bus to work with a particular slave device:

1. Select the clock frequency - anything from 125MHz to 3.8kHz
2. Determine the CS polarity - active high or low
3. Set the clock mode Mode0 thru Mode3

ESP32 SPI Interfaces

The ESP32 has four SPI controllers. SPI0 is used internally for memory access and isn't available. SPI1 can act as a master and is usually allocated to SRAM interfacing. Because of this you are restricted to using SPI2 and SPI3 which can act as master or slave.

To add to the confusion, in the case of the ESP32, SPI2 and SPI3 are also called HSPI and VSPI, terms that are sometimes used for the ESP32-S3. To make matters worse it is common for libraries, including the Arduino library and the ESP IDF, to refer to SPI2 as SPI number 0 and SPI3 as SPI number 1 as if they were the only two SPI controllers available.

The SPI pins can be connected to any GPIO pins; there is a speed advantage for the ESP32 in allowing them to work with their default pins. The reason is that the SPI hardware is connected directly to the defaults but goes via a multiplexer to other GPIO lines. As a result the default pins work at higher frequencies. The default pins can work up to 80MHz but a general GPIO line can only work at 40MHz. This isn't true for the ESP32-S3.

Default ESP32 GPIO Pins		
	SPI2 HSPI id=SPI2_HOST	SPI3 VSPI id=SPI3_HOST
SCLK	14	18
MOSI	13	23
MISO	12	19

For a full SPI interface you need to use one pin for MISO, one for MOSI and one for SCLK. The chip select lines are not really part of the SPI hardware implementation. To make use of them you have to treat them like standard GPIO lines and set them high and low to select the device under program control. What this means is that you can use as many of these lines with any SPI interface as you need.

The library abstracts the SPI hardware to make it easier to use and easier to customize to different implementations. In this chapter we are only considering using the ESP32 as a master as this is all that the Arduino library supports.

Configure The Bus

To make use of the SPI bus you need to include:

```
#include <SPI.h>
```

This loads the core SPI library on Arduino devices, but on the ESP32 it loads a library specific to the ESP32 which has some extensions to allow access to the ESP32's additional SPI hardware.

The Arduino way of working with SPI is to use the supplied SPI object. This sets up the SPI hardware to a set of defaults including which SPI controller and which GPIO pins are used. The only customization you can perform is to use the SPISettings object to control speed, data order and mode, see later. In the case of the ESP32, the SPI object defaults to using SPI2, i.e. HSPI with default GPIO lines as given in the earlier table for the ESP32 and EPS32-S3.

If you want more control over how the SPI hardware is set up then you have to go beyond the Arduino specific functions. You can create a new SPI object using the constructor:

```
SPIClass spi = SPIClass(spinumber);
```

where spinumber is HSPI or VSPI or 0 for SPI1 and 1 for SPI2 respectively.

The actual initialization of the SPI bus only happens when you call the begin method:

```
begin()
```

The version of this function in the Arduino core has no parameters and it simply sets the default GPIO lines to output and then pulls MOSI and SCK low and CS high.

The ESP32 version of the begin method has additional optional parameters allowing you to set the GPIO lines used:

```
begin(int8_t sck, int8_t miso, int8_t mosi, int8_t cs)
```

This isn't generally available in the Arduino library.

Once the bus is configured and initialized we can specify the protocol to be used via an SPISettings object which has data fields for three parameters:

```
SPISettings mySetting(speedMaximum, dataOrder, dataMode)
```

where:

- speedMaximum   Maximum speed in Hz
- dataOrder   Either MSBFIRST or LSBFIRST
- dataMode   One of SPI_MODE0, SPI_MODE1, SPI_MODE2 or SPI_MODE3

To complete the configuration it is used in a call to the `beginTransaction` method:

`beginTransaction(mySettings)`

You can call:

`SPI.endTransaction()`

to free the bus for other uses.

There are also functions to let you modify the settings without the need to create an `SPISettings` object:

- `setDataMode(mode)`
- `setBitOrder(order)`
- `setClockDivider(divider)`

Putting all this together we can write a general Arduino SPI configuration as:

```
SPI.begin();
SPI.beginTransaction(SPISettings(14000000, MSBFIRST, SPI_MODE0));
```

This sets up SPI2 to use GPIO12,13 and 14 at 14MHz, with most significant byte first and in mode 0.

An ESP32 specific configuration is:

```
SPIClass spi2 = SPIClass(0);
spi2.begin(14, 12, 13, 15);
spi2.beginTransaction(SPISettings(14000000, MSBFIRST, SPI_MODE0));
```

This sets up the same configuration, but it only works on the ESP32 and, of course, you could change the SPI control and GPIO pins to use. You can also configure the default SPI object to use different GPIO lines;

```
SPI.begin(14, 12, 13, 15);
SPI.beginTransaction(SPISettings(14000000, MSBFIRST, SPI_MODE0));
```

Data Transfer

Because of the way the SPI bus uses a full-duplex transfer, things are a little different from other buses when it comes to implementing functions to transfer data. In the core Arduino library the SPI bus supports a single transfer method that can be used in two different ways.

The first is to send a single item of data;

```
receivedVal = SPI.transfer(val)
receivedVal16 = SPI.transfer16(val16)
```

The `val` is sent to the slave and the response is stored in `receivedVal`.

The second is used to transfer a block of data:

```
transfer(buffer, size)
```

You can also choose to work in polling mode or interrupt mode, but these only differ in how they wait for a transaction to complete. In this case the received data overwrites the data in the buffer as it is transmitted.

A Loopback Example

Because of the way that data is transferred on the SPI bus, it is very easy to test that everything is working without having to add any components. All you have to do is connect MOSI to MISO so that anything sent is also received in a loopback mode.

First we have to select which pins to use and, as this is fairly arbitrary at this stage, we might as well use:

```
SPI2    MISO    GPIO 12
        MOSI    GPIO 13
        SCLK    GPIO 14
        CS      GPIO 15
```

First, connect GPIO12 to GPIO13 using a jumper wire and start a new project.

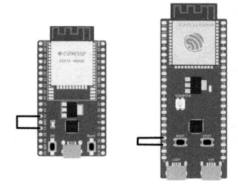

The program is very simple. First we set up the bus to use the GPIO lines listed. We are using 8-bit data and SPI mode 0. Finally we send some data and receive it without using a buffer:

```
#include <SPI.h>
void setup() {
  pinMode(15, OUTPUT);
  digitalWrite(15, 1);
  SPI.begin(14, 12, 13, 15);
  SPI.beginTransaction(SPISettings(1000000, MSBFIRST, SPI_MODE0));
  Serial.begin(9600);
}
```

```
void loop() {
  digitalWrite(15, 0);
  char receivedVal = SPI.transfer(0xAA);
  digitalWrite(15, 1);
  Serial.println(receivedVal,HEX);
  delay(1000);
}
```

Notice that we have to control the CS line explicitly and this introduces a 1μs delay between the CS changing and the clock pulse starting or stopping.

If you are using an Arduino Nano ESP32 then use pins GPIO5 to GPIO8 and change `SPI.begin(14, 12, 13, 15);` to `SPI.begin(7, 5, 6, 8);` and all references to GPIO15 to GPIO8.

The hex value `AA` is useful in testing because it generates the bit sequence `10101010`, which is easy to see on a logic analyzer.

A pure Arduino version of the program would change:

`SPI.begin(14, 12, 13, 15);`

to `SPI.begin();` and it would accept the default GPIO assignments.

If you run the program and don't get any data received back then the most likely reason is that you have connected the wrong two pins or not connected them at all.

If you connect a logic analyzer to the three GPIO lines involved you will see the data transfer:

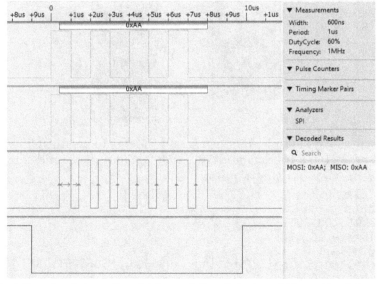

Notice that the clock is active high and the data is valid on its rising edge.

168

The MCP3008 SPI ADC

An alternative to using the ESP32's built-in ADC is to use an external chip. The MCP3000 family is a low-cost versatile SPI-based set of A-to-D converters. Although the MCP3008, with eight analog inputs at 10-bit precision, and the MCP3004, with four analog inputs at 10-bit precision, are the best known, there are other devices in the family, including ones with 12-bit and 13-bit precision and differential inputs, at around the same sort of cost, $1 to $2. In this chapter the MCP3008 is used because it is readily available and provides a good performance at low cost, but the other devices in the family work in the same way and could be easily substituted.

The MCP3008 is available in a number of different packages, but the standard 16-pin PDIP is the easiest to work with using a prototyping board. You can buy it from the usual sources including Amazon, see Resources on this book's webpage. Its pinouts are fairly self-explanatory:

```
CH0  1      16  V_DD
CH1  2      15  V_REF
CH2  3   M  14  AGND
CH3  4   C  13  CLK
CH4  5   P  12  D_OUT
CH5  6   3  11  D_IN
CH6  7   0  10  CS/SHDN
CH7  8   8   9  DGND
```

You can see that the analog inputs are on the left and the power and SPI bus connections are on the right. The conversion accuracy is claimed as 10 bits, but how many of these bits correspond to reality and how many are noise depends on how you design the layout of the circuit.

You need to take great care if you need high accuracy. For example, you will notice that there are two voltage inputs, V_{DD} and V_{REF}. V_{DD} is the supply voltage that runs the chip and V_{REF} is the reference voltage that is used to compare the input voltage. Obviously, if you want highest accuracy, V_{REF}, which has to be lower than or equal to V_{DD}, should be set by an accurate low-noise voltage source. However, in most applications V_{REF} and V_{DD} are simply connected together and the usual, low- quality, supply voltage is used as the reference. If this isn't good enough then you can use anything from a Zener diode to a precision voltage reference chip such as the TL431. At the very least, however, you should add a $1\mu F$ capacitor to ground connected to the V_{DD} pin and the V_{REF} pin.

The MC3000 family is based on the same type of ADC as the ESP32's built-in device, see the next chapter and, like it, is a successive approximation converter.

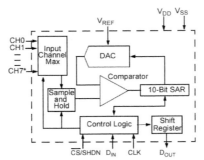

You can see that successive approximation fits in well with a serial bus as each bit can be obtained in the time needed to transmit the previous bit. However, the conversion is relatively slow and a sample-and-hold circuit has to be used to keep the input to the converter stage fixed. The sample-and-hold takes the form of a 20pF capacitor and a switch. The only reason you need to know about this is that the conversion has to be completed in a time that is short compared to the discharge time of the capacitor. So, for accuracy, there is a minimum SPI clock rate as well as a maximum.

Also, to charge the capacitor quickly enough for it to follow a changing voltage, it needs to be connected to a low-impedance source. In most cases this isn't a problem, but if it is you need to include an op amp. If you are using an op amp buffer then you might as well implement an anti-aliasing filter to remove frequencies from the signal that are too fast for the ADC to respond to. How all this works takes us into the realm of analog electronics and signal processing and well beyond the core subject matter of this book.

You can also use the A-to-D channels in pairs, i.e. in differential mode, to measure the voltage difference between them. For example, in differential mode you measure the difference between CH0 and CH1, i.e. what you measure is CH1-CH0. In most cases, you want to use all eight channels in single-ended mode. In principle, you can take 200k samples per second, but only at the upper limit of the supply voltage, i.e. V_{DD}=5V, falling to 75k samples per second at its lower limit of V_{DD}=2.7V.

The SPI clock limits are a maximum of 3.6MHz at 5V and 1.35MHz at 2.7V. The clock can go slower, but because of the problem with the sample-and-hold mentioned earlier, it shouldn't go below 10kHz. How fast we can take samples is discussed later in this chapter.

Connecting to the ESP32

The connection from the MCP3008 to the ESP's SPI bus is very simple and can be seen in the diagram below.

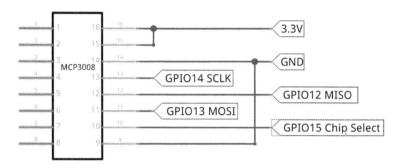

ESP32 & ESP32-S3	MCP3008
GPIO12 MISO	Pin 12
GPIO15 Chip Select	Pin 10
GPIO14 SCLK	Pin 13
GPIO13 MOSI	Pin 11
3.3v	Pins 15 and 16
GND	Pins 14 and 9

The only additional component that is recommended is a 1μF capacitor connected between pins 15 and 16 to ground, which is mounted as close to the chip as possible. As discussed in the previous section, you might want a separate voltage reference for pin 15 rather than just using the 3.3V supply.

Basic Configuration

Now we come to the configuration of the SPI bus: a clock frequency of 500kHz seems a reasonable starting point.

From the datasheet, the chip select has to be active low and, by default, data is sent most significant bit first for both the master and the slave. The only puzzle is what mode to use? This is listed in the datasheet as mode 0 0 with clock active high or mode 1 1 with clock active low. For simplicity we will use mode 0 0.

We now have enough information to initialize the slave:

```
void setup() {
  pinMode(15, OUTPUT);
  digitalWrite(15, 1);
  SPI.begin(14, 12, 13, 15);
  SPI.beginTransaction(SPISettings(1000000, MSBFIRST, SPI_MODE0));
  Serial.begin(9600);
}
```

The Protocol

Now we have the SPI initialized and ready to transfer data, but what data do we transfer? As already discussed in the previous chapter, the SPI bus doesn't have any standard commands or addressing structure. Each device responds to data sent in different ways and sends data back in different ways. You simply have to read the datasheet to find out what the commands and responses are.

Reading the datasheet might be initially confusing because it says that you have to send five bits to the slave - a start bit, a bit that selects its operating mode single or differential, and a 3-bit channel number. The operating mode is 1 for single-ended and 0 for differential.

So to read Channel 3, i.e. 011, in single-ended mode you would send the slave:

> 11011xxx

where an x can take either value. In response, the slave holds its output in a high impedance state until the sixth clock pulse, then sends a zero bit on the seventh, followed by bit 9 of the data on the eighth clock pulse.

That is, the slave sends back:

> xxxxxx0b9

where x means indeterminate and b9 means bit 9.

The remaining nine bits are sent back in response to the next nine clock pulses. This means you have to transfer three bytes to get all ten bits of data. All this makes reading the data in 8-bit chunks confusing.

The datasheet suggests a different way of doing the job that delivers the data more neatly packed into three bytes by sending a single byte:

> 00000001

At the same time, the slave transfers random data, which is ignored. The final 1 is treated as the start bit. If you now transfer a second byte with the most significant bit indicating single or differential mode, then a 3-bit channel address and the remaining bits set to 0, the slave will respond with a null and the top two bits of the conversion.

172

Now all you have to do to get the final eight bits of data is to read a third byte:

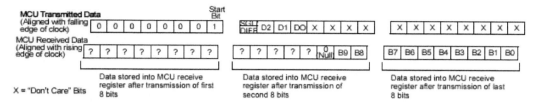

This way you get two neat bytes containing the data with all the low-order bits in their correct positions.

Using this information we can now write some instructions that read a given channel. For example, to read Channel 0 we first send a byte set to `0x01` as the start bit and ignore the byte the slave transfers. Next we send `0x80` to select single-ended and Channel 0 and keep the byte the slave sends back as the two high-order bits. Finally, we send a zero byte (`0x00`) so that we get the low-order bits from the slave:

```
char data[3];
```

```
void loop() {
  data[0] = 0x01;
  data[1] = 0x80;
  data[2] = 0x00;
  digitalWrite(15, 0);
  SPI.transfer(data,3);
  digitalWrite(15, 1);
```

Notice that the CS line is held low for the entire transaction.

To get the data out of `data` we need to do some bit manipulation:

```
int raw =  (data[1] & 0x03) << 8 |data[2];
```

The first part of the expression extracts the low three bits from the first byte the slave sent and, as these are the most significant bits, they are shifted up eight places. The rest of the bits are then ORed with them to give the full 10-bit result.

To convert to volts we use:

```
float volts=raw*3.3/1023.0;
```

assuming that V_{REF} is 3.3V.

In a real application you would also need to convert the voltage to some other quantity, like temperature or light level.

If you connect a logic analyzer to the SPI bus you will see both the commands and the response:

The complete program is:

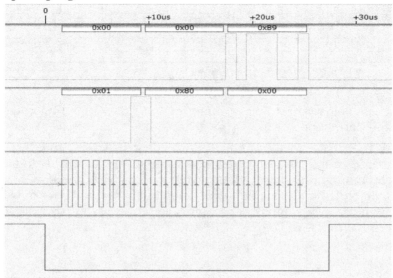

```
#include <SPI.h>
void setup() {
  pinMode(15, OUTPUT);
  digitalWrite(15, 1);
  SPI.begin(14, 12, 13, 15);
  SPI.beginTransaction(SPISettings(1000000, MSBFIRST, SPI_MODE0));
  Serial.begin(9600);
}
char data[3];
void loop() {
  data[0] = 0x01;
  data[1] = 0x80;
  data[2] = 0x00;
  digitalWrite(15, 0);
  SPI.transfer(data,3);
  digitalWrite(15, 1);
  int raw =  (data[1] & 0x03) << 8 |data[2];
  Serial.println(raw);
  float volts=raw*3.3/1023.0;
  Serial.println(volts);
  delay(1000);
}
```

If you are using an Arduino Nano ESP32 use GPIO5 to GPIO8 i.e. change SPI.begin(14,12,13,15); to SPI.begin(7,5,6,8); and all references to GPIO15 to GPIO8

Some Packaged Functions

This all works, but it would be good to have a function that read the ADC on a specified channel:

```
float readADC(uint8_t chan) {
  char data[3];
  data[0] = 0x01;
  data[1] = (0x08 | chan) << 4;
  data[2] = 0x00;
  digitalWrite(15, 0);
  SPI.transfer(data, 3);
  digitalWrite(15, 1);
  int raw = (data[1] & 0x03) << 8 | data[2];
  float volts = raw * 3.3 / 1023.0;
  return volts;
}
```

Notice that this only works if the SPI bus has been initialized and set up correctly. An initialization is something like:

```
void setup() {
  pinMode(15, OUTPUT);
  digitalWrite(15, 1);
  SPI.begin(14, 12, 13, 15);
  SPI.beginTransaction(SPISettings(1000000, MSBFIRST, SPI_MODE0));
  Serial.begin(9600);
}
```

With these two functions, the main program is very simple:

```
void loop() {
  float volts = readADC(0);
  Serial.println(volts);
  delay(1000);
}
```

If you are using an Arduino Nano ESP32 use GPIO5 to GPIO8 i.e. change `SPI.begin(14,12,13,15);` to `SPI.begin(7,5,6,8);` and all references to GPIO15 to GPIO8

How Fast?

Once you have the basic facilities working, the next question is always how fast does something work. In this case we need to know what sort of data rates we can achieve using this ADC. The simplest way of finding this out is to use the fastest read loop for a channel:

```
void loop() {
   float volts = readADC(0);
}
```

With the clock of 500 kHz the sampling rate is measured to be 16kHz. This is perfectly reasonable as it takes at least 24 clock pulses to read the data. Most of the time in the loop is due to the 24 clock pulses, so there is little to be gained from optimization.

Increasing the clock rate to 1MHz pushes the sampling rate to 27kHz, which is just fast enough to digitize audio, as long as you don't waste too much time in the loop in processing. This is about as fast as the device can work at 3.3V.

Also notice that as the clock rate goes up, you have to ensure that the voltage source is increasingly low-impedance to allow the sample-and-hold to charge in a short time.

Problems

The SPI bus is often a real headache because of the lack of a definitive standard, but in most cases you can make it work. The first problem is in discovering the characteristics of the slave device you want to work with. In general, this is solved by a careful reading of the datasheet or perhaps some trial and error. In most cases a good logic analyzer is what you need to see how the signals are interacting. Problems generally occur when you are pushing the clock speed ever higher. Fast SPI generally needs DMA to transfer the data and this is another complexity.

If you are working with a single slave then generally things work once you have the SPI bus configuration set correctly. Things are more difficult when there are multiple devices on the same bus. Typically you will find SPI devices that don't switch off properly when they are not being addressed. In principle, all SPI devices should present high impedance outputs (i.e. tri-state buffers) when not being addressed, but some don't. If you encounter a problem you need to check that the selected slave is able to control the MISO line properly.

Summary

● The SPI bus is often problematic because there is no SPI standard. Unlike other serial buses, it makes use of unidirectional connections.

● The data lines are MOSI (master output slave input) and MISO (master input slave output). In addition, there is a clock line, output from master, and a number of select lines that you have to drive under program control. Timing for the select lines is a problem as you have to include a delay that makes sure that it remains low until the end of the final clock pulse.

● Data is transferred from the master to the slave and from the slave to the master on each clock pulse, arranged as a circular buffer.

● The ESP32 has two usable SPI devices which can work with almost any of the GPIO lines.

● You can test the SPI bus using a simple loopback connection.

● Working with a single slave is usually fairly easy, working with multiple slaves can be more of a problem.

● Making SPI work with any particular device has four steps:

    1. Connect the device to the SPI pins by identifying pinouts and discovering what chip selects are supported.
    2. Configure the SPI bus to work with the device - mostly a matter of clock speed and mode.
    3. Identify the commands that you need to send to the device to get it to do something and what data it sends back as a response.
    4. Work out the relationship between the raw reading, the voltage and the quantity the voltage represents.

● The MCP3000 range of ADCs is very easy to use via SPI.

● You can read data from an MCP3000 at rates as fast as 20kHz.

Chapter 11
Using Analog Sensors

The ESP32 has a wide range of analog capabilities. It has two A-to-D converters (ADCs) and two D-to-A converters (DACs) connected to specific GPIO pins. The ESP32 S3 has the same number of ADCs but doesn't have any DACs. In addition, both have a set of capacitive input lines which can be used as touch sensors.

ESP32 ADC

The ESP32 has two 12-bit onboard ADCs, ADC1 supports 8 channels in the ESP32 and 10 channels in the ESP-S3 and ADC2 supports 10 channels. The only problem is that the WiFi uses one of the two channels, ADC2, and hence its use is best avoided unless you turn WiFi off or use it only when the WiFi is inactive.

The GPIO lines that can be used by the ADC are fixed. In the case of the ESP32, ADC 1 can use GPIO32 to 39 and ADC 2 can use GPIO 0, 2, 4, 12-15 and 25-27. In practice not all of these lines can be used. Of the eight ADC1 channels only six are available on development boards. So, even though the hardware seems to offer 18 ADC inputs, this is actually reduced to six that are easy to use. The ESP32-S3 generally offers all of the ADC channels for use. In this case ADC2 occupies GPIO11 to GPIO20.

In most cases it is better to use ADC1:

Channel	ESP GPIO	ESP-S3 GPIO
ADC1_CH0	GPIO 36	GPIO1
ADC1_CH1		GPIO2
ADC1_CH2		GPIO3
ADC1_CH3	GPIO 39	GPIO4
ADC1_CH4	GPIO 32	GPIO5
ADC1_CH5	GPIO 33	GPIO6
ADC1_CH6	GPIO 34	GPIO7
ADC1_CH7	GPIO 35	GPIO8
ADC1_CH8		GPIO9
ADC1_CH9		GPIO10

179

In the ESP32, GPIO 36 and 39 were used to read the built-in Hall sensor, but support for this has been removed in the latest version of the SDK and from the ESP32-S3.

The ADC is a successive approximation converter. You don't need to know how it works to use it, but it isn't difficult to understand. The input voltage is compared to a standard voltage, V_{REF}. First a voltage equal to $V_{REF}/2$ is generated and the input voltage is compared to this. If it is lower then the most significant bit is a 0 and if it is equal or greater then the most significant bit is a 1. At the next step the voltage generated is $V_{REF}/2 + V_{REF}/4$ and the comparison is repeated to generate the next bit. Successive approximation converters are easy to build, but they are slow.

The ESP32 ADC uses a reference voltage that is generated on-chip and varies between 1000mV and 1200mV. Since 2018, ESP32 chips have their reference voltage burned into the eFuse memory and this makes calibration a matter of reading the value and using it to correct the result. The Arduino library adapted to work with the ESP32 makes use of the calibration data without you needing to do anything but it is worth knowing how this works.

The easiest way to discover if the device you are using has calibration data is to use `espefuse.py`, which can be used to read and write the eFuse memory. This is a non-volatile write-once memory that you can use to record small amounts of configuration data, but it is better to avoid using it as there is no easy-to-use interface. It can also damage the ESP32 if you change the wrong bits as, once set to `1`, a bit cannot be changed back to `0`.

You will probably need to install `esptool` as the Arduino library does not install all of the tools. To do this you need to use `pip` to install `esptool`, but exactly how to do this depends on the nature of your Python environment.

To discover the calibration data use:

```
python espefuse.py -p COM4 adc_info
```

replacing `COM4` with the serial port that the ESP32 is connected to. If no calibration data is available you will see:

```
ADC VRef calibration: None (1100mV nominal)
```

and the best you can do is assume the middle value for the reference voltage. If there is calibration data you will see a single point calibration:

```
ADC VRef calibration: 1149mV
```

and you might also see a two-point calibration for each channel:

```
ADC readings stored in efuse BLK3:
    ADC1 Low reading  (150mV): 306
    ADC1 High reading (850mV): 3153
    ADC2 Low reading  (150mV): 389
    ADC2 High reading (850mV): 3206
```

180

The calibration value is stored as a 5-bit sign-magnitude value in increments of seven and as an offset from 1100, which is the middle of the range.

A more recent ESP32 such as the ESP-S3 should give you a four-point calibration.

This can be used to fit a correction curve.

The calibration can be used by the API to get a more accurate result, see later.

The response is non-linear near zero and the reference voltage:

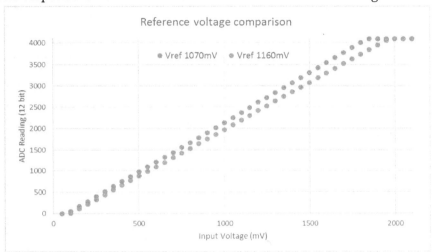

In practice, voltages less than 100mV read as zero.

In addition to calibration problems, the ADC is also sensitive to noise. You can reduce this by adding a 100nF capacitor across the input line and by averaging multiple readings:

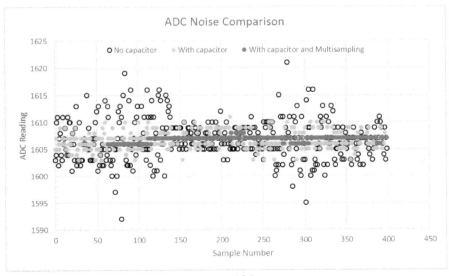

The ADC can be set to do conversions continuously, reading each of the selected inputs' Alternatively, you can simply start a conversion on a given input when you need the data.

Reading the ADC

The simplest way of using the ADC is to perform a single read of a single input under software control. You don't have to initialize anything to get started. You can simply read any of the analog pins:

```
uint16_t analogRead(uint8_t pin);
```

which returns the raw reading of the ADC. The result is in the range 0 to 4095 for 12-bit resolution or the ESP32 and 13-bit resolution for the ESP32-S3. The raw reading is an uncalibrated result from the hardware. Raw readings generally have to be scaled to turn them into physically meaningful values and they are not corrected for any calibration data available.

In most cases you are going to get more accurate and usable results via the function:

```
uint32_t analogReadMilliVolts(uint8_t pin);
```

which returns a result automatically calibrated and converted to μV.

The simplest A-to-D program you can write is:

```
void setup() {
  Serial.begin(9600);
}

void loop() {
  int16_t data = analogRead(5);
  int32_t volts = analogReadMilliVolts(5);
  Serial.println(data);
  Serial.println(volts / 1000.0);
}
```

For example, with an input at around 3V the output is:

```
4095
```

```
3.12
```

To make the ADC more useful it supports changing the input voltage range via attenuators:

- ◆ ADC.ATTEN_DB_0 : No attenuation (100mV - 950mV)
- ◆ ADC.ATTEN_DB_2_5: 2.5dB attenuation (100mV - 1250mV)
- ◆ ADC.ATTEN_DB_6:   6dB attenuation (150mV - 1750mV)
- ◆ ADC.ATTEN_DB_11: 11dB attenuation (150mV - 2450mV)

You can set attenuation for all of the analog inputs using:

```
void analogSetAttenuation(adc_attenuation_t attenuation);
```

or for a single pin using;

```
void analogSetPinAttenuation(uint8_t pin,
                    adc_attenuation_t attenuation);
```

Notice that the exact range depends on the reference voltage.

The absolute maximum input voltage to the ADC is 3.6V, but using such a high voltage risks damaging the ESP32. In practice keep the input voltage below 3.3V.

You can also set the number of bits to use with the `width` method:

```
void analogReadResolution(uint8_t bits);
```

where `bits` is between 1-16. For the ESP32 this really changes the resolution of the ADC but in other cases it simply shifts the result.

How Fast?

It is easy to get a rough estimate of how fast each of the read methods are. All we need is to use the microsecond timer function given earlier:

```
void setup() {
  Serial.begin(9600);
}

void loop() {
  int16_t data;
  unsigned long s = micros();
  for (int i = 0; i < 100000; i++) {
    data = analogRead(5);
  }
  s = micros() - s;
  Serial.println(s);
  s = micros();
  for (int i = 0; i < 100000; i++) {
    data = analogReadMilliVolts(5);
  }
  s = micros() - s;
  Serial.println(s);
}
```

The raw reads take about $30\mu s$ on an ESP32-S3 and $35\mu s$ on an ESP32. and the calibrated function takes about $1\mu s$ longer, which puts the maximum sampling rate at about 20kHz. Reducing the accuracy to 9 bits reduces the time taken by about $1\mu s$.

Continuous Conversion

The problem with using an ADC via `analogRead()`is that it blocks while the conversion is in progress. This makes it difficult to take a lot of readings without making the main loop run slow. The solution is to use interrupts and the ESP32 implementation of the ADC library provides a continuous read facility. This lets you set things up so that multiple GPIO lines are read in the background and an interrupt is generated when the data is ready. The Arduino Nano ESP32 currently does not support continuous conversion.

To use it you first have to configure it:

```
bool analogContinuous(const uint8_t pins[], size_t pins_count,
    uint32_t conversions_per_pin, uint32_t sampling_freq_hz,
        void (*userFunc)(void));
```

The pins array is simply a list of pins that need to be read and pins_count specifies how many there are. You can set the number of conversions per pin. For example, if you set `conversions_per_pin` to ten then each time a pin is measured 10 readings are taken and the mean is computed. The `sampling_freq_hz` sets the repeat sampling rate. Clearly this should be slower than the time you can process the result in. Finally `userFunc` is the call back with signature:

```
void ISR(void)
```

You can configure the attenuation of all pins using:

```
void analogContinuousSetAtten(adc_attenuation_t attenuation)
```

The measurement can be started and stopped using:

```
bool analogContinuousStart()
```

and

```
bool analogContinuousStop()
```

You can also free up the space used:

```
bool analogContinuousDeinit()
```

When the ISR is called the data is stored in an internal buffer and it can be retrieved using:

```
bool analogContinuousRead(adc_continuous_data_t ** buffer,
                                        uint32_t timeout_ms)
```

where each element of the buffer array is a struct:

```
typedef struct {
    uint8_t pin;
    uint8_t channel;
    int avg_read_raw;
    int avg_read_mvolts;
} adc_continuous_data_t;
```

The simplest program you can write to read multiple ADC channels is;

```
volatile bool adc_coversion_done = false;

void ARDUINO_ISR_ATTR adcComplete(void) {
  adc_coversion_done = true;
}

void setup() {
  uint8_t adc_pins[] = { 1, 2, 3, 4 };
  analogContinuous(adc_pins, 4, 5, 1000, &adcComplete);
  analogContinuousStart();
  Serial.begin(9600);
}

void loop() {
  adc_continuous_data_t *result = NULL;
  if (adc_coversion_done == true) {
    adc_coversion_done = false;

    if (analogContinuousRead(&result, 0)) {
      for (int i = 0; i < 4; i++) {
        Serial.printf("\nADC PIN %d data:",
                                        result[i].pin);
        Serial.printf("\n   Avg raw value = %d",
                                  result[i].avg_read_raw);
        Serial.printf("\n   Avg millivolts value = %d",
                              result[i].avg_read_mvolts);
      }
      delay(1000);
    }
  }
}
```

The setup function initializes the ADC to read pins 1 to 4 five times and average the result every thousandth of a second. The pins used are for the ESP32-S3 and need to be changed for the ESP32. When the measurement is complete it calls adcComplete which sets the flag adc_coversion_done. The main loop simply tests this flag and processes the readings when it is set to true. If you don't process the measurements after they are made they are simply overwritten by the next measurement.

Digital to Analog ESP32 Only

The ESP32 and ESP32-S2 have two 8-bit Digital-to-Analog Converters, DACs. The ESP32-S3 doesn't have any DACs and so this section only applies to the ESP32. If you need to use a DAC with the ESP32-S3 you can use a PWM signal or you can add an MCP4725 12-Bit DAC using I2C or one of the many SPI DAC chips.

The ESP32 provides two DAC outputs. These are connected to GPIO25 (GPIO17 ESP32S2) DAC channel 0 and GPIO26 (GPIO 18 ESP3S2) DAC channel 1 and this cannot be changed.

The DACs can be used in a very simple but limited way that is ESP32 specific – the Arduino doesn't have DAC support. To set a DAC output you use:

```
void dacWrite(uint8_t pin, uint8_t value);
```

where value is in the range 0-255 corresponding to 0V to 3.3V.

The only other function is

```
void dacDisable(uint8_t pin);
```

which disables the DAC output on the specified pin.

For example, to generate a ramp output you can use something like:

```
void setup() {
}

void loop() {
  for (uint8_t i = 0; i < 256; i++) {
    dacWrite(25, i);
  }
}
```

which produces:

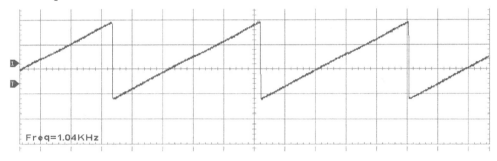

Freq=1.04KHz

The frequency is about 1kHz which is surprisingly low, but it is using the full 256 steps of resolution. You can double the frequency by halving the resolution and so on. How high a frequency you can generate depends on how much distortion you can tolerate.

For example, to use a step size of 32, change the loop to read:

```
void setup() {
}
void loop() {
  for (uint8_t i = 0; i < 256; i+= 32) {
    dacWrite(25, i);
  }
}
```

produces:

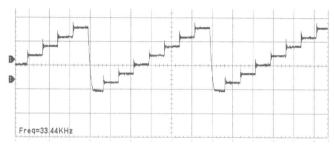

The frequency is roughly 33kHz, but the steps are clearly visible and some filtering would be required to improve the waveform.

If you want other waveforms then the standard technique is to compute a table with 256 values to write to the DAC similar to what we did with the PWM generator.

For example, to generate a sine wave you could use:

```
uint8_t wave[256];

void setup() {
   for (int i = 0; i < 256; i++) {
     wave[i] = (uint8_t)((128.0 +
            sinf((float)i * 2.0 * 3.14159 / 255.0) * 128.0));
  }
}
void loop() {
  for (int i = 0; i < 256; i++) {
    dacWrite(25, wave[i]);
  }
}
```

This creates a reasonable wave form, but at only 1kHz:

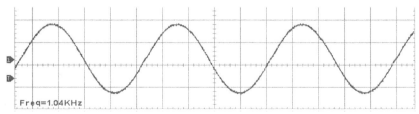

Touch Sensors

The ESP32 has the advantage of providing touch sensors, whereas with other devices you usually need to implement your own externally. The original ESP32 approach to the problem has been superseded by that used in the ESP32-S2 and -S3. The new approach is more robust and capable however it still needs careful adjustment to make work reliably. In this chapter we outline the basics.

The ESP32 has ten channels and the ESP32-S3 has 14 channels of touch sense.

	ESP32	ESP32-S3
T0	GPIO4	Not connect to a GPIO
T1	GPIO0	GPIO1
T2	GPIO2	GPIO2
T3	GPIO15	GPIO3
T4	GPIO13	GPIO4
T5	GPIO12	GPIO5
T6	GPIO14	GPIO6
T7	GPIO27	GPIO7
T8	GPIO33	GPIO8
T9	GPIO32	GPIO9
T10		GPIO10
T11		GPIO11
T12		GPIO12
T13		GPIO13
T14		GPIO14

To use a GPIO line as a touch sensor you simply have to construct a touchpad:

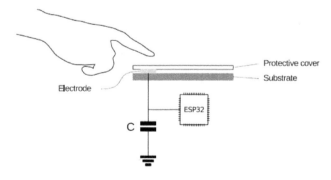

Notice that the user doesn't actually touch the electrode. The protective cover insulates the finger from the GPIO line and hence it is safe and more reliable. The principle is that when a finger, or any part of the body, is placed near the protective cover it forms the second plate of a capacitor and hence the total capacitance changes, usually by increasing. The ESP32 measures the capacitance of the touchpad.

Many projects mistake the touch sensors for resistivity sensors and the metal plate is exposed and the user is expected to actually make a connection with it. This usually works, but it isn't the correct method and it loses many of the advantages of a capacitive touch system. To use touch sensors correctly you don't actually touch the metal part of any wire from the GPIO line.

The capacitance of the sensor is measured by the ESP32 applying a varying voltage. The time to charge and discharge the capacitor depends on the size of the capacitor and a count of pulses in a given time gives an indication of whether a user is touching the sensor or not. The only real problem in using a touch sensor is knowing what the touch/no touch threshold is. This varies according to the design and implementation of the touchpad. It depends on the size of the electrode and the nature and thickness of the covering.

The biggest problem in using the touch sensors is finding a suitable configuration that works with the physical sensor you have constructed. The problem is that a given physical sensor will have an intrinsic capacitance that depends on its construction and the amount that it is changed by human presence also depends on its construction. So you have no idea what sort of capacitance indicates no human touch and how much this changes when it is touched. There is also the issue of how much noise the device is susceptible to and this depends on its construction and its location.

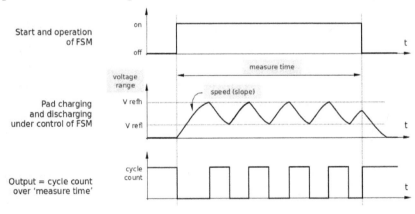

You basically have to tune the system with the real hardware and real people using it. To do this you need to know the parameters you can vary. The basic idea is that the system estimates the capacitance of the sensor by timing how long it takes to charge and discharge. The larger capacitance, the longer it takes to charge and discharge. Rather than time the event, the system simply repeats the charge/discharge cycle and counts how many times this happens in a fixed amount of time. You can vary how long the cycle goes on for, the voltages that the charge/discharge cycles between and the speed of charge/discharge.

It can be difficult to see how these relate to the quality of the measurement. The longer the measuring time the less noise in the system, but the slower it is to react to a real change. The voltage range can affect the accuracy of a reading by restricting the switching points to places where the voltage is changing rapidly rather than slowly. Finally the speed, or slope, sets how sensitive the system is to changes in capacitance. High charge rates make the system more stable, but use more current. Add to all of this the fact that there is a filtering system that can be applied to the readings to reduce the noise even further and you can see that finding an optimum setup is very difficult.

To make matters more complicated the ESP32-S3, and the ESP32-S2, implement touch sensors in a different way. The ESP32 counts how many charge/discharge cycles occur in a fixed time. The ESP32-S3 counts the time that a fixed number of charge/discharge cycles take to complete. This means that on an ESP32 the result decreases as the capacitance increases, but on the ESP32-S3 the result increases. This also results in the need for two slightly different sets of functions used to work with the touch sensors.

The most basic touch function is:

```
touch_value_t touchRead(uint8_t pin)
```

and the result is a 16-bit int for the ESP32 and a 32-bit int for the ESP32-S3.

To discover the values to use as a threshold for touch/no touch you can use a simple program that displays the current count. For the ESP32 this is:

```
void setup() {
  Serial.begin(9600);
}

void loop() {
  int touch = touchRead(4);
  Serial.println(touch);
  delay(1000);
}
```

Construct a touchpad, connect it to the GPIO line and see what readings you get when it is touched and when it is left alone. Hopefully these will be well enough separated for you to pick a threshold that gives reliable operation. If you plan to use a touchpad in a device that you deploy, you should also include a regular check on the value of the touchpad when not touched and use this to set a baseline for the threshold.

You generally don't need to modify how the touch sensors are configured, but if you do there is a single useful function:

```
void touchSetCycles(uint16_t measure, uint16_t sleep)
```

The measure sets the time to measure the touch sensor, usually 0.5ms and sleep is the time between measurements. The longer the set time, the more sensitive and accurate the results, but the more unresponsive the touch button becomes.

Once you have established a threshold that marks the difference between touched and not touched, you can use this to make the touch sensor generate an interrupt or return a 0/1 indicator. For example, if the threshold is determined to be 25000 you can respond to this:

```
void setup() {
  Serial.begin(9600);
}

void loop() {
  int touch = touchRead(4);
  if (touch > 25000) {
    Serial.println("pressed");
  }
  delay(1000);
}
```

Notice that this is for the ESP32-S3 as the value increases with touch. For an ESP32 you would have to reverse the comparison as for it the value decreases with touch.

This works, but most of the time you are likely to use an interrupt-driven approach to handling touch. You can attach an ISR to a touch button using:

```
void touchAttachInterrupt(uint8_t pin, void (*userFunc)(void),
                          touch_value_t threshold);
```

The userFunc is called when the value exceeds the threshold on an ESP32 and when it falls below the threshold on an ESP32-S3.

There is also a version of the function that allows you to pass a parameter to the ISR:

```
void touchAttachInterruptArg(uint8_t pin, void (*userFunc)(void*),
                             void *arg, touch_value_t threshold);
```

When you want to switch the interrupt off you can use:

```
void touchDetachInterrupt(uint8_t pin);
```

For example:

```
void ISR(void){
  digitalWrite(2, !digitalRead(2));
}

void setup() {
  pinMode(2, OUTPUT);
  touchAttachInterrupt(4,ISR,50000);
  Serial.begin(9600);
}

void loop() {
}
```

In this case the interrupt routine toggles GPIO2 and you can see the resulting signal when the touchpad is touched.

The touch sensors can also be used to wake up the ESP32, see Chapter 18.

Summary

- The ESP32 has two 12-bit ADCs, but only one is available for general use and it provides six easy-to-use channels in the ESP32 and eight in the ESP32-S3.

- Reading the ADC can by done in two ways, but reading it under program control is easier to get started with.

- You can also set up a regular reading of a set of ADC channels using an interrupt.

- The calibration voltage is available as a value stored in the eFuse memory. The calibration API makes use of this to correct the measurement.

- The raw and calibrated functions take roughly the same time.

- The ESP32 has two 8-bit ADC channels which use GPIO25 and GPIO26. The ESP32-S3 doesn't have any ADC channels.

- Using ESP32 ADC, you can generate a variety of waveforms at 1kHz or higher, depending on resolution.

- There are also ten touch sensors on the ESP32 and twelve on the ESP32-S3. These are capacitive sensors and do not require human contact with the GPIO line.

- The ESP32-S3 uses a slightly different approach to the touch sensors and is not software compatible with the ESP32.

- The problem in using the touch sensor is knowing the threshold and you need to establish this for any given setup.

Chapter 12

Using The I2C Bus

The I2C, standing for I-Squared-C or Inter IC, bus is one of the most useful ways of connecting moderately sophisticated sensors and peripherals to any processor. The only problem is that it can seem like a nightmarish confusion of hardware, low-level interaction and high-level software. There are few general introductions to the subject because at first sight every I2C device is different, but there are shared principles that can help you work out how to connect and talk to a new device.

The I2C bus is a serial bus that can be used to connect multiple devices to a controller. It is a simple bus that uses two active wires: one for data and one for a clock. Despite there being lots of problems in using the I2C bus, because it isn't well standardized and devices can conflict and generally do things in their own way, it is still commonly used and too useful to ignore.

The big problem in getting started with the I2C bus is that you will find it described at many different levels of detail, from the physical bus characteristics and protocol to the details of individual devices. It can be difficult to relate all of this together and produce a working project. In fact, you only need to know the general workings of the I2C bus, some general features of the protocol, and know the addresses and commands used by any particular device.

To explain and illustrate these ideas we really do have to work with a particular device to make things concrete. However, the basic stages of getting things to work, the steps, the testing and verification, are more or less the same irrespective of the device.

I2C Hardware Basics

The I2C bus is very simple from the hardware point of view. It has just two signal lines, SDA and SCL, the data and clock lines respectively. Each of these lines is pulled up by a suitable resistor to the supply line at whatever voltage the devices are working - 3.3V and 5V are common choices. The size of the pull-up resistors isn't critical, but 4.7K is typical as shown in the circuit diagram.

You simply connect the SDA and SCL pins of each of the devices to the pull-up resistors. Of course, if any of the devices have built-in pull-up resistors you can omit the external resistors. More of a problem is if multiple devices each have pull-ups. In this case you need to disable all but one.

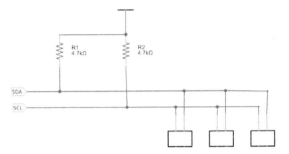

The I2C bus is an open collector bus. This means that it is actively pulled down by a transistor set to on. When the transistor is off, however, the bus returns to the high voltage state via the pull-up resistor. The advantage of this approach is that multiple devices can pull the bus low at the same time. That is, an open collector bus is low when one or more devices pulls it low and high when none of the devices is active.

The SCL line provides a clock which is used to set the speed of data transfer, one data bit is presented on the SDA line for each pulse on the SCL line. In all cases, the master drives the clock line to control how fast bits are transferred. The slave can, however, hold the clock line low if it needs to slow down the data transfer. In most cases the I2C bus has a single master device, the ESP32 in our case, which drives the clock and invites the slaves to receive or transmit data. Multiple masters are possible, but this is advanced and usually not necessary.

All you really need to know is that all communication usually occurs in 8-bit packets. The master sends a packet, an address frame, which contains the address of the slave it wants to interact with. Every slave has to have a unique address, which is usually 7 bits, but it can be 10 bits, and the ESP32 does support this in hardware. In the rest of this chapter we will use 7-bit addressing because it is commonly supported.

One of the problems in using the I2C bus is that manufacturers often use the same address, or the same set of selectable addresses, and this can make using particular combinations of devices on the same bus difficult or impossible.

The 7-bit address is set as the high-order 7 bits in the byte and this can be confusing as an address that is stated as 0x40 in the datasheet results in 0x80 being sent to the device. The low-order bit of the address signals a write or a read operation depending on whether it is a 0 or a 1 respectively. After sending an address frame it then sends or receives data frames back from the slave. There are also special signals used to mark the start and end of an exchange of packets, but the library functions take care of these.

This is really all you need to know about I2C in general to get started, but it is worth finding out more of the details as you need them. You almost certainly will need them as you debug I2C programs.

The clock (SCL) and data (SDA) lines rest high. The master signals a Start bit, S in the diagram below, by pulling the SDA line down. The clock is then pulled low by the master, during which time the SDA line can change state. The bit is read in the middle of the following high period of the clock pulse, B1, B2 and so on in the diagram. This continues until the last bit has been sent when the data line is allowed to rise while the clock is high, so sending a stoP bit, P in the diagram. Notice that when data is being transmitted the data line doesn't change while the clock is high. Any change in the data line when the clock is high sends a start or a stop bit - clock high coupled with a falling data line produces a start bit and clock high with a rising data line produces a stop bit:

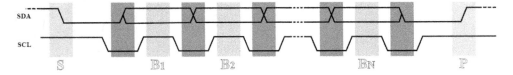

The clock speed was originally set at 100kHz, standard mode, but then increased to 400kHz in fast mode. In practice, devices usually specify a maximum clock speed that they will work with.

The ESP32 I2C Functions

The ESP32 has two I2C controllers, I2C0 and I2C1, that can work as a master or a slave. The connections from both controllers can be routed to different pins and in this sense there are no defaults despite what some pinout diagrams suggest. To use one of the controllers you have to select a pair of GPIO lines to act as SDA and SCL.

The ESP32 Arduino I2C library is based on the Arduino Core Wire library. If you restrict yourself to the defaults then the ESP works in the same way as other Arduinos. The main difference is that you can use either of the two I2C controllers. If you import the Wire library:

```
#include "Wire.h"
```

then you get two Wire objects:

`Wire` which is I2C0

and

`Wire1` which is I2C1.

The Arduino core library only defines `Wire`.

The `Wire` constructor also lets you create your own instances:

```
TwoWire myI2C=TwoWire(n)
```

where n is the number of the controller, 0 or 1 for the ESP32.

In most cases it is better to set the GPIO pins to be used. If you don't then the `Wire` objects use defaults. To set pins use:

```
bool setPins(int sdaPin, int sclPin);
```

This has to be done before calling:

```
bool begin()
```

which initializes the I2C hardware. To release the hardware call:

```
bool end()
```

If you are starting the I2C hardware in master mode you can use:

```
bool begin(int sdaPin, int sclPin, uint32_t frequency)
```

Note that a slave cannot set the frequency of the bus.

You can further customize the hardware using;

```
bool setClock(uint32_t frequency)
uint32_t getClock()
void setTimeOut(uint16_t timeOutMillis)
uint16_t getTimeOut()
```

The default time out is 50ms.

To send data on the bus you have to use three methods:

```
void beginTransmission(uint16_t address)
write(data)
uint8_t endTransmission(bool sendStop)
```

The `beginTransmission` determines the address of the slave. The data written can be a single byte, a string of bytes or an array of bytes with an additional length specifier:

```
size_t write(data, length)
```

The `beginTransmission` and `write` methods do not initiate the transmission. The data is stored in an internal buffer until the `endTransmission` method is called. The `sendStop` parameter specifies if a stop bit should be sent. The default is `true` so calling the `endTransmission` method finishes the transaction and frees the bus for another transaction. If you set this to `false` then no stop bit is sent and in principle this means that the transmission can continue with another. That is the default transaction is:

```
START|ADDR|ACK|DATA0|ACK|
            DATA1|ACK|
               ....
            DATAn|ACK|STOP
```

Notice that it is the slave that sends the ACK bit and, if the data is not received correctly, it can send NAK instead. Also notice that there is a single STOP bit at the end of the transaction.

Notice that multi-byte transfer is quite different from sending single bytes one at a time with `sendStop` set to false :

```
START|  ADDR  |ACK|DATA0|ACK|STOP
START|  ADDR  |ACK|DATA1|ACK|STOP
      ...
START|  ADDR  |ACK|DATAn|ACK|STOP
```

Notice that there are now multiple ADDR frames sent, as well as multiple START and STOP bits. What this means in practice is that you have to look at a device's datasheet and send however many bytes it needs either as a single operation or a single transaction.

The `endTransmission` method returns an error code:

> 0: Success
>
> 1: Data too long to fit in transmit buffer
>
> 2: NACK received on transmit of address
>
> 3: NACK received on transmit of data
>
> 4: Other error.
>
> 5: Timeout

To get data from a slave device you have to first use the `requestFrom` method:

```
uint8_t requestFrom(uint16_t address, uint8_t size)
uint8_t requestFrom(uint16_t address, uint8_t size, bool sendStop)
```

This immediately sends the request for data and then attempts to read the specified size bytes into a buffer. The sendStop parameter determines if a stop signal is sent at the end of the transaction. The default is true which sends a stop signal and terminates the transaction. Setting this to false keeps the bus open with the possibility of sending more data to the slave.

As in the case of a write operation, the address supplied is shifted up one bit, but now the lower-order bit is set to 1 to indicate a read operation. So, if the current slave is at address 0x40, the read sends a read address of 0x81. This is important to remember if you are viewing the transaction on a logic analyzer.

The read transaction is:

```
START|ADDR|ACK|DATA0|ACK|
             |DATA1|ACK|
             |DATA2|ACK|

         . . .
             |DATAn|NAK|STOP
```

The master sends the address frame and the slave sends the ACK after the address to acknowledge that it has been received and it is ready to send data. Then, the slave sends bytes, one at a time, and the master sends ACK in response to each byte. Finally, the master sends a NAK to indicate that the last byte has been read and then a STOP bit. That is, the master controls how many bytes are transferred.

As in the case of the write functions, a block transfer of n bytes is different from transferring n bytes one at a time. The data from the slave is stored in an internal buffer which is only 32 bytes and hence any request for data should be less than this.

Once the requestFrom method returns you can access the buffer using any of the Stream methods. The two most useful are:

- ◆ read()   Return the next byte in the buffer, -1 if no data
- ◆ readBytes(buffer,length)   Read length bytes into buffer

Notice that when you use either of these methods the data is already transferred from the slave.

Register Operations

A very standard interaction between master and slave is writing data to a register. This isn't anything special and, as far as the I2C bus is concerned, you are simply writing raw data. However, datasheets and users tend to think in terms of reading and writing internal storage locations, i.e. registers in the device. In fact, many devices have lots of internal storage, indeed some I2C devices, for example I2C EPROMS, are nothing but internal storage.

In this case a standard transaction to write to a register is:

1. Send address frame
2. Send a data frame with the command to select the register
3. Send a data frame containing the byte, or word, to be written to the register

Like writing to a register, reading from a register is a very standard operation, but it is slightly more complicated in that you need both a write and a read operation.

1. Send address frame
2. Send a data frame with the command to select the register
3. Read data associated with the register

That is, to read a register you need a write operation to send the address of the register to the device and then a read operation to get the data that the device sends as the contents of the register.

You can see that these "register" operations could be considered to be single transactions and this is indeed what some hardware does. The issue is do you send a stop bit between each part of the transaction?

In theory, and mostly in practice, a register read of this sort can work with a stop-start separating the write and the read operation, which is what you get if you use separate write and read function calls without suppressing the stop bit. That is, the transfer sequence is:

```
START|ADDR|ACK|REGADDR|ACK|STOP|
START|ADDR|ACK|DATA1|ACK|
            |DATA2|ACK|
            . . .
            |DATAn|NAK|STOP
```

If you look at the end of the write and the start of the read using a logic analyzer, you will see that there is a stop and start bit between them.

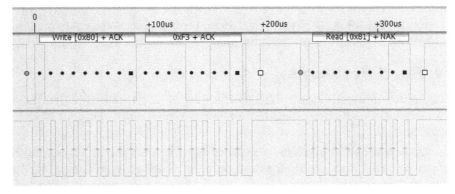

For some devices this is a problem. A stop bit is a signal that another transaction can start and this might allow another master to take over the bus. To avoid this some devices demand a repeated start bit between the write and the read and no stop bit. This is referred to as a "repeated start bit" or a "restart" transaction.

The sequence for a repeated start bit register read is:

```
START|ADDR|ACK|REGADDR|ACK|
START|ADDR|ACK|DATA0|ACK|
             |DATA1|ACK|
    . . .
             |DATAn|NAK|STOP
```

Notice that there is only one STOP.

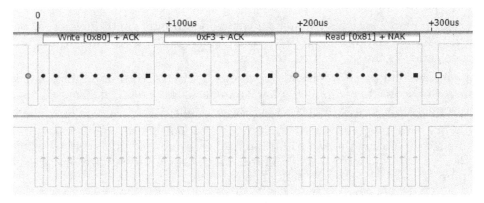

To not send a STOP between write and read you can use:

```
Wire.beginTransmission(ADDR);
Wire.write(REGADDR);
Wire.endTransmission(false);
Wire.requestFrom(ADDR,n);
```

In most cases the extra stop bit makes no difference. The documentation mentions the MLX90620 IR array needs no stop bit between write and read, but this is hardly a common peripheral.

Slow Read Protocols

The I2C clock is mostly controlled by the master and this raises the question of how we cope with the speed that a slave can or cannot respond to a request for data.

There are two broad approaches to waiting for data on the I2C bus. The first is simply to request the data and then perform reads in a polling loop. If the device isn't ready with the data, then it sends a data frame with a NAK bit set.

In this case the read function throws an exception rather than returns the number of bytes read. So all we have to do is test for an error response with a try/catch. Of course, the polling loop doesn't have to be "tight". The response time is often long enough to do other things and you can use the I2C bus to work with other slave devices while the one you activated gets on with getting the data you requested. All you have to do is to remember to read its data at some later time.

The second way is to allow the slave to hold the clock line low after the master has released it – so called "clock stretching". In most cases the master will simply wait before moving on to the next frame while the clock line is held low. This is very simple and it means you don't have to implement a polling loop, but also notice that your program is frozen until the slave releases the clock line.

Many devices implement both types of slow read protocol and you can use whichever suits your application. However, the ESP32 has a number of problems with slow reads, no matter how you decide to implement it.

A Real Device

Using an I2C device has two problems - the physical connection between master and slave and figuring out what the software has to do to make it work. Here we'll work with the HTU21D/Si7021 and the information in its datasheet to make a working temperature humidity sensor using the I2C functions we've just met.

First the hardware. The HTU21D Humidity and Temperature sensor is one of the easiest of I2C devices to use. Its only problem is that it is only available as a surface-mount package. To overcome this you could solder some wires onto the pads or buy a general breakout board. However, it is much simpler to buy the HTU21D breakout board because this has easy connections and built-in pull-up resistors. The HTU21D has been replaced by the Si7021, which is more robust than the original and works in the same way, but the HTU21D is still available from many sources.

If you decide to work with some other I2C device you can still follow the steps given, modifying what you do to suit it. In particular, if you select a device that only works at 5V you might need a level converter.

You can use a prototype board to make the connections and this makes it easier to connect other instruments such as a logic analyzer. Given that the pinouts vary according to the exact make of the device, you need to compare the suggested wiring with the breakout board you are actually using.

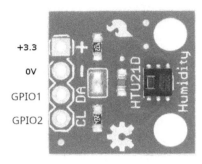

ESP32	HTU21
SDA GPIO1	SDA/DA
SCK GPIO2	SCL/CL
3.3v	VCC/VIN/+
GND	GND/-

A First Program

After wiring up any I2C device, the first question that needs to be answered is, does it work? Unfortunately for most complex devices finding out if it works is a multi-step process. Our first program aims to read some data back from the HTU21D, any data will do.

If you look at the datasheet you will find that the device address is 0x40 and that it supports the following commands/registers:

Command	Code	Comment
Trigger Temperature Measurement	0xE3	Hold master
Trigger Humidity Measurement	0xE5	Hold master
Trigger Temperature Measurement	0xF3	No Hold master
Trigger Humidity Measurement	0xF5	No Hold master
Write user register	0xE6	
Read user register	0xE7	
Soft Reset	0xFE	

The easiest of these to get started with is the Read user register command. The user register gives the current setup of the device and can be used to set the resolution of the measurement.

Notice that the codes that you send to the device can be considered as addresses or commands. In this case you can think of sending 0xE7 as a command to read the register or the read address of the register, it makes no difference. In most cases, the term "command" is used when sending the code makes the device do something, and the term "address" is used when it simply makes the device read or write specific data.

To read the user register we have to write a byte containing 0xE7 and then read the byte the device sends back. This involves sending an address frame, a data frame, and then another address frame and reading a data frame. The device seems to be happy if you send a stop bit between each transaction or just a new start bit.

A program to read the user register is fairly easy to put together. The address of the device is 0x40, so its write address is 0x80 and its read address is 0x81. Recall that bus addresses are shifted one bit to the left and the base address is the write address and the read address is base address+1.

As the I2C functions adjust the address as needed, we simply use 0x40 as the device's address, but it does affect what you see if you sample the data being exchanged:

```
#include "Wire.h"

void setup() {
  Serial.begin(9600);
  Wire.setPins(1, 2);
  Wire.begin();
}

void loop() {
  Wire.beginTransmission(0x40);
  Wire.write(0xE7);
  Wire.endTransmission(true);

  Wire.requestFrom(0x40, 1);
  char temp = Wire.read();
  Serial.printf("User Register = %X \r\n", temp);
  delay(2000);
}
```

This sends the address frame 0x80 and then the data byte 0xE7 to select the user register. Next it sends an address frame 0x81 to read the data. You might have to remove the line that sets the internal pullups to make your version of the breakout board work.

If you run the program you will see:

```
User Register = 2
```

This is the default value of the register and it corresponds to a resolution of 12 bits and 14 bits for the humidity and temperature respectively and a supply voltage greater than 2.25V.

The I2C Protocol In Action

If you have a logic analyzer that can interpret the I2C protocol connected, what you will see is:

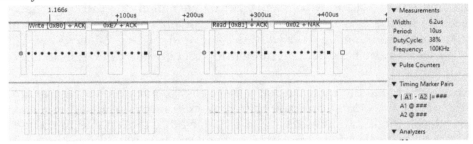

You can see that the `write_byte` function sends an address packet set to the device's 7-bit address `0x40` as the high-order bits with the low-order bit set to zero to indicate a write, i.e `0x80`. After this you get a data packet sent containing `0xE7`, the address of the register. After 60 microseconds it sends the address frame again, only this time with the low-order bit set to one to indicate a read. The gap between the operations is rather long and it slows things down. It then receives back a single byte of data from the device, `0x02`. Also notice the start and stop bits at the end of each data byte.

This all demonstrates that the external device is working properly and we can move on to getting some data of interest.

Reading Temperature Data – Clock Stretching

Now we come to reading one of the two quantities that the device measures, temperature. If you look back at the command table you will see that there are two possible commands for reading the temperature:

Command	Code	Comment
Trigger Temperature Measurement	0xE3	Hold master
Trigger Temperature Measurement	0xF3	No Hold master

What is the difference between Hold master and No Hold master? As already mentioned, the device cannot read the temperature instantaneously. To cope with this the master can either opt to be held waiting for the data, i.e. Hold master, or released to do something else and poll for the data until it is ready, i.e No Hold master.

The Hold master option works by allowing the device to stretch the clock pulse by holding the line low after the master has released it. In this mode, the master will wait until the device releases the line. Not all masters support this mode, but the ESP32 does and in theory this makes it the simpler option. To read the temperature using the Hold master mode you simply send 0xE3 and then read three bytes.

The simplest program that should work is:

```
#include "Wire.h"

void setup() {
  Serial.begin(9600);
  Wire.setPins(1, 2);
  Wire.begin();
}

void loop() {
  Wire.beginTransmission(0x40);
  Wire.write(0xE3);
  Wire.endTransmission();

  int count;
  count = Wire.requestFrom(0x40, 3);

  char msb = Wire.read();
  char lsb = Wire.read();
  char check = Wire.read();
  Serial.printf("\nmsb %d \nlsb %d \nchecksum %d \n",
                                    msb, lsb, check);
  delay(2000);
}
```

This works perfectly on an ESP32-S3:

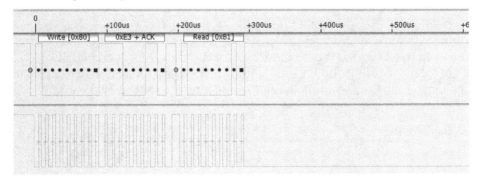

The clock is held low for around 40ms and then the slave releases it and the transaction continues.

Notice that this only works because the default for time out is 50ms – any longer and you would have to change the time out.

If you try it out on an ESP32 then you will find that the program fails without reporting any errors. The problem is that the ESP32 doesn't wait long enough for the clock stretching to complete. The reason that it times out is that the physical units used for the timeout are very small, the number of 80MHz clock pulses set by a 20-bit number. So a maximum timeout of 0xFFFFF is equivalent to about 13ms, which is nowhere near the 40ms needed by the device. So the ESP32 does support clock stretching, but only if it is less than around 13ms.

Reading Temperature Data – Polling

The alternative to clock stretching is polling. The basic idea in polling mode is that the master keeps trying to read the data from the slave but the slave responds with a NAK to indicate that data isn't ready.

The problem is that the ESP32 doesn't interpret the NAK to mean "give up this attempt to read" instead it waits for another timeout period to give the slave time to try again. What is more, once the error has occurred you cannot take control of the I2C bus without a complete reset. It works but it takes more than two seconds to read something that should take 40ms.

The ESP32-S3 implements the NAK properly, it reports an error, but doesn't try to restart the operation. As a result the following works and is reasonably fast:

```
#include "Wire.h"

void setup() {
  Serial.begin(9600);
  Wire.setPins(1, 2);
  Wire.begin();
}

void loop() {
  Wire.beginTransmission(0x40);
  Wire.write(0xF3);
  Wire.endTransmission();

  int count;
  do {
    count = Wire.requestFrom(0x40, 3);
    delay(2);
  } while (count == 0);
  char msb = Wire.read();
  char lsb = Wire.read();
  char check = Wire.read();
  Serial.printf("\nmsb %d \nlsb %d \nchecksum %d \n",
                                    msb, lsb, check);
  delay(2000);
}
```

If you try this out you will see the attempted reads. The final successful read is about 47ms after the first polling read:

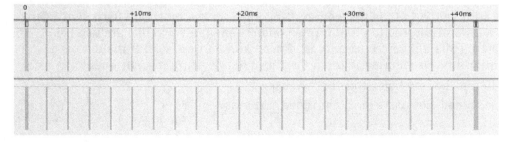

One solution to the problem of the ESP32 hardware not implementing polling correctly is to simply send the commands and then sleep for 50ms before reading the data. If the device is working correctly then the data should be available after this time and can be read without polling or clock stretching.

209

For example:

```
#include "Wire.h"

void setup() {
  Serial.begin(9600);
  Wire.setPins(1,2);
  Wire.begin();
}

void loop() {
  Wire.beginTransmission(0x40);
  Wire.write(0xF3);
  Wire.endTransmission();
  delay(50);

  int count;
  count = Wire.requestFrom(0x40, 3);
  char msb = Wire.read();
  char lsb = Wire.read();
  char check = Wire.read();
  Serial.printf("\nmsb %d \nlsb %d \nchecksum %d \n",
                msb, lsb, check);
  delay(2000);
}
```

Processing the Data

Our next task isn't really directly related to the problem of using the I2C bus, but it is a very typical next step. The device returns the data in three bytes, but the way that this data relates to the temperature isn't simple.

If you read the datasheet you will discover that the temperature data is the 14-bit value that results from putting together the most and least significant bytes and zeroing the bottom two bits. The bottom two bits are used as status bits, bit zero currently isn't used and bit one is a 1 if the data is a humidity measurement and a 0 if it is a temperature measurement.

To put the two bytes together we use:

```
unsigned int data16=((unsigned int) msb << 8) |
                                    (unsigned int) (lsb & 0xFC);
```

This zeros the bottom two bits, shifts the msb up eight bits and ORs the two together. The result is a 16-bit temperature value with the bottom two bits zeroed. Now we have a raw temperature value, but we still have to convert it to standard units. The datasheet gives the formula:

Temperature in °C = -46.85 + 175.72 * data16 / 2^{16}

The only problem in implementing this is working out 2^{16}. You can work out 2^x with the expression 1<<x, i.e. shift 1 x places to the right.

This gives:

```
float temp = (float)(-46.85 +(175.72 * data16 /(float)(1<<16)));
```

As 2^{16} is a constant that works out to 65536 it is more efficient to write:

```
float temp = (float)(-46.85 +(175.72 * data16 /(float)65536));
```

Now all we have to do is print the temperature:

```
Serial.printf("Temperature %f C \n\r", temp);
```

The full listing is at the end of this chapter.

Reading Humidity

Reading the humidity is just a little more of the same. As polling and clock stretching aren't reliable, we can simply wait for a time that gives the device the opportunity to have data ready to read. We write the 0xF5 once to the slave, wait and then read the 3-byte response. If anything goes wrong we need to reset the bus as shown earlier, but for simplicity this step is not included in the example.

Once we have the data, the formula to convert the 16-bit value to percentage humidity is:

```
RH= -6 + 125 * data16 / 2¹⁶
```

Putting all this together, and reusing some variables from the previous parts of the program, we have:

```
Wire.beginTransmission(0x40);
Wire.write(0xF5);
Wire.endTransmission();

do {
  count = Wire.requestFrom(0x40, 3);
  delay(2);
} while (count == 0);

Serial.printf("msb %d \n\r lsb %d \n\r checksum %d \n\r",
                                    msb, lsb, check);
data16 = ((unsigned int)msb << 8) | (unsigned int)(lsb & 0xFC);
float hum = -6 + (125.0 * (float)data16) / 65536;
Serial.printf("Humidity %f %% \n\r", hum);
```

Checksum Calculation

Although computing a cyclic redundancy checksum, CRC, isn't specific to I2C, it is another common task. The datasheet explains that the polynomial used is:

$$X^8+X^5+X^4+1$$

Once you have this information you can work out the divisor by writing a binary number with a one in each location corresponding to a power of X in the polynomial. In this case the 8th, 5th, 4th and 1st bit. Hence the divisor is:

```
0x0131
```

What you do next is roughly the same for all CRCs. First, you put the data that was used to compute the checksum together with the checksum value as the low-order bits:

```
uint32_t data32 = ((uint32_t)msb << 16)|
                  ((uint32_t) lsb <<8) | (uint32_t) check;
```

Now you have three bytes, i.e 24 bits, in a 32-bit variable. Next you adjust the divisor so that its most significant non-zero bit aligns with the most significant bit of the three bytes. As this divisor has a 1 at bit eight, it needs to be shifted 15 places to the right to move it to be the 24th bit:

```
uint32_t divisor = ((uint32_t) 0x0131) <<15;
```

Now that you have both the data and the divisor aligned, you step through the topmost 16 bits, i.e. you don't process the low-order 8 bits which hold the received checksum. For each bit you check to see if it is a 1. If it is, you replace the data with the data XOR divisor. In either case you shift the divisor one place to the right:

```
for (int i = 0; i < 16; i++){
  if( data32 & (uint32_t)1<<(23 - i))data32 =data32 ^ divisor;
  divisor=divisor >> 1;
};
```

When the loop ends, if there was no error, the data32 should be zeroed and the received checksum is correct and as computed on the data received.

A complete function to compute the checksum, with some optimization, is:

```
uint8_t crcCheck(uint8_t msb, uint8_t lsb, uint8_t check){
 uint32_t data32 = ((uint32_t)msb << 16)|((uint32_t) lsb <<8)|
                                         (uint32_t) check;
 uint32_t divisor = 0x988000;
 for (int i = 0 ; i < 16 ; i++){
   if( data32 & (uint32_t)1<<(23 - i) ) data32 ^= divisor;
   divisor>>= 1;
 };
 return (uint8_t) data32;
}
```

It is rare to get a CRC error on an I2C bus unless it is overloaded or subject to a lot of noise.

Complete Listing

The complete program for reading temperature and humidity, including checksum, is:

```
#include "Wire.h"
uint8_t crcCheck(uint8_t msb, uint8_t lsb, uint8_t check) {
  uint32_t data32 = ((uint32_t)msb << 16) | ((uint32_t)lsb << 8) |
                                                (uint32_t)check;
  uint32_t divisor = 0x988000;
  for (int i = 0; i < 16; i++) {
    if (data32 & (uint32_t)1 << (23 - i)) data32 ^= divisor;
    divisor >>= 1;
  };
  return (uint8_t)data32;
}

void setup() {
  Serial.begin(9600);
  Wire.setPins(1, 2);
  Wire.begin();
}

void loop() {
  Wire.beginTransmission(0x40);
  Wire.write(0xF3);
  Wire.endTransmission();

  int count;
  do {
    count = Wire.requestFrom(0x40, 3);
    delay(2);
  } while (count == 0);

  char msb = Wire.read();
  char lsb = Wire.read();
  char check = Wire.read();
  Serial.printf("\nmsb %d \nlsb %d \nchecksum %d \n",
                                      msb, lsb, check);
  unsigned int data16 = ((unsigned int)msb << 8) |
                              (unsigned int)(lsb & 0xFC);
  float temp = (float)(-46.85 + (175.72 * data16 / (float)65536));
  Serial.printf("Temperature %f C \n", temp);

  Wire.beginTransmission(0x40);
  Wire.write(0xF5);
  Wire.endTransmission(false);
```

```
  do {
    count = Wire.requestFrom(0x40, 3);
    delay(2);
  } while (count == 0);
  msb = Wire.read();
  lsb = Wire.read();
  check = Wire.read();
  Serial.printf("msb %d \n\r lsb %d \n\r checksum %d \n\r",
        msb, lsb, check);
  data16 = ((unsigned int)msb << 8) | (unsigned int)(lsb & 0xFC);
  float hum = -6 + (125.0 * (float)data16) / 65536;
  Serial.printf("Humidity %f %% \n\r", hum);

  Serial.printf("crc = %d\n\r", crcCheck(msb, lsb, check));

  delay(2000);
}
```

This works on an ESP32 and an ESP32-S3, but it takes much longer on an ESP32 and really works despite the incorrect handling of the NAK and polling in general. A better solution for the ESP32 is to simply wait 50ms before attempting a read.

Of course, this is just the start. Once you have the device working and supplying data, it is time to write your code in the form of functions that return the temperature and the humidity and generally make the whole thing more useful and easier to maintain. This is often how this sort of programming goes. First you write a lot of inline code so that it works as fast as it can, then you move blocks of code to functions to make the program more elegant and easy to maintain, checking at each refactoring that it all still works.

Not all devices used standard bus protocols. In Chapter 14 we'll look at a custom serial protocol that we have to implement for ourselves.

Summary

- The I2C bus is simple yet flexible and is one of the most commonly encountered ways of connecting devices.

- The I2C bus uses two wires – a data line and a clock.

- Arduino Wire Library allows access to the ESP32's I2C controllers.

- The ESP32 has two I2C controllers, I2C0 and I2C1, both of which can work as a master or a slave each of which can be connected to a pair of GPIO lines.

- The I2C protocol isn't standardized and you have to take account of variations in the way devices implement it.

- There are single-byte transfer operations and multi-byte transfers which differ in when a stop bit is sent.

- The low-level protocol can be made slightly more high-level by thinking of it as a single write/read a register operation.

- Sometimes a device cannot respond immediately and needs to keep the master waiting for data. There are two ways to do this, polling and clock stretching.

- The ESP32 implements clock stretching, but it has a very short timeout, 13ms, that is often too short to work. The ESP32-S3 works correctly and has a default 50ms timeout.

- The ESP32 doesn't implement polling correctly because it doesn't abort the read when it first receives a NAK but only after a one-second timeout. The ESP32-S3 treats the NAK correctly and polling works.

- The ESP32 has a problem with resetting the bus after an error.

- The HTU21D is a simple I2C device, but getting it working involves using polling with the hardware I2C or clock stretching. If you are using an ESP32-S3 then polling works. Alternatively just waiting for 50ms before reading works in all cases.

- Computing a checksum is an involved, but common, operation.

Chapter 13

One-Wire Protocols

In this chapter we make use of all the ideas introduced in earlier chapters to create a raw interface with the low-cost DHT11/22 temperature and humidity sensor and the 1-Wire bus device, the DS18B20. Both devices make good examples of how to use "bit-banging" to create a direct interface with a device.

The DHT22

The DHT22 used in this project is a more accurate version of the DHT11 The software will work with both versions and also with the AM2302, which is equivalent to the DHT22.

Model AM2302/DHT22
Power supply 3.3-5.5V DC
Output signal digital signal via 1-wire bus
Sensing element Polymer humidity capacitor
Operating range
 humidity 0-100%RH;
 temperature -40~80Celsius
Accuracy
 humidity +-2%RH(Max +-5%RH);
 temperature +-0.5Celsius
Resolution or sensitivity
 humidity 0.1%RH;
 temperature 0.1Celsius
Repeatability
 humidity +-1%RH;
 temperature +-0.2Celsius

The device will work at 3.3V and it makes use of a one-wire open collector-style bus, which makes it very easy to make the physical connection to the ESP32, however, the "one-wire bus" used isn't standard and is only used by this family of devices.

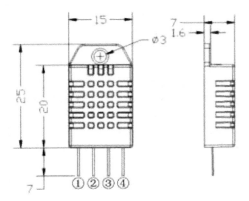

The pinouts are:
1. VDD
2. SDA serial data
3. Not used
4. GND

and the standard way of connecting the device is:

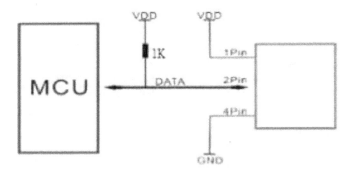

Although the recommended pull-up resistor is 1K, a higher value, typically 4.7K works better and even larger will work.

The Electronics

All you have to do is select a suitable GPIO line – any of those you are not already using will do. In our example GPIO2 is used because it is physically close to GND and 3.3V connections. Exactly how you build the circuit is a matter of preference. The basic layout can be seen below ESP32 on the left, ESP32-S3 on the right.

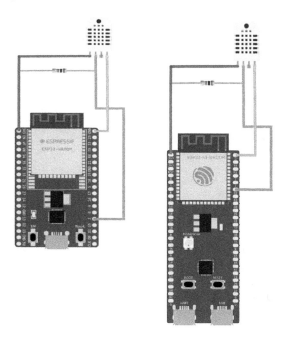

ESP32/S3	DHT22
3.3V OUT	VDD pin 1
GPIO2	SDA serial data pin 2
GND	GND pin 4

It is very easy to create this circuit using a prototyping board and some jumper wires. You can also put the resistor close to the DHT22 to make a sensor package connected to the ESP32 using three cables.

219

The Protocol

The serial protocol used by the DHT22 is fairly simple:

1. The host pulls the line low for between 0.8ms and 29ms, usually around 1ms. This is a request for data from the host to the DHT22.

2. It then releases the bus which is pulled high by the resistor.

3. After between 20μs and 200μs, usually 30μs, the device starts to send data by pulling the line down for around 80μs and then lets it float high for another 80μs. This is a "start" bit sent by the DHT22.

4. Next 40 bits of data are sent using a 70μs high for a 1 and a 26μs high for a 0 with the high pulses separated by around 50μs low periods.

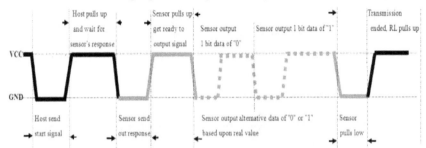

What we have to do is pull the line low for 1ms or so to start the device sending data and this is very easy. Then we have to wait for the device to pull the line down and let it pull up again for about 160μs and then read the time that the line is high or low 40 times.

A 1 corresponds to 70μs and a 0 corresponds to 26 to 28μs. This is within the range of pulse measurements that can be achieved using standard library functions. There is also a 50μs low period between each data bit and this can be used to do some limited processing. The time between falling edge transitions is therefore 120μs for a 1 and 76μs for a 0.

When trying to work out how to decode a new protocol it often helps to try to answer the question, "how can I tell the difference between a 0 and a 1?"

If you have a logic analyzer it can help to look at the waveform and see how you work it out manually. In this case, despite the complex-looking timing diagram, the difference comes down to a short versus a long pulse!

With the hardware shown on the previous page connected to the ESP32, the first thing that we need to do is establish that the system is working. The simplest way to do this is to pull the line down for 1ms and see if the device responds with a stream of pulses. These can be seen on a logic analyzer or an oscilloscope, both are indispensable tools. If you don't have access to either tool then you will just have to skip to the next stage and see if you can read in some data. The simplest code that will do the job is:

```
void setup() {
  Serial.begin(9600);
}

void loop() {
  pinMode(2, OUTPUT);
  digitalWrite(2, 1);
  delay(1000);
  digitalWrite(2, 0);
  delay(1);
  pinMode(2, INPUT);
  delay(1000);
}
```

Setting the line initially high, to ensure that it is configured as an output, we then set it low, wait for around 1ms and then change its direction to input and so allow the line to be pulled high. There is no need to set the line's pull-up mode because the ESP32 is the only device driving the line until it releases the line by changing its direction to input. When a line is in input mode it is high impedance and this is why we need an external pull-up resistor in the circuit.

As long as the circuit has been correctly assembled and you have a working device, you should see something like:

Reading the Data

With preliminary flight checks complete, it is time to read the 40-bit data stream. However, we have a problem in that we can't know how long it takes to convert a GPIO line from output to input. This means that we don't know where we are in the pulse train when the initial pulse is over. The standard solution is to use another GPIO line to signal where we are by toggling the line at the point in the program you want to identify on the logic analyzer plot.

For example, we can wait for the low that the device sends before the start bit and then wait for the start bit:

```
while (digitalRead(2) == 1) {};
while (digitalRead(2) == 0) {};
while (digitalRead(2) == 1) {};
```

The first while waits for a falling edge, the second for a rising edge and the third a falling edge.

If you look at the diagram of the protocol you should be able to see that we are now at the start of the first data bit. Next we can start to read in the data. A total of 40 bits, i.e. 5 bytes, is difficult to work with in standard variable types. A good compromise is to read in the first 32 bits into a 32-bit unsigned integer and then read the final byte into a byte variable. The reason is that the fifth byte is a checksum, so we have separated out the data and the checksum, but there are many different ways to organize this task.

First we read the 32 data bits:

```
int64_t t2;
  uint32_t data = 0;
  int64_t t1 = micros();
  for (int i = 0; i < 32; i++) {
    while (digitalRead(2) == 0) {};
    while (digitalRead(2) == 1) {};
    t2 = micros();
    data = data << 1;
    data = data | ((t2 - t1) > 100);
    t1 = t2;
  }
```

You can see the general idea is to simply find the time between falling edges and then treat anything bigger than 100 μs as a 1. In practice, the measured times between falling edges is around 80 μs for a 0 and 120 μs and 100 is a threshold halfway between the two. The bits are shifted into the variable data so that the first byte transmitted is the high-order byte.

Next we need to read the checksum byte:

```
  uint8_t checksum = 0;
  for (int i = 0; i < 8; i++) {
    while (digitalRead(2) == 0) {};
    while (digitalRead(2) == 1) {};
    t2 = micros();
    checksum = checksum << 1;
    checksum = checksum | ((t2 - t1) > 100);
    t1 = t2;
  }
```

This works in the same way. At the end of this we have 32 data bits in data and eight checksum bits in checksum and all we have to do is process the data to get the temperature and humidity.

Extracting the Data

You can process the data without unpacking it into individual bytes, but it is easier to see what is happening if we do:

```
uint8_t byte1 = (data >> 24 & 0xFF);
uint8_t byte2 = (data >> 16 & 0xFF);
uint8_t byte3 = (data >> 8 & 0xFF);
uint8_t byte4 = (data & 0xFF);
```

The first two bytes are the humidity measurement and the second two the temperature. The checksum is just the sum of the first four bytes reduced to eight bits and we can test it using:

```
Serial.printf("Checksum %X %X\n",checksum,
                     (byte1+byte2+byte3+byte4)&0xFF);
```

If you don't want to unpack the data then you can use:

```
Serial.printf("Checksum %X %X\n", checksum, ((data & 0xFF) +
            (data >> 8 & 0xFF) + (data >> 16 & 0xFF) +
                     (data >> 24 & 0xFF)) & 0xFF);
```

If the two values are different, there has been a transmission error. The addition of the bytes is done as a full integer and then it is reduced back to a single byte by the AND operation. If there is a checksum error, the simplest thing to do is get another reading from the device. Notice, however, that you shouldn't read the device more than once every two seconds.

The humidity and temperature data are also easy to reconstruct as they are transmitted high byte first and 10 times the actual value.

Extracting the humidity data is easy:

```
float humidity = (float)((byte1 <<8)| byte2) / 10.0;
Serial.printf("Humidity= %f %%\n", humidity);
```

The temperature data is slightly more difficult in that the topmost bit is used to indicate a negative temperature. This means we have to test for the most significant bit and flip the sign of the temperature if it is set:

```
float temperature;
int neg = byte3 & 0x80;
byte3 = byte3 & 0x7F;
temperature = (float)(byte3 << 8 | byte4) / 10.0;
if (neg > 0)
    temperature = -temperature;
Serial.printf("Temperature= %f C\n", temperature);
```

This completes the data processing.

The complete program is:

```
void setup() {
  Serial.begin(9600);
}

void loop() {
  pinMode(2, OUTPUT);
  digitalWrite(2, 1);
  delay(1000);
  digitalWrite(2, 0);
  delay(1);
  pinMode(2, INPUT);
  while (digitalRead(2) == 1) {};
  while (digitalRead(2) == 0) {};
  while (digitalRead(2) == 1) {};

  int64_t t2;
  uint32_t data = 0;
  int64_t t1 = micros();
  for (int i = 0; i < 32; i++) {
    while (digitalRead(2) == 0) {
    };
    while (digitalRead(2) == 1) {
    };

    t2 = micros();
    data = data << 1;
    data = data | ((t2 - t1) > 100);
    t1 = t2;
  }

  uint8_t checksum = 0;
  for (int i = 0; i < 8; i++) {
    while (digitalRead(2) == 0) {};
    while (digitalRead(2) == 1) {};
    t2 = micros();
    checksum = checksum << 1;
    checksum = checksum | ((t2 - t1) > 100);
    t1 = t2;
  }


  Serial.printf("data %ld\n", data);
  uint8_t byte1 = (data >> 24 & 0xFF);
  uint8_t byte2 = (data >> 16 & 0xFF);
  uint8_t byte3 = (data >> 8 & 0xFF);
  uint8_t byte4 = (data & 0xFF);
  Serial.printf("Checksum %X %X\n", checksum,
              (byte1 + byte2 + byte3 + byte4) & 0xFF);
  float humidity = (float)((byte1 << 8) | byte2) / 10.0;
```

```
    Serial.printf("Humidity= %f %%\n", humidity);
    float temperature;
    int neg = byte3 & 0x80;
    byte3 = byte3 & 0x7F;
    temperature = (float)(byte3 << 8 | byte4) / 10.0;
    if (neg > 0)
      temperature = -temperature;
    Serial.printf("Temperature= %f C\n", temperature);
    delay(1000);
}
```

Decoding Using Sampling

A simpler alternative way for decoding the data is to ignore the fact that it is
the width of each bit's frame that defines a zero, a short frame, or a one a
long frame. Instead notice that if you sample at a suitable fixed time from
the rising edge of a pulse then you will get a 0 in a zero frame and a 1 in a
one frame:

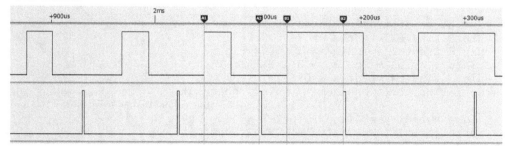

You can see the sampling times from the pulses on the lower trace of the
logic analyzer and the fact that you do indeed get a 0 in a zero frame and a 1
in a one frame. You can also see that the time to sample from the rising edge
is constant, even if the sampling period varies.

Using this decoding approach the two data loops can be written:

```
void setup() {
  Serial.begin(9600);
}

void loop() {
  pinMode(2, OUTPUT);
  digitalWrite(2, 1);
  delay(1000);
  digitalWrite(2, 0);
  delay(1);
  pinMode(2, INPUT);
  while (digitalRead(2) == 1) {};
  while (digitalRead(2) == 0) {};
  while (digitalRead(2) == 1) {};
```

225

```
  uint32_t data = 0;
  for (int i = 0; i < 32; i++)
  {
    while (digitalRead(2) == 0) {};
    delayMicroseconds(50);
    data = data << 1;
    data = data | digitalRead(2);
    while (digitalRead(2) == 1) {};

  }
  uint8_t checksum = 0;
  for (int i = 0; i < 8; i++)
  {
    while (digitalRead(2) == 0) {};
    delayMicroseconds(50);
    checksum = checksum << 1;
    checksum = checksum | digitalRead(2);
    while (digitalRead(2) == 1) {};
  }
  Serial.printf("data %ld\n", data);
  uint8_t byte1 = (data >> 24 & 0xFF);
  uint8_t byte2 = (data >> 16 & 0xFF);
  uint8_t byte3 = (data >> 8 & 0xFF);
  uint8_t byte4 = (data & 0xFF);
  Serial.printf("Checksum %X %X\n", checksum,
                      (byte1 + byte2 + byte3 + byte4) & 0xFF);
  float humidity = (float)((byte1 << 8) | byte2) / 10.0;
  Serial.printf("Humidity= %f %%\n", humidity);
  float temperature;
  int neg = byte3 & 0x80;
  byte3 = byte3 & 0x7F;
  temperature = (float)(byte3 << 8 | byte4) / 10.0;
  if (neg > 0)
    temperature = -temperature;
  Serial.printf("Temperature= %f C\n", temperature);
  delay(1000);
}
```

The delay of 50us is close to optimal based on a logic analyzer trace.

The 1-Wire Bus and the DS1820

The 1-Wire bus is a proprietary bus, but it has a lot in common with the I2C and SPI buses. It defines a general bus protocol that can be used with a range of different devices. There are many useful devices you can connect to it, including the iButton security devices, memory, data loggers, fuel gauges and more. However, probably the most popular of all 1-Wire devices is the DS18B20 temperature sensor - it is small, very cheap and very easy to use. This chapter shows you how to work with it, but first let's deal with the general techniques needed to work with the 1-Wire bus.

The Hardware

One-wire devices are very simple and only use a single wire to transmit data:

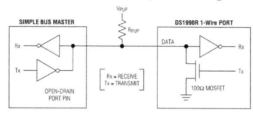

The 1-Wire device can pull the bus low using its Tx line and can read the line using its Rx line. The reason for the pull-up resistor is that both the bus master and the slave can pull the bus low and it will stay low until they both release the bus.

The device can even be powered from the bus line by drawing sufficient current through the pullup resistor, so-called parasitic mode. Low-power devices work well in parasitic mode, but some devices have such a heavy current draw that the master has to provide a way to connect them to the power line, referred to as strong pullup. In practice, parasitic mode can be difficult to make work reliably for high-power devices.

In normal-powered mode there are just three connections – V, usually 3.3V for the ESP32, Ground and Data. The pullup resistor varies according to the device, but anything from 2.2K to 4.7kΩ works. The longer the bus, the lower the pullup resistor has to be to reduce "ringing". There can be multiple devices on the bus and each one has a unique 64-bit lasered ROM code, which can be used as an address to select the active devices.

DS18B20 Hardware

The most popular 1-Wire device is the DS18B20. It is available in a number of formats, but the most common makes it look just like a standard BJT (Bipolar Junction Transistor) which can sometimes be a problem when you are trying to find one. You can also get them made up into waterproof sensors complete with cable.

No matter how packaged, they will work at 3.3V or 5V.

The basic specification of the DS18B20 is:

- Measures temperatures from -55°C to +125°C (-67°F to +257°F)
- ±0.5°C accuracy from -10°C to +85°C
- Thermometer resolution is user-selectable from 9 to 12 bits
- Converts temperature to 12-bit digital word in 750ms (max)

It can also be powered from the data line, allowing the bus to operate with only two wires, data and ground. However, this parasitic power mode is difficult to make work reliably and is best avoided in an initial design.

There are also the original DS1820 and the DS18S20, which too are best avoided in new applications.

To supply the DS18B20 with enough power during a conversion, the host has to connect it directly to the data line by providing a "strong pullup", essentially replicating a transistor. In normal-powered mode there are just three connections:

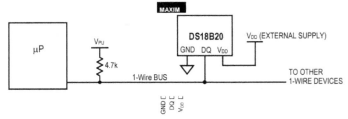

Ground needs to be connected to the system ground, VDD to 3.3V and DQ to the pull-up resistor of an open collector bus.

While you can have multiple devices on the same bus, for simplicity it is better to start off with a single device until you know that everything is working.

You can build the circuit in a variety of ways. You can solder the resistor to the temperature sensor and then use some longer wires with clips to connect to the ESP32.

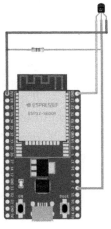

ESP32

ESP32-S3

The 1-Wire Protocol

Every transaction with a 1-wire device starts with an initialization handshake. This is simply a low pulse that lasts at least 480μs, a pause of 15μs to 60μs follows and then any and all of the devices on the bus pull the line low for 60μs to 240μs. The suggested timings set the line low for 480μs and read the line after 70μs followed by a pause of 410μs.

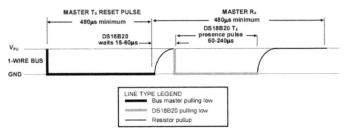

This is fairly easy to implement:

```
int presence(int pin) {
  pinMode(pin, OUTPUT |OPEN_DRAIN);
  digitalWrite(pin, 1);
  delayMicroseconds(1000);
  digitalWrite(pin, 0);
  delayMicroseconds(480);
  digitalWrite(pin, 1);
  delayMicroseconds(70);
  int res = digitalRead(pin);
  delayMicroseconds(410);
  return res;
}
```

The timings in this case are not critical as long as the line is read while it is held low by the slaves, which is never less than 60μs and is typically as much as 100μs. Notice that the line is set to open drain and input/output. When it is set high other devices on the bus can still pull it low and the GPIO line can be read.

If you try this partial program and have a logic analyzer with a 1-wire protocol analyzer you will see something like:

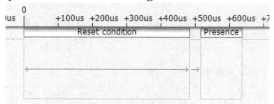

Seeing a presence pulse is the simplest and quickest way to be sure that your hardware is working.

Our next task is to implement the sending of some data bits to the device. The 1-Wire bus has a very simple data protocol. All bits are sent using a minimum of 60 μs for a read/write slot. Each slot must be separated from the next by a minimum of 1 μs.

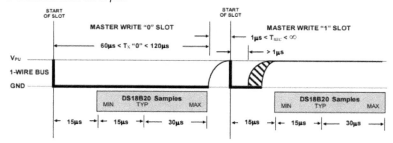

230

The good news is that timing is only critical within each slot. You can send the first bit in a slot and then take your time before you send the next bit as the device will wait for you. This means you only have to worry about timing within the functions that read and write individual bits.

To send a 0 you have to hold the line low for most of the slot. To send a 1 you have to hold the line low for just between 1μs and 15μs and leave the line high for the rest of the slot.

As the only time critical operations are the actual setting of the line low and then back to high, there is no need to worry too much about the speed of operation of the entire function so we might as well combine writing 0 and 1 into a single writeBit function:

```
void writeBit(uint8_t pin, int b) {
  int delay1, delay2;
  if (b == 1) {
    delay1 = 6;
    delay2 = 64;
  } else {
    delay1 = 60;
    delay2 = 10;
  }
  digitalWrite(pin, 0);
  delayMicroseconds(delay1);
  digitalWrite(pin, 1);
  delayMicroseconds(delay2);
}
```

The code at the start of the function simply increases the time between slots slightly.

You can see a zero followed by two ones in the following logic analyzer trace:

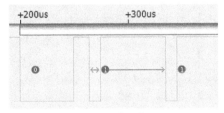

You can use this function to write an 8-bit byte:

```
int readByte(uint8_t pin) {
  int byte = 0;
  for (int i = 0; i < 8; i++) {
    byte = byte | readBit(pin) << i;
  };
  return byte;
}
```

231

We already know how the master sends a 1 and a 0. The protocol for the slave device is exactly the same, except that the master still provides the slot's starting pulse. That is, the master starts a 60 μs slot by pulling the bus down for at least 1 μs. Then the slave device either holds the line down for a further 15 μs minimum or it simply allows the line to float high. See below for the exact timings:

So all we have to do to read bits is to pull the line down for more than 1 μs and then sample the bus after pausing long enough for the line to be pulled up or held low. The datasheet gives 6 μs for the master's pulse and a 9 μs pause.

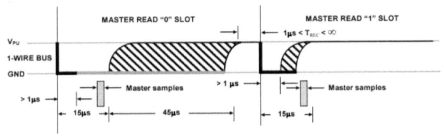

In practice, a final delay of 8 μs seems to work best and allows for the time to change the line's direction:

```
uint8_t readBit(uint8_t pin) {
  digitalWrite(pin, 0);
  delayMicroseconds(2);
  digitalWrite(pin, 1);
  delayMicroseconds(5);
  uint8_t b = digitalRead(pin);
  delayMicroseconds(60);
  return b;
}
```

The start of the slot pulse is just less than 3μs.

You can use the readBit function to implement reading a byte:

```
int readByte(uint8_t pin) {
  int byte = 0;
  for (int i = 0; i < 8; i++) {
    byte = byte | readBit(pin) << i;
  };
  return byte;
}
```

Match or Skip ROM

After discovering that there is at least one device connected to the bus, the master has to issue a ROM command. In many cases the ROM command used first will be the Search ROM command, which enumerates the 64-bit codes of all of the devices on the bus. After collecting all of these codes, the master can use Match ROM commands with a specific 64-bit code to select the device the master wants to talk to. Having to find and use the ROM codes is often a nuisance and unnecessary if you only have a single device of a known type connected to the bus. If there is only one device then we can use the Skip ROM command, 0xCC, to tell all the devices, i.e. the only device, on the bus to be active. It is a good and easy exercise to create a class that will read a single device and this also demonstrates how to read the temperature.

The steps to read the temperature from the only DS18B20 connected to the bus are:

1. Send a reset
2. Send a Skip ROM, 0xCC, command
3. Send a Convert, 0x44, command
4. Wait for the temperature to be read
5. Send a Read Scratchpad, 0xBE, command and then read the nine bytes that the device returns

The Convert command, 0x44, starts the DS18B20 making a temperature measurement. Depending on the resolution selected, this can take as long as 750ms. How the device tells the master that the measurement has completed depends on the mode in which it is operating, but using an external power line, i.e. not using parasitic mode, the device sends a 0 bit in response to a bit read until it is completed, when it sends a 1.

This is how 1-Wire devices that need time to get data ready slow down the master until they are ready.

The master can read a single bit as often as it likes and the slave will respond with a 0 bit until it is ready with the data. As we already have a readBit method, this is easy. The software polls for the completion by reading the bus until it gets a 1 bit:

```
int convert(uint8_t pin) {
  writeByte(pin, 0x44);
  int i;
  for (i = 0; i < 500; i++) {
    delayMicroseconds(10000);
    if (digitalRead(pin) == 1)
      break;
  }
  return i;
}
```

You can, of course, test the return value to check that the result has been obtained. If the `convert` returns `500` then the loop times out. When the function returns, the new temperature measurement is stored in the device's scratchpad memory and now all we have to do is read it.

The scratchpad memory has nine bytes of storage in total and does things like control the accuracy of conversion and provide status information.

SCRATCHPAD

BYTE 0	TEMPERATURE LSB (50h)		
BYTE 1	TEMPERATURE MSB (05h)		EEPROM
BYTE 2	T$_H$ REGISTER OR USER BYTE 1*	◄──►	T$_H$ REGISTER OR USER BYTE 1*
BYTE 3	T$_L$ REGISTER OR USER BYTE 2*	◄──►	T$_L$ REGISTER OR USER BYTE 2*
BYTE 4	CONFIGURATION REGISTER*	◄──►	CONFIGURATION REGISTER*
BYTE 5	RESERVED (FFh)		
BYTE 6	RESERVED		
BYTE 7	RESERVED (10h)		
BYTE 8	CRC*		

In our simple example the only two bytes of any interest are the first two, which hold the result of a temperature conversion. However, as we are going to check the CRC for error detection, we need to read all nine bytes.

All we have to do is issue a Read Scratchpad, `0xBE`, command and then read the nine bytes that the device returns. To send the new command we have to issue a new initialization pulse and a Skip ROM, `0xCC`, command followed by a Read Scratchpad command, `0xBE`:

```
presence(pin);
writeByte(pin, 0xCC);
writeByte(pin, 0xBE);
```

Now the data is ready to read.

```
uint8_t data[9];
for (int i = 0; i < 9; i++) {
  data[i] = readByte(pin);
}
```

We can read all nine bytes of it or just the first two that we are interested in. The device will keep track of which bytes have been read. If you come back later and read more bytes you will continue the read from where you left off. If you issue another initialization pulse then the device aborts the data transmission.

Computing the CRC

We have already encountered the idea and implementation of a CRC (Cyclic Redundancy Checksum) in Chapter 13. The 1-Wire bus uses the same CRC for all its devices and therefore we need to implement it just once. This is perhaps not in the most efficient way, but it will work. For low data rate applications high efficiency isn't needed and you can make use of a direct implementation. The 1-Wire datasheet specifies the CRC used in 1-wire devices as a shift register as well as a polynomial equation:

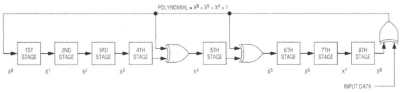

However, this is equivalent to a generator polynomial that defines the CRC as it is simply the hardware implementation of the calculation.
In this case it is:

$X^8 + X^5 + X^4 + 1$

The first question to answer is, what is the connection between binary values, polynomials and shift-registers? The answer is that you can treat a binary number as the coefficients of a polynomial, for example 101 is $1*X^2+0*X+1$. Each bit position corresponds to a power of X.
Using this notation creates a very simple relationship between multiplying by X and a left-shift.
For example:
$(1*X^2 + 0*X+ 1)*X = 1*X^3 + 0*X^2 + 1X + 0$
corresponds to:
101 <<1 == 1010
You can see that this extends to multiplying one polynomial by another and even polynomial division, all accomplished by shifting and XOR (eXclusive OR).
The CRC is the remainder when you divide the polynomial that represents the data by the generator polynomial. The computation of the remainder is what the shift register specified on the datasheet does. The fact that the division can be implemented so simply in hardware is what makes this sort of CRC computation so common. All the hardware has to do is zero the shift register and feed the data into it. When all the data has been shifted in, what is left in the shift register is the CRC, i.e. the remainder.

To check the data you have received, all you have to do is run it through the shift register again and compare the computed CRC with the one received. A better trick is also to run the received CRC through the shift register. If there have been no errors, this will result in 0.

You can look into the theory of CRCs, bit sequences and polynomials further, it is interesting and practically useful, but we now know everything we need to if we want to implement the CRC used by 1-Wire devices. All we have to do is implement the shift register in software.

From the diagram, what we have to do is take each bit of the input data and XOR it with the least significant bit of the current shift register. If the input bit is 0, the XORs in the shift register don't have any effect and the CRC just has to be moved one bit to the right. If the input bit is 1, we have to XOR the bits at positions 3 and 4 with 1 and put a 1 in at position 7 to simulate shifting a 1 into the register, i.e. XOR the shift register with 10001100.

So the algorithm for a single byte is:

```
for (int j = 0; j < 8; j++) {
        temp = (crc ^ databyte) & 0x01;
        crc >>= 1;
        if (temp)
                crc ^= 0x8C;
                databyte>>= 1;
        }
}
```

First we XOR the data with the current CRC and extract the low-order bit into temp. Then we right-shift the CRC by one place. If the low-order result stored in temp was a 1, we have to XOR the CRC with 0x8C to simulate the XORs in the shift register and shift in a 1 at the most significant bit. Then shift the data one place right and repeat for the next data bit.

With this worked out, we can now write a crc8 function that computes the CRC for the entire eight bytes of data:

```
uint8_t crc8(uint8_t *data, uint8_t len) {
        uint8_t temp;
        uint8_t databyte;
        uint8_t crc = 0;
        for (int i = 0; i < len; i++) {
                databyte = data[i];
                for (int j = 0; j < 8; j++) {
                        temp = (crc ^ databyte) & 0x01;
                        crc >>= 1;
                        if (temp)
                        crc ^= 0x8C;
                        databyte >>= 1;
                }
        }
        return crc;
}
```

With this in place we can now check the CRC of any data a 1-Wire bus device sends us.

Decoding Temperature

To obtain the temperature measurement we need to work with the first two bytes, which are the least and most significant bytes of the 12-bit temperature reading:

```
int t1 = data[0];
int t2 = data[1];
```

t1 holds the low-order bits and t2 the high-order bits.

All we now have to do is to put the two bytes together as a 16-bit two's complement integer. As the ESP32 supports a 16-bit int type, we can do this very easily:

```
int16_t temp1 = (t2 << 8 | t1);
```

Notice that this only works because int16_t really is a 16-bit integer. If you were to use:

```
int temp1= (t2<<8 | t1);
```

temp1 would be correct for positive temperatures, but it would give the wrong answer for negative values because the sign bit isn't propagated into the top 16 bits. If you want to use a 32-bit integer, you will have to propagate the sign bit manually:

```
if(t2 & 0x80) temp1=temp1 | 0xFFFF0000;
```

Finally, we have to convert the temperature to a scaled floating-point value. As the returned data gives the temperature in centigrade with the low-order four bits giving the fractional part, it has to be scaled by a factor of 1/16:

```
float temp = (float) temp1 / 16;
```

Now we can print the CRC and the temperature:

```
Serial.printf("CRC %hho \n\r ", crc);
Serial.printf("temperature = %f C \n", temp);
```

A Temperature Function

Packaging all of this into a single function is easy:

```
float getTemperature(uint8_t pin) {
  if (presence(pin) == 1) return -1000;
  writeByte(pin, 0xCC);
  if (convert(pin) == 500) return -3000;
  presence(pin);
  writeByte(pin, 0xCC);
  writeByte(pin, 0xBE);
  uint8_t data[9];
  for (int i = 0; i < 9; i++) {
    data[i] = readByte(pin);
  }
```

```
    uint8_t crc = crc8(data, 9);
    if (crc != 0) return -2000;
    int t1 = data[0];
    int t2 = data[1];
    int16_t temp1 = (t2 << 8 | t1);
    float temp = (float)temp1 / 16;
    return temp;
}
```

Notice that the function returns -1000 if there is no device, -2000 if there is a CRC error and -3000 if the device fails to provide data. These values are outside the range of temperatures that can be measured.

The Complete Program

The complete program to read and display the temperature is:

```
uint8_t readBit(uint8_t pin) {
  digitalWrite(pin, 0);
  delayMicroseconds(2);
  digitalWrite(pin, 1);
  delayMicroseconds(5);
  uint8_t b = digitalRead(pin);
  delayMicroseconds(60);
  return b;
}

void writeBit(uint8_t pin, int b) {
  int delay1, delay2;
  if (b == 1) {
    delay1 = 6;
    delay2 = 64;
  } else {
    delay1 = 60;
    delay2 = 10;
  }
  digitalWrite(pin, 0);
  delayMicroseconds(delay1);
  digitalWrite(pin, 1);
  delayMicroseconds(delay2);
}

int readByte(uint8_t pin) {
  int byte = 0;
  for (int i = 0; i < 8; i++) {
    byte = byte | readBit(pin) << i;
  };
  return byte;
}
```

```
void writeByte(uint8_t pin, int byte) {
  for (int i = 0; i < 8; i++) {
    if (byte & 1) {
      writeBit(pin, 1);
    } else {
      writeBit(pin, 0);
    }
    byte = byte >> 1;
  }
}
int presence(int pin) {
  pinMode(pin, OUTPUT |OPEN_DRAIN);
  digitalWrite(pin, 1);
  delayMicroseconds(1000);
  digitalWrite(pin, 0);
  delayMicroseconds(480);
  digitalWrite(pin, 1);
  delayMicroseconds(70);
  int res = digitalRead(pin);
  delayMicroseconds(410);
  return res;
}
int convert(uint8_t pin) {
  writeByte(pin, 0x44);
  int i;
  for (i = 0; i < 500; i++) {
    delayMicroseconds(10000);
    if (digitalRead(pin) == 1)
      break;
  }
  return i;
}
uint8_t crc8(uint8_t* data, uint8_t len) {
  uint8_t temp;
  uint8_t databyte;
  uint8_t crc = 0;
  for (int i = 0; i < len; i++) {
    databyte = data[i];
    for (int j = 0; j < 8; j++) {
      temp = (crc ^ databyte) & 0x01;
      crc >>= 1;
      if (temp)
        crc ^= 0x8C;

      databyte >>= 1;
    }
  }
  return crc;
}
```

```
float getTemperature(uint8_t pin) {
  if (presence(pin) == 1) return -1000;
  writeByte(pin, 0xCC);
  if (convert(pin) == 500) return -3000;
  presence(pin);
  writeByte(pin, 0xCC);
  writeByte(pin, 0xBE);
  uint8_t data[9];
  for (int i = 0; i < 9; i++) {
    data[i] = readByte(pin);
  }
  uint8_t crc = crc8(data, 9);
  if (crc != 0) return -2000;
  int t1 = data[0];
  int t2 = data[1];
  int16_t temp1 = (t2 << 8 | t1);
  float temp = (float)temp1 / 16;
  return temp;
}

void setup() {
  Serial.begin(9600);
}

void loop() {
  float temp = getTemperature(2);
  Serial.printf("temperature=%f\n", temp);
  delay(1000);
}
```

Other Commands

As well as the commands that we have used to read the temperature, the DS18B20 supports a range of other commands. Two commands concerned with when there are more devices on the bus are Search ROM, 0xF0, which is used to scan the bus to discover what devices are connected and Match ROM, 0x55, which is used to select a particular device.

You can also read the unique 64-bit code of a device using the Read ROM command, 0x33. In this case, the slave transmits eight bytes, consisting of a single-byte device family code, 0x28 for the DS18B20, six bytes of serial number and a single CRC byte. Notice that the first byte of the ID identifies the type of the device. For example, a DS18B20 starts with 0x10.

There is also a select_rom method which will select a device according to its ID. This uses a MatchROM command to select the device and following this all data transfer is between the selected device and the controller until the next reset.

As well as the Read ScratchPad command, `0xBE,` that we used to read the temperature, there is also a Write ScratchPad command, `0x4E`.

The format of the scratchpad is:

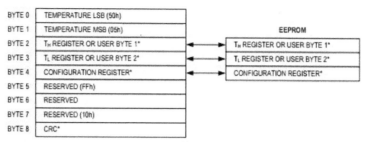

SCRATCHPAD

BYTE 0	TEMPERATURE LSB (50h)	
BYTE 1	TEMPERATURE MSB (05h)	EEPROM
BYTE 2	T_H REGISTER OR USER BYTE 1*	T_H REGISTER OR USER BYTE 1*
BYTE 3	T_L REGISTER OR USER BYTE 2*	T_L REGISTER OR USER BYTE 2*
BYTE 4	CONFIGURATION REGISTER*	CONFIGURATION REGISTER*
BYTE 5	RESERVED (FFh)	
BYTE 6	RESERVED	
BYTE 7	RESERVED (10h)	
BYTE 8	CRC*	

The first two bytes are the temperature that we have already used. The only writable entries are bytes 2, 3 and 4. The Write ScratchPad command transfers three bytes to these locations. Notice that if there is a transmission error, there is no CRC and no error response. The datasheet suggests that you read the scratchpad after writing it to check that you have been successful in setting the three bytes.

The third byte written to the scratchpad is to the configuration register:

BIT 7	BIT 6	BIT 5	BIT 4	BIT 3	BIT 2	BIT 1	BIT 0
0	R1	R0	1	1	1	1	1

Essentially the only thing you can change is the resolution of the temperature measurement.

Configuration Register	Resolution	Time
`0x1F`	9 bits	93ms
`0x3F`	10 bits	175ms
`0x5F`	11 bits	375ms
`0x7F`	12 bits	750ms

The time quoted is the maximum for a conversion at the given precision. You can see that the only real advantage of decreasing precision is to make the conversion faster. The default is `0x7F` and 12 bits of precision.

The first two bytes of the write scratchpad set a high and low temperature alarm. This feature isn't much used, but you can set two temperatures that will trigger the device into alarm mode. Notice you only set the top eight bits of the threshold temperatures. This is easy enough, but the alarm status is set with every read so if the temperature goes outside the set bounds and then back in the alarm is cleared. Notice that you have to use the device's ROM code even if it is the only device on the bus.

The second problem is that, to discover which devices are in alarm mode, you have to use the Alarm Search command, 0xEC. This works like the Search ROM command, but the only devices that respond are the ones with an alarm state. The alarm feature might be useful if you have a lot of devices and simply want to detect an out-of-band temperature. You could set up multiple devices with appropriate temperature limits and then simply repeatedly scan the bus for devices with alarms set.

You may notice that the scratchpad also has an EEPROM memory connected. You can transfer the three bytes of the scratchpad to the EEPROM using Copy Scratchpad, 0x48, and transfer them back using the Recall EEPROM command, 0xB8. You can use this to make the settings non-volatile.

Finally there is the Read Power Supply command, 0xB4. If the master reads the bus after issuing this command, a 0 indicates that there are parasitic powered devices on the bus. If there are such devices the master has to run the bus in such a way that they are powered correctly.

Many one-wire buses can be implemented using a UART. As long as the bit cell is a fixed size, it will work. You can see an example of reading a DS18B20 in Chapter 14.

The S3 RGB LED NeoPixel

A very simple one-wire protocol is used with the NeoPixel style of lighting strip. What follows is applicable to a general NeoPixel array, but it is specific to the RGB LED built-in to most ESP32-S3 development boards.

The task is to make use of the RGB LED that is standard on an ESP32-S3. This is an addressable LED in the WS2812 family and you can run this program on an ESP32 by connecting a WS2312 "NeoPixel" device to a GPIO line. In simple terms, the timing requirements are such that the ESP32 is only just fast enough to cope.

In the most general case you can daisy-chain NeoPixels to produce linear strips of LEDs:

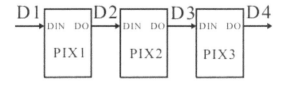

To set an LED to a color you have to send a 24-bit value on the data line using a coding:

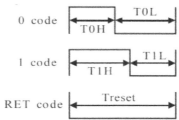

The data line rests low and a 0 is sent with a high time of 350ns and a 1 is sent with a high time of 700ns and a total pulse width of 1.25μs, all timings are ±150ns. The RET code is just a minimum low time between groups of 24-bit signals. If you have multiple LEDs daisy chained you can control each one individually by sending groups of 24 bits at a time. Each LED consumes 24 bits of the signal and passes the remaining bits on to the next LED in the chain. In this way each LED in the chain gets its own 24 bits specifying the color. The LEDs process the stream of bits until the line is held low for at least 50μs, i.e. the RET code. At this point all of the LEDs transfer the data to a latch and display the specified color. The format used to set the color is:

Composition of 24bit data:

G7	G6	G5	G4	G3	G2	G1	G0	R7	R6	R5	R4	R3	R2	R1	R0	B7	B6	B5	B4	B3	B2	B1	B0

As already mentioned, you can connect a NeoPixel device to any GPIO line to act as the data line, but the ESP32-S3 has a single NeoPixel connected to either GPIO38 or GPIO48 depending on the development board. Some boards also have a solder pad next to the LED that has to be connected before the LED can be used. You can connect them with a small blob of solder:

A Simple RMT NeoPixel Driver

When dealing with bit streams the RMT Remote Control Transceiver is very useful but of course it is ESP32 specific. At the time of writing support is a work in progress. While it works in both transmit and receive modes and hence can help with processing of bit streams in both "directions" currently it is only fully working in transmit mode. Using the ESP32 IDF both the ESP32 and the ESP32-S3 are fast enough to generate a bit stream to control a NeoPixel LED – but using the Arduino library they are not. If we want to generate a bit stream with shorter pulses we have no choice but to use the RMT.

The RMT Remote Control Transceiver was designed to implement a serial protocol for infrared and ultrasonic remote controllers. This may seem like a very niche application, but it is covered here as it has to be programmable to create and read arbitrary bit streams. The way that it does this is to simply record how long a pulse stream is high and low. It accepts and returns an array of structs of the form:

```
typedef struct {
    struct {
        uint16_t duration0 : 15; /*!< Duration of level0 */
        uint16_t level0 : 1;     /*!< Level of the first part */
        uint16_t duration1 : 15; /*!< Duration of level1 */
        uint16_t level1 : 1;     /*!< Level of the second part */
    };
} rmt_data_t;
```

Each element of the array has two 16-bit fields with the low bit giving the state of the line, high or low, and the top 15 bits giving how long, in RMT clock ticks, it has been in that state. You can see that you could set up an array that would specify that the line was high for so long, then low for so long, then high for so long and so on. Similarly, if the RMT receives a bit stream it will convert it into how long the line was high, then how long low, how long high and so on. The RMT can be used to produce any bit stream and it can record the details of any input bit stream. In this case we are going to use it to generate a pulse stream needed to control an RGB LED or a string of such LEDs.

We can set up a receive channel or a transmit channel but we need to transmit bits to the LED. To create a channel we need to use:

```
bool rmtInit(int pin, rmt_ch_dir_t channel_direction,
        rmt_reserve_memsize_t mem_size, uint32_t frequency_Hz) {
```

where the parameters are:

- pin   GPIO line
- channel_direction   RMT_TX_MODE or RMT_RX_MODE
- mem_size   RMT_MEM_NUM_BLOCKS_n where n varies from 1 to 8 depending on model
- frequency_Hz   Clock frequency, in Hz

Each memory block has space for 48 rmt_data_t structs and each ESP32 type has:

ESP32 has 8 MEM BLOCKS shared with Reading and/or Writing

ESP32-S2 has 4 MEM BLOCKS shared with Reading and/or Writing

ESP32-S3 has 4 MEM BLOCKS for Reading and 4 MEM BLOCKS for Writing

ESP32-C3 has 2 MEM BLOCKS for Reading and 2 MEM BLOCKS for Writing

To start sending data we use:

```
bool rmtWrite(int pin, rmt_data_t *data, size_t num_rmt_symbols,
                                uint32_t timeout_ms) {
```

So to setup a transmit channel with a 100ns clock:

```
rmtInit(pin,RMT_TX_MODE,1,1000000)
```

The only remaining problem is that we need to code up the pulse widths that we need into an array of rmt_data_t structs. This is what the convertGRB function does. It takes a color coded using Green, Red, Blue as specified by each four bits of a 12-bit representation and converts it into an element of the array specified as how long the line should be high or low. The complete program to set the onboard NeoPixel LED on the EP32 S3 is;

```
void convertGRB(int GRB, rmt_data_t *rawdata) {
  int mask = 0x800000;
  for (int j = 0; j < 24; j++) {
    if ((GRB & mask)) {
      rawdata[j].level0 = 1;
      rawdata[j].duration0 = 7;
      rawdata[j].level1 = 0;
      rawdata[j].duration1 = 12 - 7;
    } else {
      rawdata[j].level0 = 1;
      rawdata[j].duration0 = 3;
      rawdata[j].level1 = 0;
      rawdata[j].duration1 = 12 - 3;
    }
    mask = mask >> 1;
  }
}
```

```
rmt_data_t raw_symbols[100];
int pin =  48;

void setup() {
  Serial.begin(9600);
  rmtInit(pin, RMT_TX_MODE, RMT_MEM_NUM_BLOCKS_1, 10000000);
}

void loop() {
  int color = 0x00FFFF;
  convertGRB(color, raw_symbols);
  rmtWrite(pin, raw_symbols,
            24 * sizeof(rmt_data_t), RMT_WAIT_FOR_EVER);
  delay(1000);
}
```

The convertGRB function takes a 32-bit GRB value and encodes it as a rmt_symbol_word_t array. Each element stores the state of the line, high or low, and how long the line is to be high or low in tenths of a microsecond. This is as fast a clock as we can use and it results in 0 pulses with a high time of 300ns and 1 pulses with a high time of 700ns and a total width of 1200ns, which is within the tolerance of the specification.

You can use this as the basis for a more general NeoPixel function. To drive more than one pixel at a time, all you need to do is increase the number of bits to a multiple of 24 and make sure that you leave at least 50µs between each setting.

Summary

- The DHT22 is a low-cost temperature and humidity sensor. It uses a custom single wire bus which is not compatible with the well known 1-Wire bus. Its asynchronous protocol is easy to implement directly.

- The 1-Wire bus is a proprietary, but widely-used, bus. It is simple and very capable. As its name suggests, it makes use of a single data wire and usually a power supply and ground.

- Implementing the 1-Wire protocol is mostly a matter of getting the timing right.

- There are three types of interaction: presence pulse, which simply asks any connected devices to reply and make themselves known, read and write.

- The 1-Wire protocol is easier to implement than you might think because each bit is sent as a "slot" and while timing is critical within the slot, how fast slots are sent isn't and the master is in control of when this happens.

- The DS18B20 temperature sensor is one of the most commonly encountered 1-Wire bus devices. It is small, low-cost and you can use multiple devices on a single bus.

- After a convert command is sent to the device, it can take 750ms before a reading is ready. To test for data ready you have to poll on a single bit. Reading a zero means data not ready and reading a one means data ready. When the data is ready, you can read the scratchpad memory where the data is stored.

- The DS18B20 has other commands that can be used to set temperature alarms etc, but these are rarely used.

- The RMT is useful in transmit mode as a way of generating a pulse stream and it can be used to control a NeoPixel array.

Chapter 14

The Serial Port

The serial port is one of the oldest of ways of connecting devices together, but it is still useful as it provides a reasonably fast communication channel that can be used over a longer distance than most other connections, such as USB. Today, however, its most common and important use is in making connections with small computers and simple peripherals. It can also be used as a custom signal decoder, see later.

Serial Protocol

The serial protocol is very simple. It has to be because it was invented in the days when it was generated using electromechanical components, motors and the like. It was invented to make early teletype machines work and hence you will find abbreviations such as TTY used in connection with it. As the electronic device used for serial communication is called a Universal Asynchronous Receiver/Transmitter, the term UART is also often used to refer to the protocol.

The earliest standards are V24 and RS232. Notice, however, that early serial communications worked between plus and minus 24V and later ones between plus and minus 12V. Today's serial communications work at logic, or TTL, levels of 0V to 5V or 0V to 3.3V. This voltage difference is a problem we will return to later. What matters is that, irrespective of the voltage, the protocol is always the same.

For the moment let's concentrate on the protocol. As already mentioned, it's simple. The line rests high and represents a zero. When the device starts to transmit it first pulls the line low to generate a start bit. The width of this start bit sets the transmission speed as all bits are the same width as the start bit. After the start bit there are a variable number, usually seven or eight, data bits, an optional single parity bit, and finally one or two stop bits.

Originally the purpose of the start bit was to allow the motors etc to get started and allow the receiving end to perform any timing corrections. The stop bits were similarly there to give time for the motors to come back to their rest position. In the early days the protocol was used at very slow speeds; 300 baud, i.e. roughly 300 bits per second, was considered fast enough.

Today the protocol is much the same, but there is little need for multiple stop bits and communication is often so reliable that parity bits are dispensed with. Transmission speeds are also higher, typically 9600 or 115200 baud.

To specify what exact protocol is in use, you will often encounter a short form notation. For example, 9600 baud, 8 data bits, no parity, one stop bit, will be written as 9600 8n1. Here you can see the letter 0 (`01101111` or `0x6F`) transmitted using 8n1:

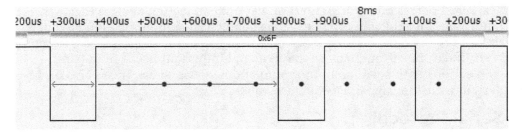

Notice that the signal is sent least significant bit first. The first low is the start bit, then the eight dots show the ideal sampling positions for the receiver. The basic decoding algorithm for receiving serial data is to detect the start of the start bit and then sample the line at the center of each bit time. Notice that the final high on the right is the stop bit. Notice also that the sampling points can be put to use on custom protocols. As long as the data is transmitted in fixed time "cells" indicated by a start bit, you can use a serial port to read individual bits – see later.

For a serial connection to work, it is essential that the transmitter and the receiver are set to the same speed, data bits and parity. Serial interfaces most often fail because they are not working with the same settings. A logic analyzer with a serial decoder option is an essential piece of equipment if you are going to do anything complicated with serial interfacing.

What is a baud? Baud rate refers to the basic bit time. That is, 300 baud has a start bit that is 1/300s wide. This means that for 9600 baud a bit is 1/9600 wide or roughly 104μs and at 115200 baud a bit is 1/115200 or roughly 8.6μs. Notice that baud rate doesn't equate to the speed of sending data because of the overhead in stop, start and perhaps parity bits to include in the calculation.

UART Hardware

A simple serial interface has a transmit pin, Tx, and a receive pin, Rx. That is, a full serial interface uses two wires for two-way communications. Typically you connect the Tx pin on one device to the Rx pin on the other and vice versa. The only problem is that some manufacturers label the pins by what they should be connected to not what they are and then you have to connect Rx to Rx and Tx to Tx. If you are in any doubt you need to check with a meter, logic probe or oscilloscope which pin is which.

In addition to the Tx and Rx pins, a full serial interface also has a lot of control lines. Most of these were designed to help with old-fashioned teleprinters and they are not often used. For example, RTS - Request To Send is a line that is used to ask permission to send data from the device at the other end of the connection, CTS - Clear To Send is a line that indicates that it is okay to send data and so on. Usually these are set by the hardware automatically when the receive buffer is full or empty.

You can use RTS and CTS as a hardware flow control. There is also a standard software flow control involving sending XON and XOFF characters to start and stop the transmission of data. For most connections between modern devices you can ignore these additional lines and just send and receive data. If you need to interface to something that implements a complex serial interface you are going to have to look up the details and hand-craft a program to interact with it.

The ESP32 has three UARTs which can be used with any GPIO lines that support input and output but there are default assignments:

	UART0	UART1	UART2
Tx	1	10	17
Rx	3	9	16

On most development boards you cannot use UART1 without changing the default pin allocations as GPIO9 and GPIO10 are generally used to interface flash memory. Also notice that UART0 is mapped to the USB port by default, but if you don't want to use it while your program is running you can use it as a general UART.

Each UART shares a hardware-implemented 1024-byte buffer which by default is allocated as 128 bytes to a receive and transmit FIFO (first in, first out) for each UART.

There is a problem with making the connection to the ESP32's Rx and Tx pins in that devices work at different voltages. PC-based serial ports usually use +13V to -13V and all RS232-compliant ports use a + to - voltage swing, which is completely incompatible with most microprocessors which work at 5V or 3.3V.

If you want to connect the ESP32 to a PC or other standard device then you need to use a TTL-to-RS232 level converter. In this case it is easier to use the PC's USB port as a serial interface with a USB-to-TTL level converter. All you have to do is plug the USB port into the PC, install a driver and start to transmit data. Remember when you connect the ESP32 to another device, that Tx goes to the other device's Rx and Rx goes to the other device's Tx pin. Also remember that the signaling voltage is 0V to 3.3V.

Setting Up the UART

There are four UART objects defined for the ESP32:

Serial   USB Serial
Serial0   UART0
Serial1   UART1
Serial2   UART2

The core Arduino library only supports Serial and Serial1.

To configure a UART you need to use the begin function which has been extended for the ESP32:

```
begin(unsigned long baud, uint32_t config,
       int8_t rxPin, int8_t txPin,
           bool invert, unsigned long timeout_ms,
                      uint8_t rxfifo_full_thrhd)
```

The parameters are:

- ◆ baud   Baud rate
- ◆ config   One of:

SERIAL_5N1	SERIAL_5E1	SERIAL_5O1
SERIAL_6N1	SERIAL_6E1	SERIAL_6O1
SERIAL_7N1	SERIAL_7E1	SERIAL_7O1
SERIAL_8N1	SERIAL_8E1	SERIAL_8O1
SERIAL_5N2	SERIAL_5E2	SERIAL_5O2
SERIAL_6N2	SERIAL_6E2	SERIAL_6O2
SERIAL_7N2	SERIAL_7E2	SERIAL_7O2
SERIAL_8N2	SERIAL_8E2	SERIAL_8O2

     where the first character is the number of data bits, the second the parity, N(one), E(ven) or O(dd) and the third the number of stop bits. The default is 8N1.

- ◆ invert   Invert output when true
- ◆ timeout_ms   Timeout for auto-baud detect, defaults to 20s
- ◆ rxfifo_full_thrhd   FIFO buffer full threshold

In most cases you can ignore invert, timeout_ms and the FIFO buffer full threshold setting as they are rarely useful.

If you call `begin` with the `rxPin` or `txPin` pins set to -1 then any existing assignments are not changed and the pins are not reinitialized.

If you set `baud` to 0 the device will attempt to set an auto-baud rate by examining signals being received. Obviously for this to work the connected device has to be using a valid baud rate and transmitting data. The `timeout_ms` parameter sets how long the ESP32 will attempt to determine the baud rate with a default of 20 seconds.

Notice that the only two forms of `begin` that are compatible with the core Arduino library are:

```
begin(speed)
begin(speed, config)
```

You can release the UART hardware and GPIO lines using:

```
end()
```

Additional functions let you set individual parameters:

- ◆ `setTimeout(unsigned long timeout)`
- ◆ `updateBaudRate(unsigned long baud)`
- ◆ `setRxInvert(bool);`
- ◆ `setRxBufferSize(size_t new_size)`
- ◆ `setTxBufferSize(size_t new_size)`

The buffer sizes have to be set before `begin` is called and cannot be changed until the hardware is released by calling `end` and then reinitialized by calling `begin` again. The buffer size has to be larger than the FIFO buffer size, usually 128.

Only the `setTimeout` function is part of the Arduino library, the rest are specific to the ESP32. There are some more advanced parameters which are described in detail later.

Data Transfer

After you have set up the UART you can start sending and receiving data using methods. The `Serial` object inherits from `Stream` and hence has all of the same methods, but some are modified to improve efficiency. All of the methods read and write a buffer rather than working directly with the UART hardware.

There is a `write` function which has three general forms:

- ◆ `Serial.write(val)`   Writes a single byte
- ◆ `Serial.write(str)`   Writes a string as a series of bytes
- ◆ `Serial.write(buf, len)`   Writes a buffer as a series of bytes

All three forms block until the data has been loaded into the transmit buffer. Notice that this means that the function could return before all of the data has actually been transmitted. The `tx_buffer` is slowly processed by an interrupt routine until it is empty.

You can also use print, println and even the standard C printf with the Serial object. These are slightly more sophisticated and will convert the data types to a stream of bytes. The printf method will also accept a standard format string that lets you control how the conversion is carried out.

The usual Stream set of read methods is supported:

- read()
  Returns the next byte in the buffer or -1 if no data is available
  Notice that -1 cannot occur when reading a valid byte as an int is returned and it sets a timeout of 0, i.e. it returns at once.
- peek()
  As for read(), but it doesn't move the buffer on to the next character
- readBytes(char *buffer, size_t length)
  Reads a maximum of length bytes from the buffer into buffer and returns number of bytes read and blocks for the set timeout
- readBytesUntil(char terminator,char *buffer, size_t length)
  Same as readBytes, but stops when it encounters terminator or reaches length bytes. The terminator is not included in the result.
- ReadString()
  Returns a C++ string of all characters until a timeout occurs
- readStringUntil(char terminator)
  As for ReadString, but stops if it detects a terminator character in the stream

All of the read functions block until either the number of characters specified has been read or a timeout as set by setTimeout.

There is also a flush() method which simply waits for the tx buffer to be empty – it doesn't remove any data in the buffer.

Loopback Test

If you connect GPIO12 to GPIO13 we can use these pins to perform some loopback tests that demonstrate how things work:

```
void setup() {
  Serial.begin(9600);
  Serial1.begin(9600, SERIAL_8N1, 12, 13);
  Serial1.setTimeout(30);
}
void loop() {
  char buffer[100];
  Serial1.write("Hello World\n");
  int len = Serial1.readBytes(buffer, 100);
  buffer[len] = NULL;
  Serial.printf("\nreceived data: %s\n", buffer);
  delay(1000);
}
```

If you try this out without the 30ms timeout you will find that it doesn't work. The reason is that the write method stores the data in a buffer which returns almost at once and the data is sent by the UART later, which at 9600 baud takes around 13.5ms. The problem is that the read function tries to read the data even before the first character has arrived.

This is another example of input being harder than output. To send data via a serial port you simply write the data to the buffer and wait while it is sent. To read data from a serial port you need to know when to read it.

There are a number of ways around this problem and which one you use depends on the agreed protocol between the transmitter and the receiver. As the UART has buffers, it is ready to receive data at any time without the intervention of the program and, as long as the buffer doesn't fill up, you can delay reading until you are ready to process the data. You might think that given the transmitted data only takes 13.5ms, we only need a delay that long to get the data. In fact, you need a delay of at least 24ms and its length depends on when the data is transferred to the Rx buffer.

Instead of inserting an estimated delay we can arrange to poll for the data in the buffer.

Serial Polling

The key method in implementing UART polling is:

```
available()
```

which returns the number of characters in the Rx ring buffer waiting to be read.

It is easy to see that you can use the `available` function to write polling loops which test to see if there is anything to read. For example, to create a blocking read:

```
void setup() {
  Serial.begin(9600);
  Serial1.begin(9600, SERIAL_8N1, 12, 13);
  Serial1.setTimeout(30);
}
void loop() {
  char buffer[100];
  Serial1.write("Hello World\n");

  if (Serial1.available()) {
    char byte;
    byte = Serial1.read();
    Serial.print(byte);
  }
  delay(10);
}
```

This waits for there to be at least one byte in the ring buffer and then reads it and returns it. The advantage this offers is that you can do other work within the while loop and check that reading hasn't been waiting too long. In this sense it isn't a blocking serial read. You can easily extend it to include a timeout. However, there are still problems with this blocking function. It waits for data to be ready to read, but how can you know that all of the data that you are expecting has been read?

There are three general solutions to this problem:

1. Work in fixed sized blocks so that everything that is exchanged between transmitter and receiver has the same number of bytes. If you want to send something smaller then you need to pad the block with null bytes. Of course, this only works if you can identify a code to use as a null byte.

2. Use a terminator such as a line feed or a carriage return. This is what the readline method is for. Again you have to have a suitable code to use as a terminator.

3. Rely on timing to tell you when a transmission is complete. This is typically how interactions with users take place if they are not line-oriented. The algorithm is – wait till the first character arrives, keep waiting for additional characters until an inter-byte timeout is up. The idea is that a transmission is a continuous flow of bytes separated by a maximum time interval.

Serial Interrupts

The Arduino library provides a very simple way to deal with serial input using interrupts, but it doesn't work on the ESP32. Instead you have to use:

```
void onReceive(OnReceiveCb function, bool onlyOnTimeout)
```

The interrupt function has the signature void function(void) and it is called when there is data ready to be read in the ring buffer. For example:

```
int count;
char buffer[100]={0};
void recieveData(void){
    int nr=Serial1.readBytes(buffer,100);
    buffer[nr]=0;
};
void setup() {
  Serial.begin(9600);
  Serial1.begin(9600, SERIAL_8N1, 12, 13);
  Serial1.setTimeout(5);
  Serial1.onReceive(recieveData);
}
```

```
void loop() {
  Serial.print(count++);
  Serial.println(buffer);
  buffer[0]=0;
  Serial1.write("Hello World\n");
  delay(2000);
}
```

Although there is no read in the main loop you will see Hello World printed
after the first time through the loop. What happens is that the interrupt
routine is called after the write and before the loop repeats and this reads
the data into the buffer. There is also an:

void onReceiveError(OnReceiveErrorCb *function*)

which will call the function when a receive error occurs.

Both of these functions are not part of the core Arduino library and are
specific to the ESP32.

Buffers

If you read the specifications for the ESP32's UART you will discover that it
has a 1-kbyte buffer shared between the three UARTs in 128-byte blocks.
The documentation suggests that the buffer size can be varied, but in
practice the driver does not implement this and each of the UARTs gets a
128-byte buffer for its Rx and Tx channels.

What is more difficult to discover is that the UART driver implements a ring
buffer for both Rx and Tx channels in addition to the 128-byte FIFO buffer
implemented by the hardware. You can change the size of this software
buffer and, in general, this is all you need to do because the 128-byte FIFO
buffer is serviced by a regular interrupt and shouldn't fill up unless the ring
buffer does so first.

The read and write functions transfer data directly to and from the ring
buffer which in turn transfers data to the FIFO buffer as space or data
become available. This all works transparently as long as the data doesn't
overflow the buffers. If it does then the result might not be what you expect
due to the way the two buffers interact.

The write method is only effectively non-blocking if there is space in the
ring buffer for it to write its data and return. If the ring buffer is full the
write method blocks and waits for space to become free.

Notice that data written to the Tx FIFO is transmitted out at a steady rate
determined by the baud rate irrespective of whether there is anything
receiving that data – i.e. by default there is no flow control. What this means
is that the Tx ring buffer is filled at the rate that the program can submit
data and the Tx FIFO buffer empties at the baud rate which is much slower.

For the Rx buffers things are the other way round – the FIFO buffer fills at the baud rate and is transferred to the ring buffer at a much higher rate.

Clearly in any given situation the size of the buffers matters. This all sounds complicated, but it is easier to understand after a few extreme examples. First consider what happens when the Tx ring buffer is too small for the amount of data being sent, but the Rx buffer is more than big enough:

```
void setup() {
  Serial.begin(9600);
  delay(2000);
  Serial.begin(9600);
  Serial1.setTxBufferSize(256);
  Serial1.setRxBufferSize(1024);
  Serial1.begin(9600, SERIAL_8N1, 12, 13);
  Serial1.setTimeout(30);
  int n = 1000;
  char SendData[n];
  for (int i = 0; i < n; i++) {
    SendData[i] = 'A';
  }
  SendData[n - 1] = 0;

  Serial1.flush();
  unsigned long s = micros();
  Serial1.write(SendData, n);
  s = micros() - s;
  Serial.printf("t= %f\n", s / 1000.0);
}

void loop() {
}
```

Note: At the time of writing there is a problem with the initialization of the USB `Serial` object that makes it unresponsive until the `loop` function has been called. A simple fix is to wait for it to finish initialization and then make a change to it – in this case by initializing it a second time – at the start of the `setup` function.

The Tx ring buffer is 256 bytes and the Rx ring buffer is 1024 bytes. If you send only 252 characters then the buffer just copes and the `write` takes around 0.136us. If you increase this to 253 characters then the `write` has to wait for the buffer to be free and takes 50.65ms. Notice that the Rx buffer is large enough to store all of the data sent and, as long as you leave a long enough delay before reading the data or arranging polling, no data is lost. For example, if you send 1000 bytes the time to write goes up to 780ms and the time to send the data at 9600 baud is around 1 second. Remember, the write returns as soon as it has written its last byte to the buffer, but the buffer still has around 250 bytes to send at this point.

So, if we wait around 300ms, all of the data should be in the receive buffer and you will see all of the data printed if you add the following code to the previous program:

```
char RecData[n+1];
int nr = Serial1.readBytes(RecData,n+1);
RecData[nr + 1] = 0;
Serial.printf("%s\n", RecData);
Serial.printf("%d    %d\n", nr, sizeof(SendData));
}
```

Now consider what happens if the receive buffer is too small. If we arrange to send 1000 bytes with a large enough Tx buffer, then the write returns in about 0.1 ms and the data then takes just over a second to be transmitted. With an Rx buffer of 512 bytes only 613 bytes are ever received:

```
void setup() {
  Serial.begin(9600);
  delay(2000);
  Serial.begin(9600);
  Serial1.setTxBufferSize(2048);
  Serial1.setRxBufferSize(512);
  Serial1.begin(9600, SERIAL_8N1, 12, 13);
  Serial1.setTimeout(30);
  int n = 1000;
  char SendData[n];
  for (int i = 0; i < n; i++) {
    SendData[i] = 'A' + i / 40;;
  }
  SendData[n - 1] = 0;

  Serial1.flush();
  unsigned long s = micros();
  Serial1.write(SendData, n);
  s = micros() - s;
  Serial.printf("t= %f\n", s / 1000.0);
  delay(3000);
  char RecData[n+1];
  int nr = Serial1.readBytes(RecData,n+1);
  RecData[nr + 1] = 0;
  Serial.printf("%s\n", RecData);
  Serial.printf("%d    %d\n", nr, sizeof(SendData));
}

void loop() {
}
```

The extra 100 or so bytes are presumably due to the hardware-provided 128-byte FIFO buffer. The program prints blocks of AAA, BBB and so on and if you look at the display you will find that it is alphabetical until around MM and then it jumps to WW, That is, the end of the transmitted data has overwritten the middle of the sequence with the end. The reason is the way that the ring buffer interacts with the FIFO buffer. When the ring buffer is full it refuses more data but the FIFO buffer continues to receive data and when the transmission is complete the ring buffer has the first part of the transmission and the FIFO buffer has the last part.

To summarize:

- Data is not lost when buffers fill up during writing and all that happens is that the write method will take longer to complete.

- Data is lost when buffers fill up while receiving data and the lost data isn't necessarily at the end of the transmission.

- The statement that data isn't lost when writing data has occasional exceptions, but none that are repeatable.

If you want to avoid problems with serial data, make sure that the Rx buffer is large enough not to fill up, and read data from it often. The size of the Tx buffer is less critical, but it can slow your program down.

Timeouts

From the previous section you should be able to see that the usual way that a transmitter and receiver interact is that the transmitter, after perhaps a longish silence, "decides" to send some data. This is usually sent as a block and, as long as the transmitter isn't overloaded, each character follows the next with minimum delay. What this means is that, from the receiver's point of view, there might be a long wait before being able to start reading data, but after that there should be only a short interval between each character. If the receiver finds itself waiting for a long time for the next character then the chances are the transmitter has finished sending a block of data.

Thus there are two sorts of timeout we need to specify. An initial timeout, which is how long to wait before the first character is received, and an inter-character timeout, which is the maximum time the receiver should wait between characters before concluding that in all probability the transmitter has finished.

The `timeout` int in the read function is the time that the function will wait to see if there is a new character in the buffer. That is, when you call `uart_read_bytes` it will read characters into the buffer until either the buffer is full or no new characters have been received for the specified timeout.

It is easy to create a function that works in a more complex way:

```
int uart_read_chars(char *buf, int length,
                     int timeout, int timeout_char) {
  Serial1.setTimeout(timeout);
  int nr = Serial1.readBytes(buf,1);
  if (nr == -1) return 0;
  Serial1.setTimeout(timeout_char);
  nr = Serial1.readBytes(&buf[1], length - 1);
  return nr+1;
}
```

The first read only waits for timeout ms and either times out or reads a single character. If it times out it returns a 0 to indicate that no characters were read. If it doesn't time out it tries to read as many characters as the buffer can hold waiting for up to timeout_char between characters.

The time to wait for the first character is usually set by a combination of how much time the receiver can devote to waiting in a polling loop and how often the transmitter sends data. The inter-character time is usually low if the transmitter manages to keep the Rx FIFO buffer topped up. It should be set to less than the characteristic time between data blocks from the transmitter.

Polling On Write

Writing data to the UART is much simpler than reading it. Data is written to the Tx ring buffer as fast as it can be and the only thing that can go wrong is having to wait because it is full. If so then the call to the write method will block until there is space to accept all of the data. If your program has nothing else to do while the transmission is underway, there is no problem. If, however, your program has to service a polling loop doing a range of other things, then it can be a big problem.

The function:

```
availableForWrite()
```

which returns the number of characters free in the Tx ring buffer.

You can use this to decide when to send additional data.

Alternatively you can use:

```
flush()
```

which blocks until the Tx FIFO buffer is empty.

Flow Control

The problem of buffers filling up is usually dealt with by flow control, i.e. signaling whether or not it is okay to send more data. The ESP32 supports both software and hardware flow control. The difference is that under software flow of control the program has to set the control lines, but hardware control sets them automatically based on the state of the buffers.

Hardware flow control is based on two control lines, Request To Send (RTS) and Clear To Send (CTS). For the ESP32, RTS is an output and CTS is an input and you can configure any suitable GPIO line to act as either. Exactly how the RTS and CTS lines are actually used depends on what you are connecting to and what control lines it has.

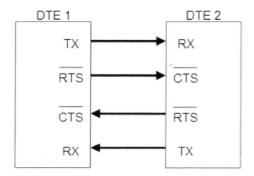

A lot of the jargon and procedures involved have their origins back in the days of the mechanical teletype and the non-digital phone system. What matters today is to know that the RTS line is low when there is space in the ESP32's Rx FIFO buffer and high when it is full to a specified level – usually 80% or 90% of the buffer capacity. What this means is that the transmitter can use this to determine if it is "clear to send" data to the receiver. That is, if RTS is low you can send data and if RTS is high you should stop sending data. This is exactly what happens if you connect the RTS line to the CTS line. That is, if the CTS line is low the ESP32 will send any data in its Tx FIFO buffer and if the CTS line is high it will hold the data in the Tx FIFO buffer.

What this means is if you have two ESP32-like devices, traditionally referred to as DTE, Data Terminal Equipment, then you can connect them together to implement flow control on TX and RX using:

The only complication is that some devices are regarded as DCE, Data Communication Equipment, which are always connected to a DTE and have their RTS and CTS line labels swapped over. This allows the connections to be specified as "connect RTS to RTS and CTS to CTS". In practice, you need to make sure that RTS is an output connected to line marked CTS, which is an input on the other device, or to a line marked RTS, which is also an input on the other device.

As the ESP32 is acting as both DCE1 and DCE2, to test flow control we can simply connect the RTS line on the ESP32 to the CTS line on the ESP32. In the examples given below, it is assumed that GPIO4 is RTS and GPIO5 is CTS and they are connected together in loopback mode.

The biggest complication in using flow control with the ESP32 is that the RTS signal is linked to the Rx FIFO buffer and not the Rx ring buffer. What this means is that the ESP32 will send a signal to stop the transmission when its FIFO buffer is full, even though there might be lots of space in the ring buffer. Another complication is that data is transferred to the Rx Ring buffer, which has to be at least as big as the FIFO buffer, usually 128 bytes, and the FIFO buffer starts sending data at once. This means that the RX FIFO buffer is emptying as incoming data is trying to fill it. This means that the number of bytes it can receive before reaching the threshold is more than you might have guessed.

To configure flow control you need to configure the pins to use:

```
bool setPins(int8_t rxPin, int8_t txPin,
                    int8_t ctsPin = -1, int8_t rtsPin = -1)
```

Any pins set to -1 are not used. Once you have allocated pins you can set the flow control mode:

```
bool setHwFlowCtrlMode(SerialHwFlowCtrl mode, uint8_t threshold)
```

where threshold is the number of bytes used in the RX FIFO buffer before RTS is set high usually between 1 and 127 and mode is one of:

- UART_HW_FLOWCTRL_DISABLE Disable hardware flow control
- UART_HW_FLOWCTRL_RTS Enable RX hardware flow control
- UART_HW_FLOWCTRL_CTS Enable TX hardware flow control
- UART_HW_FLOWCTRL_CTS_RTS Enable hardware flow control

You can see that this is the case in the following example:

```
void setup() {
  Serial.begin(9600);
  delay(2000);
  Serial.begin(9600);
  Serial1.setTxBufferSize(2000);
  Serial1.setRxBufferSize(130);
  Serial1.begin(115200, SERIAL_8N1, 12, 13);
  Serial1.setPins(12, 13, 5, 4);
  Serial1.setHwFlowCtrlMode(UART_HW_FLOWCTRL_CTS_RTS, 10);
```

```
    int n = 1000;
    char SendData[n];
    for (int i = 0; i < n; i++) {
      SendData[i] = 'A' + i / 40;
    }
    SendData[n - 1] = 0;
    Serial1.write(SendData, n);

    char RecData[2000];
    int nr = 0;
    int nt = 0;
    Serial1.setTimeout(1);
    do {
      delay(100);
      nt = Serial1.readBytes(&RecData[nr], sizeof(RecData) - nr);
      nr = nr + nt;
      Serial.printf("%d    %d\n", nt, nr);
    } while (nt != 0);

    RecData[nr + 1] = 0;
    Serial.printf("%s\n", &RecData[1]);
    Serial.printf("%d    %d\n", nr, sizeof(SendData));
}

void loop() {
}
```

This program sets up the UART to use flow control on GPIO4 and GPIO5 and to use a high baud rate. The higher the baud rate the less the effect of the system emptying the Rx FIFO buffer. It then sends 1000 bytes and attempts to read them back in. The while loop reads new data until 1000 bytes have been received. Notice that we have set a Tx ring buffer large enough to take all of the data to be transmitted. This is important because, in a loopback configuration, if the data could not be sent at once the program would stall at the write method, waiting forever for the ESP32 to read data in after its Rx FIFO buffer was full and it had set RTS to low to halt transmission. With all of the data stored in the ring buffer, the write returns and the program can continue to try to read the data back in. This is not a consideration when the transmitter and receiver are different devices running different programs. In this case, the transmitter can just wait till the receiver has read enough to clear its Rx FIFO buffer.

Also notice that the way that the FIFO and ring buffers interact complicates the picture. The data from the Rx FIFO buffer is transferred to the ring buffer, which has to fill before the Rx FIFO buffer fills and sets RTS low. The result is that the data is received in blocks of 250 bytes rather than 128 bytes.

You can see the pattern of start/stop transmission on the logic analyzer:

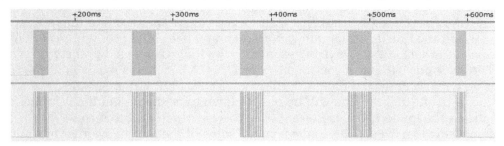

The top trace is the Tx line and the bottom trace is the CTS line. You can see that transmission is stopped on a regular basis. The actual pattern of data transfer is complicated. The big gaps are caused by the 100ms delay in the loop and it shows that every 250 characters it takes longer than 1ms to get the next character. Within each of these transfer blocks the CTS line goes high every 10 characters corresponding to the filling of the Rx FIFO buffer.

If you change the configuration to:

`UART_HW_FLOWCTRL_DISABLE`

and run the program again you will discover that the transmission occurs in one block and you do lose data as the Rx ring buffer isn't large enough.

You can discover more about the way flow control works using the loopback configuration, but keep in mind that the fact that the same machine is doing the sending and receiving makes things a little different. For example, as already mentioned, if you drop the size of the Tx ring buffer down below the amount of data to be sent the program will hang – this doesn't happen if the data is being transmitted by another device.

Using a UART to Decode Data

As an exercise in using a UART to decode a general serial protocol, we can implement the temperature-reading function given in Chapter 14 to read the DS18B20 one-wire device. This is worthwhile as it provides access to the device using hardware.

The first thing we have to do is deal with the electronics. The default configuration of the UART TX pin seems to work reliably with a pullup. If you are unhappy about this you can use a transistor buffer to act as an open drain output.

The basic idea is that we can use the UART to send an initial stop pulse which pulls the line down. After this we can send data on the line for a write or just allow the DS18B20 to pull the line low. Of course, we have to get the timing right. Let's start with the presence/reset pulse.

If we use a speed of 9600 baud, the start bit pulls the line down for 104.2μs, the next four zero bits holds the line low for 502μs and then the final four one bits allow it to be pulled up. If there is a device connected to the line, it will pull the line down for a few microseconds. The serial port will read the line at the same time it is being written as the Rx is connected to the Tx. The Tx sends 0xF0, and you might expect this to be what is received. If there is no device connected then RX will receive 0xF0, but if there is an active device connected the line will be pulled down for some part of the last four bits. As the low-order bits are sent first, this causes the RX to receive something like 0xE0, 0xD0, and so on, i.e. some of the four high-order bits are zeroed by the device pulling the line low. You can use this to detect the device.

Assuming that the serial line is set to 9600 baud, the presence/reset pulse can be implemented as a function to perform this task:

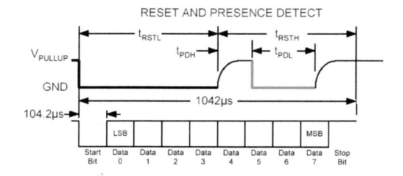

```
int presence() {
  Serial1.updateBaudRate(9600);
  Serial1.write(0xF0);
  char byte;
  Serial1.readBytes(&byte, 1);
  Serial1.updateBaudRate(115200);
  if (byte == 0xF0) return -1;
  return 0;
}
```

To read and write a single bit we need to increase the baud rate to 115200. In this case the start bit, which acts as the initial pulse to read or write a single bit, lasts 8.7μs.

To write a zero we simply write `0x00`, which holds the line low for eight bits, about 78μs. To write a one we let the line be pulled up after the start bit, which leaves it high for 78μs. To make things slightly faster, we can deal with a single byte at a time:

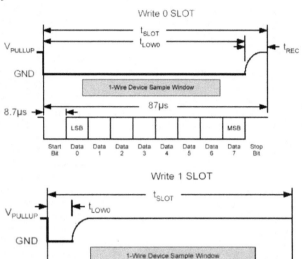

To do this programatically:

```
void writeByte(int byte) {
  char buf[8];
  for (int i = 0; i < 8; i++) {
    if ((byte & 1) == 1) {
      buf[i] = 0xFF;
    } else {
      buf[i] = 0x00;
    }
    byte = byte >> 1;
  };
  Serial1.write(buf, 8);
  Serial1.readBytes(buf, 8);
}
```

We have to remember to read the bytes back in otherwise they would still be in the Rx buffer.

Reading a bit works in the same way. If you write `0xFF` then the line is allowed to be pulled high and the remote device can pull it low for a zero or let it remain high to signal a one. That is, if you write `0xFF` and read back `0xFF` then you have read a one:

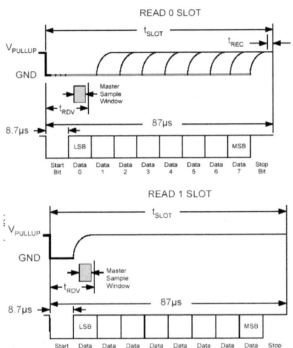

The code to implement this is:

```
char readByte(void) {
  char buf[8];
  for (int i = 0; i < 8; i++) {
    buf[i] = 0xFF;
  }
  Serial1.write(buf, 8);
  Serial1.readBytes(buf, 8);
  char result = 0;
  for (int i = 0; i < 8; i++) {
    result = result >> 1;
    if (buf[i] == 0xFF) result = result | 0x80;
  }
  return result;
}
```

Again we can read in a whole byte rather than a bit at a time. With these modified readByte and writeByte functions, we can use the program developed in Chapter 13 to read the device.

The complete program is:

```
int presence() {
  Serial1.updateBaudRate(9600);
  Serial1.write(0xF0);
  char byte;
  Serial1.readBytes(&byte, 1);
  Serial1.updateBaudRate(115200);
  if (byte == 0xF0) return -1;
  return 0;
}

void writeByte(int byte) {
  char buf[8];
  for (int i = 0; i < 8; i++) {
    if ((byte & 1) == 1) {
      buf[i] = 0xFF;
    } else {
      buf[i] = 0x00;
    }
    byte = byte >> 1;
  };
  Serial1.write(buf, 8);
  Serial1.readBytes(buf, 8);
}

char readByte(void) {
  char buf[8];
  for (int i = 0; i < 8; i++) {
    buf[i] = 0xFF;
  }
  Serial1.write(buf, 8);
  Serial1.readBytes(buf, 8);
  char result = 0;
  for (int i = 0; i < 8; i++) {
    result = result >> 1;
    if (buf[i] == 0xFF) result = result | 0x80;
  }
  return result;
}
```

```
void setup() {
  Serial.begin(9600);
  Serial1.begin(115200, SERIAL_8N1, 12, 13);
}

void loop() {
  Serial.printf("\n%d\n", presence());
  writeByte(0xCC);
  writeByte(0x44);
  Serial.printf("%d\n", presence());
  writeByte(0xCC);
  writeByte(0xBE);

  char data[9];
  for (int i = 0; i < 9; i++) {
    data[i] = readByte();
  }

  int t1 = data[0];
  int t2 = data[1];
  int temp1 = (t2 << 8 | t1);
  if (t2 & 0x80) temp1 = temp1 | 0xFFFF0000;
  float temp = temp1 / 16.0;
  Serial.printf("temp =%f\n", temp);
  delay(2000);
}
```

You can use the readByte and writeByte functions within other one-wire functions with minor modifications.

You can use the UART approach whenever a signaling protocol uses an initial start bit to signal that the data bits that follow use a fixed size "cell". However, you cannot use the UART approach with the DHT22 temperature and humidity sensor because, although it sends each bit with a start bit, the time to the next start bit varies.

Summary

- The serial port is one of the oldest ways of connecting devices together, but it is still very much in use.

- The serial protocol is asynchronous, but simple. A start bit gives the timing for the entire exchange.

- Many of the control lines once used with telephone equipment are mostly ignored in computer use and the original ±12V signaling has been mostly replaced by 5V and even 3.3V signaling.

- The standard hardware that implements a serial connection is usually called a UART.

- The ESP32 contains three UARTs, one of which is used for the USB serial connection. Each UART has a 128-element FIFO send and receive buffer and a resizable ring buffer.

- The API provides functions for initializing and sending and receiving data.

- You can use the read and write functions to send and receive byte buffers of data to and from the ring buffer.

- The write method is blocking but as it writes to the ring buffer it returns at once as long as there is free space. Also as the write method waits for space in the ring buffer, data is never lost in transmission.

- As the read method relies on the ring buffer, data can be lost if it fills up.

- If the ring buffer does fill up then the order of the received data might not be what you expect because the FIFO keeps receiving data.

- The ESP32 supports simple flow control using the RTS and CTS lines, but exactly how these work is complicated by the use of the FIFO and ring buffers.

- You can use a UART to implement a range of serial data protocols that uses a fixed data cell time.

Chapter 15
Using WiFi

The ESP32 comes complete with a radio capable of 2.4GHz WiFi and Bluetooth. Most of the time you can ignore the technical details as there are easy-to-use functions which enable you to connect to a WiFi network and exchange data. In this chapter we look at the basics and how to create and use a WiFi connection. The libraries involved are many and extensive due to the need to cover a wide range of different protocols. A consequence is that there is no way to cover all of them in a reasonable space. This chapter is about getting started and understanding the basic structure of the WiFi and IP infrastructures. When you understand this the rest of the API becomes much easier to understand. The topic of Bluetooth is omitted as it is so varied that it deserves a book to itself.

ESP32 Architecture

You don't really need to know anything about the ESP32's WiFi hardware to make use of it. Indeed there is very little information available apart from how to use the WiFi drivers in the C development kit. The ESP32 usually has two processor cores, which are used to run the WiFi and applications simultaneously. This means that WiFi has little impact on the running of your application. The two cores, CPU 0 and CPU 1, are the Protocol CPU (PRO_CPU) and Application CPU (APP_CPU) respectively. The PRO_CPU processor handles the WiFi, Bluetooth and other internal peripherals like SPI, I2C, ADC etc. The APP_CPU runs the application code, including your programs.

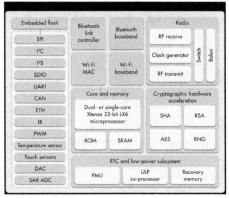

The WiFi Stack

The Arduino library has all of the general functions you need to configure the WiFi stack and use it to make HTTP connections in client or server mode.

The WiFi can be configured to work as an access point AP or a station STA that connects to an access point. In this chapter we concentrate on making a connection to an existing access point as this is the most common requirement.

To get the WiFi started we have to first configure it and make a connection to an AP:

```
WiFi.begin(ssid)
WiFi.begin(ssid, pass)
WiFi.begin(ssid, keyIndex, key)
```

where ssid is the name of the network, pass is the WPA password and keyIndex and key are the keys to use with WEP security.

Connection can take seconds to complete and generally you need to wait for the connection to complete. To do this you can use the status function which returns one of:

- WL_NO_SHIELD   = 255
- WL_STOPPED   = 254
- WL_IDLE_STATUS   = 0
- WL_NO_SSID_AVAIL   = 1
- WL_SCAN_COMPLETED   = 2
- WL_CONNECTED   = 3
- WL_CONNECT_FAILED   = 4
- WL_CONNECTION_LOST   = 5
- WL_DISCONNECTED   = 6

The simplest WiFi connection program is:

```
#include <WiFi.h>
void setup() {
  Serial.begin(9600);delay(2000);Serial.begin(9600);
  int status = WiFi.begin("ssid", "password");
  delay(100);
  while (WiFi.status() != WL_CONNECTED) {
    delay(100);
    Serial.println(WiFi.status());
  };
}
```

This should print 6, then 0 and finally 3 as it transitions from disconnected to connected. A practical connection function should also deal with any errors that might occur.

You can end a connection with:

```
disconnect()
```

The `begin` method assumes that a DHCP server will be available to set the IP addess, subnet, gateway and DNS server. If you want to set any of these manually then you need to call the `config` method:

```
config(ip, dns, gateway, subnet)
```

You can omit the gateway and it will be set to the same IP address, but ending in 1 and the subnet defaults to 255.255.255.0. To set both primary and secondary DNS server you can use:

```
setDNS(dns_server1, dns_server2)
```

and you can leave `server2` unspecified.

If you want details of the current connection you can use;

```
SSID()
BSSID(bssid)    Not supported by Nano ESP32
RSSI()
```

The `ssid` is the name of the connected AP, the `bssid` is its 6 character MAC address, the `RSSI` is the signal strength in `db` and the encryption type is one of:

- TKIP (WPA)   = 2
- WEP   = 5
- CCMP (WPA)   = 4
- NONE   = 7
- AUTO   = 8

At the time of writing `encryptionType()` is not implemented for the ESP32. If you want to get the MAC address of the ESP32 you can use:

```
macAddress(mac)
```

To find out about the IP address of the ESP32 you need to use the `IPAddress` class:

```
localIP()
subnetMask()
gatewayIP()
```

These all return `IPAddress` objects. For example to find out the details of the connection:

```
#include <WiFi.h>
void setup() {
  Serial.begin(9600);
  delay(2000);
  Serial.begin(9600);
  int status = WiFi.begin("ssid", "password");
  delay(100);
  while (WiFi.status() != WL_CONNECTED) {
    delay(100);
    Serial.println(WiFi.status());
  };
```

```
  String ssid = WiFi.SSID();
  Serial.printf("ssid %s \n", ssid);
  unsigned char bssid[6];
  WiFi.BSSID(bssid);
  Serial.printf("bssid  %X %X %X %X %X %X \n",
      bssid[0], bssid[1], bssid[2], bssid[3], bssid[4], bssid[5]);
  Serial.printf("RSSI %d\n", WiFi.RSSI());
  Serial.print("Local IP ");
  Serial.println(WiFi.localIP());
  Serial.print("Subnet mask ");
  Serial.println(WiFi.subnetMask());
  Serial.print("Gateway IP ");
  Serial.println(WiFi.gatewayIP());
}

void loop() {
}
```

The output should be something like:

```
ssid dlink3
bssid  0 1F 1F 24 48 70
RSSI -34
Local IP 192.168.253.65
Subnet mask 255.255.255.0
Gateway IP 192.168.253.1
```

IPAddress

Notice that in the previous example the print method displays the IP addresses in their usual "dotted" form. The reason this works is that the print method doesn't actually do the printing. Instead the IPAddress object has a method that prints it in the correct format. If you want to implement this function in a class that you are creating, myclass, all you have to do is ensure that myclass inherits from Printable, then implement:

```
size_t myclass::printTo(Print& p) const
```

which calls p.print() to print itself correctly and returns the total number of bytes printed. For example, the IPAddress class implements printTo as:

```
size_t IPAddress::printTo(Print& p) const
{
  size_t n = 0;
  for (int i =0; i < 3; i++)
  {
    n += p.print(_address.bytes[IPADDRESS_V4_BYTES_INDEX + I],DEC);
    n += p.print('.');
  }
  n += p.print(_address.bytes[IPADDRESS_V4_BYTES_INDEX + 3],DEC);
  return n;
}
```

276

The `IPAddress` class has a range of methods and operators that allow you to manipulate IP addresses.

You can create an IP address using any of the constructors:

- ```
  IPAddress(uint8_t first_octet, uint8_t second_octet,
                  uint8_t third_octet, uint8_t fourth_octet)
  ```
- `IPAddress(uint32_t address)`
- `IPAddress(const char *address)`

For example:

```
#include <IPAddress.h>

  IPAddress ip("1.2.3.4");
  Serial.println(ip);
  IPAddress ip2(192,168,253,1);
  Serial.println(ip2);
```

There are some type conversion functions:

- `String toString() const`
- `bool fromString(const char *address)`
- `bool fromString(const String &address)`

For example:

```
ip2.fromString("0.0.0.0");
```

sets `ip2` to the specified string.

The assignment, equality and indexing operators have also been defined so you can write things like:

```
IPAddress ip2 = ip;
Serial.println(ip == ip2);
ip2[3] = 255;
Serial.println(ip2);
```

You can also use an `IPAddress` wherever an `uint32_t` would be acceptable.

The IP Address library handles IPv6 as well as IPv4 and there are corresponding functions for IPv6 addresses.

All of the above functions are core Arduino functions, but there are some specific to the ESP32 to allow conversion between the Arduino `IPAddress` class and ESP IDF IP address types:

- `IPAddress(const ip_addr_t *addr);`
  Constructs an IP address from an IDF IP address
- `void to_ip_addr_t(ip_addr_t *addr) const;`
  Converts an IPAddress to an IDF IP address
- `IPAddress &from_ip_addr_t(const ip_addr_t *addr);`
  Converts from an IDF IP address to an IP address.
```

ESP WiFi

There are many ESP specific WiFi functions the most important is the enhanced `begin` function:

```
wl_status_t begin(const char* ssid, const char *passphrase = NULL,
             int32_t channel = 0, const uint8_t* bssid = NULL,
                                      bool connect = true);
```

This lets you set the connection channel, `bssid` of the AP, and causes WiFi to auto-connect. When used in AP mode these set the AP's parameters used by clients.

Alternatively you can use:

```
bool config(IPAddress local_ip, IPAddress gateway,
        IPAddress subnet, IPAddress dns1 = (uint32_t)0x00000000,
                           IPAddress dns2 = (uint32_t)0x00000000);
```

to configure the client and then use:

```
wl_status_t begin();
```

to make the connection.

To disconnect you can use:

```
bool disconnect(bool wifioff = false, bool eraseap = false);
```

If you turn the WiFi off it saves power. The `eraseap` parameter removes details of the AP from memory disabling auto-connect. To control auto-connect:

```
bool setAutoReconnect(bool autoReconnect);
```

To manually reconnect use:

```
bool reconnect();
```

but this depends on the stored credentials.

To check that you have a connection use;

```
bool isConnected();
```

As security settings often make the WiFi unable to connect, an important function is:

```
bool setMinSecurity(wifi_auth_mode_t minSecurity);
```

where `minSecurity` is one of:
- WIFI_AUTH_OPEN
- WIFI_AUTH_WEP
- WIFI_AUTH_WPA_PSK
- WIFI_AUTH_WPA2_PSK
- WIFI_AUTH_WPA_WPA2_PSK
- WIFI_AUTH_ENTERPRISE
- WIFI_AUTH_WPA2_ENTERPRISE

- WIFI_AUTH_WPA3_PSK
- WIFI_AUTH_WPA2_WPA3_PSK
- WIFI_AUTH_WAPI_PSK
- WIFI_AUTH_OWE
- WIFI_AUTH_WPA3_ENT_192

These specify the minimum security protocol in use. If you set
WIFI_AUTH_OPEN then in principle you should be able to connect with any
AP as long as you provide the appropriate credentials.

There are also some general configuration methods:

- `setHostname(const char *hostname);`
- `const char *getHostname();`
  Sets or gets the host name, must be called before begin
- `static void useStaticBuffers(bool bufferMode);`
  If bufferMode is true then static buffers are used

Bear in mind that while dynamic buffers save memory, static buffers are
faster.

If you have an ESP32 module that supports two WiFi antennas, you can
configure them using:

```
bool setDualAntennaConfig(uint8_t gpio_ant1, uint8_t gpio_ant2,
              wifi_rx_ant_t rx_mode, wifi_tx_ant_t tx_mode)
```

There are also a set of methods concerned with using an AP rather than a
client. To setup the AP use:

- `WiFi.softAP(ssid, password)bool softAP(const char* ssid,`
      `const char* passphrase = NULL,`
          `int channel = 1, int ssid_hidden = 0,`
              `int max_connection = 4,`
                  `bool ftm_responder = false)`
- `bool softAPConfig(IPAddress local_ip, IPAddress gateway,`
                  `IPAddress subnet)`

To disconnect use:

```
bool softAPdisconnect(bool wifioff = false);
```

A range of functions enable you to find out or set the configuration:

`IPAddress softAPIP()`	Get the AP's IP
`softAPSSID()`	Get AP's ssid
`softAPBroadcastIP()`	Get the broadcast IP
`IPAddress softAPNetworkID()`	Get the network ID
`softAPmacAddress()`	Get or set the mac address
`softAPgetHostname()`	Get the hostname
`softAPsetHostname()`	Set the hostname
`softAPSubnetCIDR()`	Get the CIDR
`uint8_t softAPgetStationNum()`	Get the station number
`IPAddress softAPSubnetMask()`	Get the subnet mask

ESP32 WiFi Events

In addition to a set of extended WiFi methods the ESP32 also supports WiFi events as an alternative way of establishing a connection. You can register a callback to handle WiFi events with:

`onEvent(WiFiEventCb, arduino_event_id_t = ARDUINO_EVENT_MAX)`

The callback has three options:
- ◆ `void WiFiEventCb(arduino_event_id_t id)`
  which accepts just the event number as a parameter
- ◆ `void WiFiEventCb(arduino_event_t *event)`
  where event is a pointer to a struct with fields:
  `event_id` and `event_info`
- ◆ `void WiFiEventCb(event_id, event_info)`
  which accepts both the event number and `event_info` as parameters

In practice the first form is usually sufficient and you can register different event handlers for different events by using more than one `onEvent` call.

There are functions to remove events for each type of callback. The default, `ARDUINO_EVENT_MAX` means that the event handler will be called for every possible event.

The list of possible events is long:
- ◆ `ARDUINO_EVENT_WIFI_READY`
- ◆ `ARDUINO_EVENT_WIFI_SCAN_DONE`
- ◆ `ARDUINO_EVENT_WIFI_STA_START`
- ◆ `ARDUINO_EVENT_WIFI_STA_STOP`
- ◆ `ARDUINO_EVENT_WIFI_STA_CONNECTED`
- ◆ `ARDUINO_EVENT_WIFI_STA_DISCONNECTED`
- ◆ `ARDUINO_EVENT_WIFI_STA_AUTHMODE_CHANGE`
- ◆ `ARDUINO_EVENT_WIFI_STA_GOT_IP`
- ◆ `ARDUINO_EVENT_WIFI_STA_LOST_IP`
- ◆ `ARDUINO_EVENT_WPS_ER_SUCCESS`
- ◆ `ARDUINO_EVENT_WPS_ER_FAILED`
- ◆ `ARDUINO_EVENT_WPS_ER_TIMEOUT`
- ◆ `ARDUINO_EVENT_WPS_ER_PIN`
- ◆ `ARDUINO_EVENT_WIFI_AP_START`
- ◆ `ARDUINO_EVENT_WIFI_AP_STOP`
- ◆ `ARDUINO_EVENT_WIFI_AP_STACONNECTED`
- ◆ `ARDUINO_EVENT_WIFI_AP_STADISCONNECTED`
- ◆ `ARDUINO_EVENT_WIFI_AP_STAIPASSIGNED`
- ◆ `ARDUINO_EVENT_WIFI_AP_PROBEREQRECVED`
- ◆ `ARDUINO_EVENT_WIFI_AP_GOT_IP6`
- ◆ `ARDUINO_EVENT_WIFI_STA_GOT_IP6`
- ◆ `ARDUINO_EVENT_ETH_GOT_IP6`
- ◆ `ARDUINO_EVENT_ETH_STARTARDUINO_EVENT_ETH_STOP`
- ◆ `ARDUINO_EVENT_ETH_CONNECTED`
- ◆ `ARDUINO_EVENT_ETH_DISCONNECTED`
- ◆ `ARDUINO_EVENT_ETH_GOT_IPARDUINO_EVENT_ETH_GOT_IP6`

For example, the simplest event handling WiFi setup program is:

```
#include <WiFi.h>

void WiFiEvent(WiFiEvent_t event) {
  Serial.printf("[WiFi-event] event: %d\n", event);

  switch (event) {
    case ARDUINO_EVENT_WIFI_READY:
        Serial.println("WiFi interface ready"); break;
    case ARDUINO_EVENT_WIFI_SCAN_DONE:
        Serial.println("Completed scan for access points"); break;
    case ARDUINO_EVENT_WIFI_STA_START:
        Serial.println("WiFi client started"); break;
    case ARDUINO_EVENT_WIFI_STA_STOP:
        Serial.println("WiFi clients stopped"); break;
    case ARDUINO_EVENT_WIFI_STA_CONNECTED:
      Serial.println("Connected to access point"); break;
    case ARDUINO_EVENT_WIFI_STA_DISCONNECTED:
      Serial.println("Disconnected from WiFi access point"); break;
    case ARDUINO_EVENT_WIFI_STA_GOT_IP:
      Serial.print("Obtained IP address: ");
      Serial.println(WiFi.localIP());
      break;
    case ARDUINO_EVENT_WIFI_STA_LOST_IP:
       Serial.println("Lost IP address"); break;
    default: break;
  }
}

void setup() {
  Serial.begin(9600);
  delay(2000);
  Serial.begin(9600);
  WiFi.onEvent(WiFiEvent);
  int status = WiFi.begin("ssid", "password");
};

void loop() {
}
```

If you run the program you will see the main program end and messages from the event handler will be displayed as the WiFi connects.

281

A Practical Connect Function

Connecting to WiFi is a standard operation and it makes sense to package it in a function.

```
#include <WiFi.h>

int wifiConnect(char* ssid, char* password) {
  int status = WiFi.begin(ssid, password);
  while (status != WL_CONNECTED) {
    switch (status) {
      case WL_NO_SSID_AVAIL:
        Serial.printf("No AP with name %s can be found", ssid);
        return status;
      case WL_CONNECT_FAILED:
        Serial.printf("Connection failed");
        return status;
      case WL_CONNECTION_LOST:
        Serial.printf("Connection lost possible security problem");
        return status;
    }
    delay(100);
    status = WiFi.status();
  }
  return status;
}
```

Using the functions connection becomes easy:

```
void setup() {
  Serial.begin(9600);delay(2000);Serial.begin(9600);
  int status=wifiConnect("ssid", "password");
  Serial.println(status);
};
```

You can clearly customize the connection to include parameters to control the IP address, host name and authentication type. The delay in the while loop allows other tasks to run while waiting.

Alternatively you could use the ESP32 event system to make the connection asynchronous and to handle status changes after the connection:

```
#include <WiFi.h>
int status;
void WiFiEvent(WiFiEvent_t event) {
  status = event;
  Serial.println();
  switch (event) {
    case ARDUINO_EVENT_WIFI_READY:
      Serial.println("WiFi interface ready");
      break;
```

```
          case ARDUINO_EVENT_WIFI_SCAN_DONE:
            Serial.println("Completed scan for access points");
            break;
          case ARDUINO_EVENT_WIFI_STA_START:
            Serial.println("WiFi client started");
            break;
          case ARDUINO_EVENT_WIFI_STA_STOP:
            Serial.println("WiFi clients stopped");
            break;
          case ARDUINO_EVENT_WIFI_STA_CONNECTED:
            Serial.println("Connected to access point");
            break;
          case ARDUINO_EVENT_WIFI_STA_DISCONNECTED:
            Serial.println("Disconnected from WiFi access point");
            break;
          case ARDUINO_EVENT_WIFI_STA_GOT_IP:
            Serial.print("Obtained IP address: ");
            Serial.println(WiFi.localIP());
            break;
          case ARDUINO_EVENT_WIFI_STA_LOST_IP:
            Serial.println("Lost IP address");
            break;
          default: break;
      }
  }


  void wifiConnect(char* ssid, char* password) {
    WiFi.onEvent(WiFiEvent);
    status = WiFi.begin(ssid, password);
  }
```

Notice that the variable, status, is used to communicate with the rest of the program:

```
  void setup() {
    Serial.begin(9600);
    delay(2000);
    Serial.begin(9600);
    wifiConnect("ssid", "password");
  };
  void loop() {
    while (status != ARDUINO_EVENT_WIFI_STA_GOT_IP) {
      delay(1000);
    };
    Serial.println(status);
    delay(1000);
  }
```

The event approach is more sophisticated and can detect additional states, but it is highly ESP-specific.

WiFi Scan

The `scanNetworks` method can be used to survey what access points are available. It returns the number of APs available. This in itself isn't of much use, but behind the scenes it fills in a table of values that provide more information about each AP. This table can be accessed using the usual information functions by passing an integer signifying the AP that the data is needed for.

For example:

```
#include <WiFi.h>
void setup() {
  Serial.begin(9600);
  delay(2000);
  Serial.begin(9600);
  int nNet = WiFi.scanNetworks();
  Serial.println(nNet);
  for (int i = 0; i < nNet; i++) {
    Serial.printf("ssid %s  rssi %d channel %d encryption %d\n",
        WiFi.SSID(i), WiFi.RSSI(i),WiFi.channel(i),
                                    WiFi.encryptionType(i));
  }
  Serial.println("Scan complete");
};
void loop(){}
```

This will print the SSID, RSSI and encryption type for each of the detected networks. The `scanNetworks` method blocks until the scan is complete.

The ESP32 adds some additional features to the scan including an asynchronous version – which of course only works on the ESP32. In this case the `scanNetworks` function is:

```
int16_t scanNetworks(bool async = false, bool show_hidden = false,
      bool passive = false, uint32_t max_ms_per_chan = 300,
                                    uint8_t channel = 0)
```

The most important is the `async` parameter which, if set to `true`, causes the scan to be performed in the background. This returns at once and you can check on the progress using:

```
int16_t scanComplete()
```

which returns the number of networks acquired. If it returns a negative value then it is still scanning or an error has occurred. You can test for the error using `WIFI_SCAN_FAILED`.

The results of the scan can be accessed in the same way as for the synchronous scan:

```
#include <WiFi.h>
void setup() {
  Serial.begin(9600);
  WiFi.scanNetworks(true);
};
void loop() {
  delay(1000);
  int16_t nNet = WiFi.scanComplete();
  if (nNet  >= 0) {
    for (int i = 0; i < nNet; i++) {
      Serial.printf("ssid %s  rssi %d channel %d encryption %d\n",
          WiFi.SSID(i), WiFi.RSSI(i), WiFi.channel(i),
                                    WiFi.encryptionType(i));
    }
  }
 WiFi.scanDelete();
}
void loop(){}
```

There is also an alternative way of getting the data:

```
bool getNetworkInfo(uint8_t networkItem, String &ssid,
    uint8_t &encryptionType, int32_t &RSSI,
      uint8_t* &BSSID, int32_t &channel)
```

which simply loads the data into the variables indicated by the pointers.

A Web Client

Now that we have a WiFi connection we can start using it. The lowest-level way of making a network connection is to use sockets. This is a standard and very flexible way of making connections using a range of different protocols, however, in practice, most connections are TCP/IP which is used by the internet and the web in particular. You can use sockets if you want to, but this isn't part of the Arduino library. Instead you can make use of the WiFiClient class to implement a client TCP/IP socket without having to delve into how sockets work.

To create a client you simply create an instance of WiFiClient:

```
WiFiClient client;
```

and then use its connect method to connect to a server either via its IP address or its URL. For example:

```
client.connect("www.example.com", 80);
```

or:

```
client.connect("93.184.215.14", 80);
```

285

The second parameter is the port to use to connect and, for web pages using HTTP, this is usually port 80.

As long as there is no error, the method returns true if the connection is good, we can start to send and receive data.

But what data? The answer is that it all depends on the protocol you are using. There is nothing about a connection that tells you what to send. It is a completely general I/O mechanism using TCP/IP to transport data. You can send anything, but if you don't send what the server is expecting, you won't get very far.

The web uses the HTTP protocol and this is essentially a set of text headers that tell the server what to do, and a set of headers that the server sends back to tell you what it has done.

The most basic transaction the client can have with the server is to send a GET request for the server to send a particular file.

This means that the simplest set of headers we can send the server is:

```
GET /index.html HTTP/1.1
HOST:example.com
```

An HTTP request always ends with a blank line. If you don't send the blank line then you will get no response from most servers. In addition the HOST header has to have the domain name with no additional syntax - no slashes and no http: or similar.

With the headers defined we can send our first HTTP request using the println method of the client class:

```
client.println("GET /index.html HTTP/1.1");
client.println("HOST:example.com");
client.println();
```

The server receives the HTTP request and should respond by sending the data corresponding to the file specified, i.e. index.html. We can read the response just as if the client was a stream:

```
void loop() {
  if (client.available()) {
    char c = client.read();
    Serial.print(c);
  }
}
```

You can make this more complicated by checking the number of bytes read and reading more if the buffer is full, but this is a simple and direct way to get the HTML.

In fact, you get more than the HTML as you get the entire HTTP response including the response headers:

```
HTTP/1.1 200 OK
Accept-Ranges: bytes
Age: 343832
Cache-Control: max-age=604800
Content-Type: text/html; charset=UTF-8
Date: Mon, 18 Nov 2024 17:54:20 GMT
Etag: "3147526947+gzip"
Expires: Mon, 25 Nov 2024 17:54:20 GMT
Last-Modified: Thu, 17 Oct 2019 07:18:26 GMT
Server: ECAcc (nyd/D169)
Vary: Accept-Encoding
X-Cache: HIT
Content-Length: 1256

<!doctype html>
<html>
```

and so on...

Notice the blank line marking the end of the header and signaling that the data payload follows.

The complete program is:

```
#include <WiFi.h>
#include <WiFiClient.h>

int wifiConnect(char* ssid, char* password) {
  int status = WiFi.begin(ssid, password);
  while (status != WL_CONNECTED) {
    switch (status) {
      case WL_NO_SSID_AVAIL:
        Serial.printf("No AP with name %s can be found", ssid);
        return status;
      case WL_CONNECT_FAILED:
        Serial.printf("Connection failed");
        return status;
      case WL_CONNECTION_LOST:
        Serial.printf("Connection lost possible security problem");
        return status;
    }
    delay(100);
    status = WiFi.status();
  }
  return status;
}

WiFiClient client;
```

```
void setup() {
  Serial.begin(9600);
  int status = wifiConnect("ssid", "password");
  Serial.println(status);

  client.connect("www.example.com", 80);
  client.println("GET /index.html HTTP/1.1");
  client.println("HOST:example.com");
  client.println();
};

void loop() {
  if (client.available()) {
    char c = client.read();
    Serial.print(c);
  }
}
```

Of course, we can do much better than this simple example. For one thing, each operation needs to be checked for errors.

ESP32 HTTPS Client

Creating an HTTP client is easy, but creating an HTTPS client requires more processing power that most Arduino processors can muster. As a result HTTPS is only possible on more modern devices such as the ESP32. In this case there is a modified WiFiClient class that makes switching to HTTPS very easy.

The key point about HTTPS is encryption. If you connect to an HTTPS server then the data is encrypted before transmission. The key used for the encryption is exchanged using Public Key Cryptography with the help of one or more certificates. If the client and the server have certificates then it is possible for the client to confirm that the server is what it claims to be and the server can confirm that the client is what it claims to be. This can be used to restrict access to clients that have a particular certificate that proves their identity. In many cases this is unnecessary and the encryption key can be exchanged just using the server's certificate. This is referred to as "unsafe", but its encryption is perfectly secure, it is only the identity of the client which is not determined. This is the mode that most browsers work in, unless you upload a specific client certificate.

To create a certificate-less HTTPS client all you have to do is to make the following changes to increase security:

From	To
`#include <WiFiClient.h>`	`#include <WiFiClientSecure.h>`
`WiFiClient client;`	`WiFiClientSecure client;`
`client.connect("www.example.com",80);`	`client.setInsecure();` `client.connect("www.example.com",443);`

Apart from setting "insecure" mode you also have to change the port to 443, which is the usual port for an HTTPS connection.

The complete program is:

```
#include <WiFi.h>
#include <WiFiClientSecure.h>
int wifiConnect(char* ssid, char* password) {
  int status = WiFi.begin(ssid, password);
  while (status != WL_CONNECTED) {
    switch (status) {
      case WL_NO_SSID_AVAIL:
        Serial.printf("No AP with name %s can be found", ssid);
        return status;
      case WL_CONNECT_FAILED:
        Serial.printf("Connection failed");
        return status;
      case WL_CONNECTION_LOST:
        Serial.printf("Connection lost possible security problem");
        return status;
    }
    delay(100);
    status = WiFi.status();
  }
  return status;
}
WiFiClientSecure client;

void setup() {
  Serial.begin(9600);
  int status = wifiConnect("ssid", "password");
  Serial.println(status);
  client.setInsecure();
  client.connect("www.example.com", 443);
  client.println("GET /index.html HTTP/1.1");
  client.println("HOST:example.com");
  client.println();
};
```

```
void loop() {
  if (client.available()) {
    char c = client.read();
    Serial.print(c);
  }
}
```

If you have a client certificate that the server needs to make the connection then you can supply it using:

```
client.setCACert(cert);
```

where `cert` is a C string representation of the certificate, see ESP HTTPS Server Component for an example of how to specify a certificate.

Request Methods

HTTP supports a number of request methods which transfer data. Usually these are described in terms of what they do to resources hosted by a web server, but from our point of view what matters is what happens to the data.

The HTTP request methods available are:

GET	Transfers data from server to client
HEAD	Transfers HTTP headers for the equivalent GET request
PUT	Transfers data from the client to the server
POST	Transfers data from the client to the server
PATCH	Transfers data from the client to the server
DELETE	Specifies that the data on the server should be deleted
OPTIONS	Transfers data from the client to the server

If you know about HTTP request methods you will find the above list disconcerting. If you don't know about HTTP requests then you will be wondering why there are so many requests that transfer data from the client to the server? The answer is that in the HTTP model the server stores the master copy of the resource – usually a file or a database entry. The client can request a copy of the resource using GET and then ask the server to modify the resource using the other requests. For example, the PUT request sends a new copy of the resource for the server to use, i.e. it replaces the old copy. POST does the same thing, but PUT should be idempotent which means if you repeat it the result is as if you had done it just once. With POST you are allowed side effects. For example, PUT 1 might just store 1 but POST 1 might increment a count.

Another example is where you send some text to the server to save under a supplied file name. For this you should use a PUT as repeating the request with the same text changes nothing. If, on the other hand, you supply text to the server and allow it to assign a name and store it then you should use a POST as you get a new file each time you send the data, even if it is the same.

Similarly the PATCH request should be used by the client to request that that server makes a change to part of an existing resource. Exactly how the change is specified depends on the server. Usually a key/value scheme is used, but this isn't part of the specification.

Notice that all of these interpretations of the HTTP request methods are "optional" in the sense that it is up to you and the server you are using to interpret them and implement them. If you write your own server, or server application, then you can treat POST as if it was PUT and vice versa. Also notice that the only difference between client and server is which one initiates the transaction. A client always contacts a server, but once the connection is made data can be transferred in either direction – a GET sends data to the client and a PUT sends data to the server.

This is true but a GET can also send some additional data to the server, usually used to determine what the server returns, using a query string. A query string is a set of key/value pairs that are added to the end of the URL. For example:

```
http://example.com/page?key1=value1&key2=value2...
```

The server will parse the key/value pairs and make use of them to customize the page that it returns.

A Sensor Client

The standard approach to implementing a sensor device that makes its readings available to other devices is to implement a web server or a custom protocol on the ESP32 that allows other devices to connect. A simpler solution is to implement an HTTP client and allow the sensor device to send data to a server, using PUT or POST, which other devices can then connect to as required.

The main program only needs minor modification. The method needs to be changed to PUT or POST and the server is specified using its IP address, path and port. Notice that the path is supplied to the server, but it can be ignored. The data to be sent to the server is placed in the body of the request after the headers in exactly the same way that data is sent from the server to the client in response to a GET. The only complication is that you usually have to supply some additional headers to let the server work out how to interpret the data in the body of the request.

The only difficult part is making up the Content-Length header with the variable length of the string representing the temperature. The Content-Type header is optional, but if you are connecting to a full server then it will tell the server how to make the data available to any program that uses it.

The main program is;

```
#include <WiFi.h>
#include <WiFiClient.h>
int wifiConnect(char* ssid, char* password) {
  int status = WiFi.begin(ssid, password);
  while (status != WL_CONNECTED) {
    switch (status) {
      case WL_NO_SSID_AVAIL:
        Serial.printf("No AP with name %s can be found", ssid);
        return status;
      case WL_CONNECT_FAILED:
        Serial.printf("Connection failed");
        return status;
      case WL_CONNECTION_LOST:
        Serial.printf("Connection lost possible security problem");
        return status;
    }
    delay(100);
    status = WiFi.status();
  }
  return status;
}

WiFiClient client;

void setup() {
  Serial.begin(9600);
  int status = wifiConnect("ssid", "password");
  Serial.println(status);

  Serial.print(client.connect("192.168.253.75", 8080));
  float temp = 20.5;

  int len = snprintf(NULL, 0, "%f", temp);
  char *text = (char*)malloc(len + 1);
  snprintf(text, len + 1, "%f", temp);

  client.println("PUT /index.html HTTP/1.1");
  client.println("Content-Type:text/plain");
  client.print("Content-Length: ");
  client.println(len);
  client.println();
  client.println(text);
};
```

```
void loop() {
  if (client.available()) {
    char c = client.read();
    Serial.print(c);
  }
}
```

You need to change the IP address for the IP address or URL of the server and its port number. To try the program out we can easily put together a small server in Python using port 8080, which is a common alternative for slightly non-standard HTTP servers.

The server simply has to respond to the PUT request and convert the bytes to a string and then a float.

A Python program that acts as a basic server is simple:

```python
from http.server import HTTPServer, BaseHTTPRequestHandler
from io import BytesIO

class SimpleHTTPRequestHandler(BaseHTTPRequestHandler):

    def log_message(self,*args, **kwargs):
        pass

    def do_PUT(self):
        content_length = int(self.headers['Content-Length'])
        body = self.rfile.read(content_length)
        bodyString= body.decode(encoding="utf-8")
        temp=float(bodyString)
        print(temp)
        self.send_response(200)
        self.end_headers()

httpd = HTTPServer(('', 8080), SimpleHTTPRequestHandler)
httpd.serve_forever()
```

As before, it is simple enough to convert the server and the client to HTTPS. You can appreciate that this architecture works well if you can allocate a simple device to act as a server that everything else can connect to.

The HTTP Server

As well as an HTTP client class, there is a server class which is very easy to use.

To create a server you use the constructor:

```
WiFiServer server(port)
```

In this case the port is the port that connections are accepted on, usually 80 for a web server. This creates the server but doesn't activate it. To start it listening for incoming connections on the port you use the begin method:

```
begin()
```

The main problem with a server is that you don't control when a client might connect. A polling solution to this problem is:

```
client = available()
```

This returns a client if there is one waiting for data. If there isn't, then the returned client object behaves like false in an if statement. The client inherits from Stream and so you can use the standard stream methods read, readBytes, write, print and println to send and receive data from the client.

When you are finished with the client you can remove it by closing the stream using close(). You can also check that the client is still connected using connected().

Once you have setup a WiFiServer object you simply wait for a client to connect. When you have the client object you can read and write it as if it was a stream and exchange data with the client. Notice that you have to process all of the headers explicitly in code. That is, the server simply provides a communication channel whereas you have to decode the GET, PUT or POST etc request and sort out what should be sent to the client, if anything.

Here's a simple program to service a basic GET request:

```
#include <WiFi.h>
#include <WiFiClient.h>
int wifiConnect(char* ssid, char* password) {
  int status = WiFi.begin(ssid, password);
  while (status != WL_CONNECTED) {
    switch (status) {
      case WL_NO_SSID_AVAIL:
        Serial.printf("No AP with name %s can be found", ssid);
        return status;
      case WL_CONNECT_FAILED:
        Serial.printf("Connection failed");
        return status;
```

```
      case WL_CONNECTION_LOST:
        Serial.printf("Connection lost possible security problem");
        return status;
    }
    delay(100);
    status = WiFi.status();
  }
  return status;
}

WiFiServer server(80);

void setup() {
  Serial.begin(9600);
  int status = wifiConnect("ssid", "password");
  Serial.println(status);

  server.begin();
};

void loop() {
  int buflen = 100;
  char buffer[100];

  WiFiClient client = server.available();
  if (client) {
    if (client.connected()) {
      Serial.println("connected");
      while (client.available()) {
        char c = client.read();
        Serial.print(c);
      }

      char page[] = "<html><Body>Temperature =
                          20.5C</Br></body></html>";
      int len = strlen(page);
      client.println("HTTP/1.1 200 OK");
      client.println("Content-Type: text/html; charset=UTF-8");
      client.println("Content-Length: ");
      client.println(len);
      client.println();
      client.println(page);
    }
  }
  client.stop();
}
```

You can see that all that happens is that we wait for a client and then read
the request headers. Notice that the data sent by the client is in the receive
buffer and you can read this data at any point in the transaction. In principle

you would process the headers to find out what file the client wanted from the URL and the request header to find out if this is a GET, PUT or whatever. Once the headers are processed we then send the fewest headers possible and then some HTML as a payload.

ESP IDF HTTPS Server Component

There is no standard way to implement an HTTPS server using the Arduino core library and it isn't even supported in the ESP32 version. There are a number of third party libraries that make use of the ESP IDF SDK to add HTTP to the Arduino ESP32 library, but at the time of writing the most commonly recommended of them simply don't work with the new Arduino IDE and the latest ESP IDF SDK. The only reasonable solution is to use the ESP IDF directly and mostly abandon the Arduino library. You can still use it to make the WiFi connection and other tasks, but the actual server is provided by the ESP IDF SDK.

It is important to realize that making an HTTPS connection is a very computational-intensive task. Being an HTTPS client is demanding, but being a server uses a lot of memory and it tends to be slow. If you can avoid it, by using the ESP32 as a client, then this is likely to be a much better solution.

We need to use the ESP IDF HTTPS server component. This adds SSL encryption on top of the existing HTTP server component. So, what you know about the HTTP server is still useful and all you really have to do is supply and configure a certificate.

The next problem is getting a certificate, which can be an involved process. Even popular free certificate-issuing sites like Let's Encrypt require proof that you own the domain that the certificate applies to. To do this you have to write code which generates a new key pair and then either create a specific DNS record or store a file on the website. This is easy enough for production purposes, but not so easy when you are in the process of creating a program.

The usual solution is to create a self-signed certificate. If the operating system has OpenSSL installed, and most versions of Linux do, then you can create a key and certificate pair using:

```
openssl req -newkey rsa:2048 -nodes -keyout iopress.key -x509
                 -days 365 -out iopress.crt
```

changing *iopress* to the name of your server. You will be asked a set of questions for information that is included in the certificate. How you answer these questions only modifies what the user sees if they ask to inspect the certificate so you can simply accept the defaults.

The `openssl` command creates two files, a .key file and a .crt file, which need to be processed to create strings that can be used in a C program. There are many ways to get a simple certificate into a program, but the most direct way is to quote it as a string literal. It is very easy to write a standard Python program to do the job of converting the contents of the files to a C literal string complete with variable declaration:

```python
with open("iopress.key", 'rb') as f:
    lines = f.readlines()
lines=b'"'.join(lines)
lines=lines.decode("ascii")
lines=lines.replace("\n",'\\n"\n')
print("static const unsigned char key[]="+'"', lines+";")

with open("iopress.crt", 'rb') as f:
    lines = f.readlines()
lines=b'"'.join(lines)
lines=lines.decode("ascii")
lines=lines.replace("\n",'\\n"\n')
print("static const unsigned char cert[]="+'"', lines+";")
```

If you run this program, with the names of the .key and .crt files corrected to apply to the certificate you have generated, then it will read in each file, add quotes and line endings to create a multi-line C string literal:

```c
static const unsigned char key[]=" -----BEGIN PRIVATE KEY-----\n"
"MIIEvQIBADANBgkqhkiG9w0BAQEFAASCBKcwggSjAgEAAoIBAQC5zxoZHid/tAtR\n"
                    ...
"EVzn7XZ781QWSSBer5/vcQM=\n"
"-----END PRIVATE KEY-----\n"
;
static const unsigned char cert[]=" -----BEGIN CERTIFICATE-----\n"
"MIIDazCCAlOgAwIBAgIUA+lvUf9wMrNvaz9DuKnfx4TCoeQwDQYJKoZIhvcNAQEL\n"
                    ...
"mjqAoUl1y8um2Iw5koON\n"
"-----END CERTIFICATE-----\n"
;
```

where the multiple lines of text that make up each literal have been omitted to save space.

You can simply copy and paste these two blocks to get the certificate you have generated into the program.

Once we have the certificates in the program the rest is fairly straightforward in that we simply have to set up the server. One big difference between the Arduino and the IDF server is that it uses handlers for each response method and file target. These have to be registered with the server and they are automatically called when the server receives that request from a client. This means that much of the routine processing is done for you.

For example to register a GET handler for a request for /temp we would first create a struct and then register it:

```
 httpd_uri_t uri_get = {
    .uri = "/temp",
    .method = HTTP_GET,
    .handler = get_handler,
    .user_ctx = NULL
    };
httpd_register_uri_handler(server, &uri_get);
```

When the server receives a GET request for /temp it automatically calls the get_handler function:

```
esp_err_t get_handlertemp(httpd_req_t* req)
{
    /* Send a simple response */
    const char resp[] = "Temperature is 20.3";
    httpd_resp_send(req, resp, HTTPD_RESP_USE_STRLEN);
    return ESP_OK;
}
```

You can register multiple handlers for each of the response methods and files you want to support.

The complete details of how the HTTPS server works can be found in *Programming the ESP32 in C Using the Espressif IDF*, ISBN:978-1871962918, but reading the complete program should inform you of how to extend it to handle other requests:

```
#include "esp_https_server.h"
#include <WiFi.h>

int wifiConnect(char* ssid, char* password) {
  int status = WiFi.begin(ssid, password);
  while (status != WL_CONNECTED) {
    switch (status) {
      case WL_NO_SSID_AVAIL:
        Serial.printf("No AP with name %s can be found", ssid);
        return status;
      case WL_CONNECT_FAILED:
        Serial.printf("Connection failed");
        return status;
      case WL_CONNECTION_LOST:
        Serial.printf("Connection lost possible security problem");
        return status;
    }
    delay(100);
    status = WiFi.status();
  }
  return status;
}
```

```c
esp_err_t get_handlertemp(httpd_req_t* req)
{
    /* Send a simple response */
    const char resp[] = "Temperature is 20.3";
    httpd_resp_send(req, resp, HTTPD_RESP_USE_STRLEN);
    return ESP_OK;
}
esp_err_t get_handlerhum(httpd_req_t* req)
{
    /* Send a simple response */
    const char resp[] = "Humidity is 80%";
    httpd_resp_send(req, resp, HTTPD_RESP_USE_STRLEN);
    return ESP_OK;
}

void setup() {
  Serial.begin(9600);
  int status = wifiConnect("ssid", "password");
  Serial.println(status);

static const unsigned char cert[] = "-----BEGIN CERTIFICATE-----\n"
"MIIDazCCAlOgAwIBAgIUA+lvUf9wMrNvaz9DuKnfx4TCoeQwDQYJKoZIhvcNAQEL\
n"
                              . . .
"mjqAoUl1y8um2Iw5koONN\n"
"-----END CERTIFICATE-----\n";
static const unsigned char key[] = " -----BEGIN PRIVATE KEY-----\n"
"MIIEvQIBADANBgkqhkiG9w0BAQEFAASCBKcwggSjAgEAAoIBAQC5zxoZHid/tAtR\
n"
                              . . .
"EVzn7XZ781QWSSBer5/vcQM=\n"
"-----END PRIVATE KEY-----\n";

    httpd_ssl_config_t config = HTTPD_SSL_CONFIG_DEFAULT();
    config.servercert = cert;
    config.servercert_len = sizeof(cert);
    config.prvtkey_pem = key;
    config.prvtkey_len = sizeof(key);

    httpd_handle_t server = NULL;
    httpd_uri_t uri_get = {
    .uri = "/temp",
    .method = HTTP_GET,
    .handler = get_handlertemp,
    .user_ctx = NULL
    };
```

```
    if (httpd_ssl_start(&server, &config) == ESP_OK) {
        httpd_register_uri_handler(server, &uri_get);
        uri_get.uri = "/hum";
        uri_get.handler = get_handlerhum;
        httpd_register_uri_handler(server, &uri_get);
    }
};

void loop() {
}
```

The server is set up to serve two pages /temp and /hum and these are unchanged from the previous HTTP server.

If you want the full program, including the certificates, the listing is on this book's page at www.iopress.info, along with all the other substantial programs.

If you try this program you will find that connecting with a browser using https:// *ip of server* causes a security warning to pop-up due to the use of a self-signed certificate. This is what you will see using Chrome.

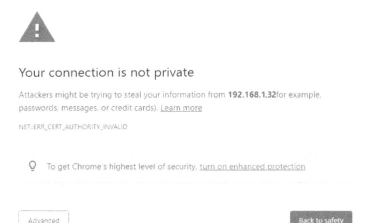

Your connection is not private

Attackers might be trying to steal your information from **192.168.1.32**(for example, passwords, messages, or credit cards). Learn more

NET::ERR_CERT_AUTHORITY_INVALID

To get Chrome's highest level of security, turn on enhanced protection

Advanced   Back to safety

Messages like this are because browsers don't trust self-signed certificates. However, if you allow the page to download, it will use SSL encryption. To do this click on Advanced and then confirm that you want to proceed. You can force a browser to accept the certificate by adding it to its trusted root certification authorities tab. However, for most testing purposes this isn't necessary. If you have a valid certificate and key for a particular web server you can substitute it for the self-signed certificates.

It is worth saying that making an SSL connection is not fast. The ESP32 is being asked to do significant computation to implement the cryptography and the handshake process is involved and hence time-consuming. You will also see a number of exceptions caused by the client aborting the connection due to the self-signed certificate, which is perfectly normal.

Firefox is a much more friendly browser to use when testing SSL connections. Chrome tends to want to lock things down as soon as it detects a problem with the certificate.

Also notice that a browser will generally attempt to negotiate the cryptographic protocol to exchange keys. If the server or the client don't support the proposed method then an error is reported at the server and a different protocol is tried. As a result it can take some time to make a SSL connection and you will see errors similar to:

```
W (68737) httpd: httpd_server: error accepting new connection
I (68737) esp_https_server: performing session handshake
E (69467) esp-tls-mbedtls: mbedtls_ssl_handshake returned -0x7780
E (69467) esp_https_server: esp_tls_create_server_session failed
E (69467) httpd: httpd_accept_conn: session creation failed
```

As long as everything works out and a connection is finally made, you can ignore these errors.

Summary

- Connecting to a WiFi network is a matter of using the WiFi object configured as a station to connect to an access point

- The ESP version of the WiFi object has extensions to make it more sophisticated, including events to allow it to work asynchronously.

- You can use the IPAddress class to work with IP addresses.

- Implementing error handling for a WiFi connection can be challenging.

- You can scan to discover what networks are available.

- An HTTP client can both send and receive data to the server depending on the request it makes.

- You can create a client or a server using the WiFiClient

- The most common request is GET which accepts data from the server.

- Both POST and PUT can be used to send data to the server.

- The only difference between a client and server is that a client can only make a connection whereas a server can accept a connection.

- It is possible to avoid having to implement a server on the ESP32 by allowing a client to connect to a server running on another machine and send its data using a PUT or POST request.

- The HTTP client is easy use, but in most cases you are going to want to use the HTTPS WiFiClientSecure class which doesn't need a custom certificate to work. This is ESP-specific.

- The HTTP WiFiServer server works in a very simple way and you have to manually generate all of the headers needed to implement any of the request methods,

- There is no Arduino core way of implementing an HTTPS server and the best solution is to fall back to the ESP IDF.

The ESP supports both internal and external file systems stored on flash memory. There is no support for flash memory in the Arduino core library but it is well supported in the ESP32 version of the Arduino library. In this chapter we look at partitions, Non-Volatile storage, the internal FAT file system and supporting external SD cards.

This chapter is specific to the ESP32 Arduino library.

Flash Memory

There are a number of different objects and methods that allow you to work with the ESP32's built-in flash memory, non-volatile computer storage that can be electrically erased and reprogrammed. You can also easily add external removable flash memory in the form of an SD card reader.

Flash memory is treated much like a disk drive in that you can create and use partitions. There are some very low-level functions that can create and modify partitions. Flash memory is divided up into partitions for different uses. There are two general types of partition:

```
ESP_PARTITION_TYPE_APP
ESP_PARTITION_TYPE_DATA
```
These roughly correspond to programs and data.

You can find out what partitions are present in your ESP32 using:

```
void setup() {
  Serial.begin(9600);
  delay(2000);
  Serial.begin(9600);
  Serial.println();
  esp_partition_iterator_t partit =
    esp_partition_find(ESP_PARTITION_TYPE_DATA,
                       ESP_PARTITION_SUBTYPE_ANY, NULL);
  while (partit != NULL) {
    const esp_partition_t* part = esp_partition_get(partit);
    Serial.printf("DATA label= %s Address= %lX  size = %ld \n",
           part->label, part->address, part->size);
    partit = esp_partition_next(partit);
  };
  esp_partition_iterator_release(partit);
  Serial.printf("\n");
```

303

```
  partit = esp_partition_find(ESP_PARTITION_TYPE_APP,
                              ESP_PARTITION_SUBTYPE_ANY, NULL);
  while (partit != NULL) {
    const esp_partition_t* part = esp_partition_get(partit);
    Serial.printf("APP label= %s Address= %lX  size = %ld \n",
          part->label, part->address, part->size);
    partit = esp_partition_next(partit);
  };
  esp_partition_iterator_release(partit);
}

void loop() {
}
```

Typically you will see:

```
DATA label= nvs Address= 9000  size = 20480
DATA label= otadata Address= E000  size = 8192
DATA label= spiffs Address= 290000  size = 1441792
DATA label= coredump Address= 3F0000  size = 65536

APP label= app0 Address= 10000  size = 1310720
APP label= app1 Address= 150000  size = 1310720
```

The APP partition, factory, stores your current program. The DATA partition nvs, hosts the Non Volatile Storage system.

To work with a partition you create a partition struct using:

```
part = esp_partition_find_first(type, subtype, id)
```

where id is the label of the block.

For example, to work with the nvs partition you could use:

```
part = esp_partition_find_first(ESP_PARTITION_TYPE_DATA,
                                ESP_PARTITION_SUBTYPE_ANY,"nvs")
```

followed by the functions:
  ◆   esp_partition_read(&part, offset, buf, size)
  ◆   esp_partition_write(&part, offset, buf, size)
  ◆   esp_partition_erase_range(&part, offset, size)

The read and write use the partition from the specified offset and either read or write data into the buffer. You have to erase the same region of the flash. Notice that you work with a raw partition in terms of bytes offset from the start of the partition – there are no files.

You probably only need to get involved in partition management if you want to use OTA (Over The Air) updates. This involves creating a flash layout that has two partitions ota_0 and ota_1 which can be used to store a complete version of your app. The OTA update works by downloading the new version of your app to the free OTA partition. Exactly how to implement this is beyond the scope of this book.

You can use the read/write blocks methods to load and store data, but you would have to keep track of which blocks were in use. This is usually the task of a file system and the API supports the FAT (File Allocation Table) filing system.

Creating Partitions – Adding FAT

If you are familiar with the way that hard disk partitions work on desktop machines, you may think that they are something that are set up when you first install the disk and they remain the same for the rest of its life, unless something odd happens. Partitions are installed on flash memory whenever a new application is flashed. The partition table, which is also located on flash memory, is updated when you install a program. As such, flash partition tables can be easily changed.

To change the partition table use the menu command Tools, Partition Scheme:

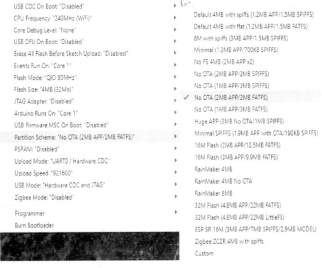

You can select one of the standard configurations or a custom table which is defined by a CSV file.

Non-Volatile Storage

To make it even easier to use flash storage for saving state, the ESP32 implements Non-Volatile Storage, NVS. This isn't anything new in the sense you could just write a file with the same data, but NVS, which is usually provided by the partition called nvs, is easier to use as it provides key/value storage. Keys have to be unique and are ASCII strings no larger than 15 characters and values are either integers, binary blobs or strings.

Start with:

```
nvs_open(namespace, open_mode, pout_handle)
```

You can think of *namespace* as a sort of file name and if it doesn't already exist it is created. The open_mode parameter is one of NVS_READONLY or NVS_READWRITE and pout_handle is a pointer to a returned handle. This works with the partition named nvs. You can use any partition as a nonvolatile storage using nvs_open_from_partition.

You save key/integer-value pairs using:

- ◆ nvs_set_i8(handle,key,value)
- ◆ nvs_set_i16(handle,key,value)
- ◆ nvs_set_i32(handle,key,value)
- ◆ nvs_set_i64(handle,key,value)

and there are similar functions for unsigned values replacing i with u and a set of load functions with set replaced by get.

You can save a string using:

```
nvs_set_str (handle, key, str);
```

and a blob using:

```
nvs_set_blob(handle, key, pbuf, length);
```

where pbuf is a pointer to a void buffer. There are corresponding get functions.

Finally:

```
nvs_erase_key(handle,key);
```

erases a key/value pair and

```
nvs_erase_all(handle)
```

erases all key/value pairs in the namespace.

It is important to notice that any setting of key/value pairs is postponed until you use:

```
nvs_commit(handle)
```

For example, to save and retrieve a simple value from a new namespace:

```
#include "nvs_flash.h"
void setup() {
    Serial.begin(9600);
    delay(2000);
    Serial.begin(9600);
    Serial.println();
    nvs_flash_init();
    nvs_handle_t my_handle;

    nvs_open("localstorage", NVS_READWRITE, &my_handle);
    char key[] = "mykey";
    int32_t myvalue = 42;
    int32_t myretrievedvalue;
    nvs_set_i32(my_handle, key, myvalue);
    nvs_commit(my_handle);
    nvs_get_i32(my_handle, key, &myretrievedvalue);
    Serial.printf("stored value = %ld\n", myretrievedvalue);
}
```

Notice that the NVS namespace is called localstorage and we can have other namespaces if we need to. The storage persists over program and processor restarts.

The FAT File System

For storage, the ESP32 supports a traditional FAT (File Allocation Table) system. You can create a FAT file system on any available partition, such as the one created in the section on creating partitions. The actual structure of file system support is quite complicated, but if you start at the topmost level it is fairly easy to use. The FAT system is implemented by the fatfs open source library as the fatfs component. You can use this directly, but it is easier to use it wrapped by the VFS (Virtual File System). The VFS can be used to integrate any file system with the standard C library functions such as fopen, fprintf and so on. Even if you plan to do complicated low-level file operations, it is still easier to get started with VFS FAT. However, the Arduino ESP32 library has an even easier way to get started.

There is an ESP32 Arduino implementation of a FAT file system which is much easier to use than the ESP IDF implementation. It is a fairly light wrapper over the fatfs component.

To use this you first have to create a FAT partition. To do this use the Tools,Partition Scheme menu command and select "Default 4MBytes with ffat". This creates a 1.5MB partition labeled ffat. If you have a more flash memory than 4MBytes then select 16M Flash or 32M Flash with the appropriate allocation to the FAT partition.

If you used the previous program to find what partitions have been created, you should find a line something like:

```
DATA label= ffat Address= 290000  size = 1441792
```

Before you can use the FAT partition it has to be formatted:

```
#include "FS.h"
#include "FFat.h"
void setup() {
  Serial.begin(9600);
  Serial.println();
  Serial.println(FFat.format(true,"ffat"));

}

void loop() {
}
```

The first parameter is `true` for a full erase and `false` for a quick format. The second parameter is the label of the partition you want to format, `ffat` by default.

To mount the partition so that you can work with it you use the FFAT object's `begin` method:

```
bool begin(bool formatOnFail, const char *basePath,
        uint8_t maxOpenFiles, const char *partitionLabel)
```

If the first parameter causes the partition to be reformatted if it cannot be read. The second gives the path to start the file system at, `maxOpenFiles` sets the memory limit on open files and the final parameter specifies the partition to use. When you are finished with the file system use the `end()` method.

There are a two useful methods for finding out about the state of the storage:

- ◆ `totalBytes()` Returns the total bytes available
- ◆ `usedBytes()` Returns the number of byes used

After a successful call to `begin` the FFAT object can be used to open files:

```
File f = FFat.open("/hello.txt", mode);
```

where `mode` is `FILE_READ`, `FILE_WRITE` or `FILE_APPEND`.

The File object isn't a standard C file object, instead it inherits from Stream and adds a few additional methods:

- close()　　　　　　　　　Closes file
- seek(pos, mode)　　　　Seeks to pos relative to:
　　　　　　　　　　　　　　SEEK_SET: Beginning of the file
　　　　　　　　　　　　　　SEEK_CUR: Current position of file pointer
　　　　　　　　　　　　　　SEEK_END: End of the file
- position()　　　　　　　Current position of file pointer
- size()　　　　　　　　　Size of file
- setBufferSize(size)　Sets buffer to size
- path()　　　　　　　　　Returns path as string
- name()　　　　　　　　　Returns name as string
- exists(path)　　　　　true if file exists
- remove(path)　　　　　Deletes file
- rename(path1,path2)　Renames path1 to path2
- mkdir(path)　　　　　　Makes directory
- rmdir(path)　　　　　　Removes directory
- isDirectory　　　　　　true if file is a directory
- seekDir(pos)　　　　　Moves to position pos in directory
- openNext(mode)　　　　Opens next file in directory
- getNextFileName()　　Gets name of the next file in the directory
- rewindDirectory()　　Sets directory pointer back to starting

For example, assuming that a partition called FFAT exists and has been formatted, then reading and writing a file is easy:

```
#include "FS.h"
#include "FFat.h"
void setup() {
  Serial.begin(9600);
  delay(2000);
  Serial.begin(9600)
  Serial.println();
  FFat.begin(false, "", 2, "ffat");
  Serial.printf("Total space: %10u\n", FFat.totalBytes());
  Serial.printf("Free space: %10u\n", FFat.freeBytes());
  File f = FFat.open("/hello.txt", FILE_WRITE);
  f.println("Hello world");
  f.close();
  f = FFat.open("/hello.txt",FILE_READ);
  while (f.available()) {
    char c = f.read();
    Serial.write(c);
  }
  f.close();
  Serial.println("File Closed");
}
void loop() {}
```

You can see that, apart from mounting the partition using `begin` and opening the file, this is similar to using an Arduino `Stream` object.

For an example of working with directories, the following program lists the contents of a single directory:

```
#include "FS.h"
#include "FFat.h"
void setup() {
  Serial.begin(9600);
  delay(2000);
  Serial.begin(9600);
  FFat.begin(false, "", 2, "ffat");
  Serial.printf("Total space: %10u\n", FFat.totalBytes());
  Serial.printf("Free space: %10u\n", FFat.freeBytes());

  File root=FFat.open("/");
  File file = root.openNextFile();
  while(file){
    Serial.println(file.name());
    file = root.openNextFile();
  }
}

void loop() {
}
```

If you want a full listing of directories, including sub-directories, then you need to implement a recursive function.

External SD

Although the ESP32 generally doesn't have an external SD card reader, it is fairly easy to add one. Add-on SD card readers are available to order at very reasonable prices, see the Resources section of the book's webpage for stockists. In principle you don't need one as you can connect directly to the pins on the card – but this is usually not a good idea.

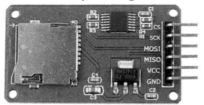

The only problem is that most have zero documentation or specification and they lack a card-detect and a write-protect pin. Connection to the ESP32 is fairly easy via one of the two SPI buses. The only complication is that most of the devices need a 5V supply. They work at 3.3V logic levels and so can be directly connected to the ESP32 and have an onboard voltage regulator to reduce the supply to 3.3V. Most claim to work if powered from 3.3V, but this depends on the regulator used and some fail or become unreliable. The ESP32 has a suitable 5V supply pin and in most cases this is the VCC connection to use. The ESP32 S3 often cannot supply enough 5V current to operate a card reader.

As we have already discussed, there are four SPI interfaces, but two are dedicated to SD use and it is easier to use one of the remaining two, i.e. SPI2 HSPI or SPI3 VSPI. The following pin assignments work with the ESP32 or the ESP32 S3, as should any other reasonable selection:

SCK	18
CS	5
MISO	4
MOSI	15

You can use any GPIO line for any of the SPI signals, but in the case of the ESP32 the default assignments are faster. The connections are as shown below:

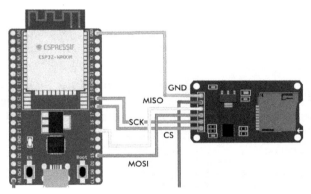

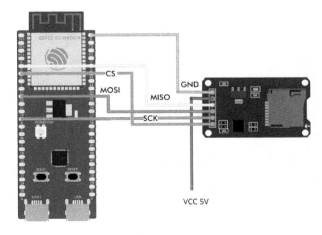

The ESP32 has enough power to supply 5V to most card adapters, but the ESP32 S3 generally hasn't and you need to provide a separate 5V supply unless the adapter works at 3.3V. If the software reports a timeout and the SD card is good and the wiring correct then the most likely reason is an inadequate power supply. If the software reports a CRC error then the connecting cables are too long and you need to reduce the clock speed.

Once you have this wired up you need an SD card, freshly formatted using FAT, and a single partition, which is what you get if you use a new, just out of the packet, formatted SD card. If the card isn't new, then partition and format it in another machine. You can partition and format cards using the ESP32, but getting started is easier with a pre-formatted card. Make sure the card is correctly inserted before moving on to the software and if you can, check that it can be read in another system.

The ESP32 version of the Arduino library supports external SD cards either using the SPI bus or the MMC bus. In this example the SPI bus is used because it is easier to setup from a hardware point of view. The MMC bus software is more or less identical. The Arduino library is much easier to use than the ESP32 IDF SPI SD card system which it wraps.

To get started you need to use the SD object's begin method:

```
bool begin(uint8_t ssPin = SS, SPIClass &spi = SPI,
    uint32_t frequency = 4000000, const char *mountpoint = "/sd",
    uint8_t max_files = 5, bool format_if_empty = false);
```

You can see that this is like the begin method of the FFAT object, the only difference is that you have to specify the SPI controller to use and the GPIO pin to use for the CS pin. You can accept the defaults for these or you can set up the SPI bus before you call begin:

```
SPI.begin(sck, miso, mosi, cs);
```

You also need to set the cs line on the SD object:

```
SD.begin(cs);
```

The SD object has set up useful and obvious methods:

```
  sdcard_type_t cardType();
  uint64_t cardSize();
  size_t numSectors();
  size_t sectorSize();
  uint64_t totalBytes();
  uint64_t usedBytes();
  bool readRAW(uint8_t *buffer, uint32_t sector);
  bool writeRAW(uint8_t *buffer, uint32_t sector);
```

where `cardType` is one of:

- ◆ CARD_NONE
- ◆ CARD_MMC
- ◆ CARD_SD
- ◆ CARD_SDHC
- ◆ CARD_UNKNOWN

Once you have initialized the SD object you can use it as if it was an FS object, which it inherits from. It has all of the methods described for FFAT earlier. This means you can use SD to open and close files and use Stream to read and write files and directories. In other words, everything works as for the FAT file system described earlier.

To prove that things are working this program prints the details of the card and then creates and reads a file:

```
#include "FS.h"
#include "SD.h"
#include "SPI.h"
void setup() {
  Serial.begin(9600);
  delay(2000);
  Serial.begin(9600);
  Serial.println();

  SPI.begin(18, 4, 15, 5);
  SD.begin(5);
  uint64_t cardSize = SD.cardSize() / (1024 * 1024);
  Serial.printf("SD Card Size: %lluMB\n", cardSize);

  File f = SD.open("/hello.txt", FILE_WRITE);
  f.println("Hello world");
  f.close();

  f = SD.open("/hello.txt",FILE_READ);
  while (f.available()) {
    char c = f.read();
    Serial.write(c);
  }
  f.close();
  Serial.println("File Closed");
}

void loop() {
}
```

For the Arduino Nano ESP32 use GPIO14 in place of GPIO15.

313

Summary

- You can work with the ESP32's internal flash memory as partitions.

- You can install file systems onto partitions and then work with files.

- The NVS file system allows you to save key/value pairs to the internal flash memory.

- You can also setup FAT partitions on the internal flash memory and format and use them as if they were standard disk drives.

- To use the FAT partition you work with the `FFAT` object which inherits from `File`, which in turn inherits from `Stream`

- The `File` object isn't a C or a C++ file. It is an Arduino `Stream` with some additional methods to work with files and directories.

- If you add an external SD card reader, you can work with an SD card using the same techniques as used for the internal flash memory.

Chapter 17
Direct To The Hardware

The Arduino library is easy to use, but it doesn't deliver the full potential of any hardware it runs on because of compromises it makes in order to run on a wide range of hardware. Versions of the library targeted at particular hardware do a better job, but there will generally be features that are unsupported. Even dedicated SDKs created by the manufacturers of the hardware, such as the ESP IDF, will lack support for some obscure features of the hardware.

All libraries and SDKs that make hardware easier to use are simply software wrappers over the hardware's implementation. The actual limit on what can be achieved is the hardware, not the software. Of course, you are always at liberty to refer to the hardware's documentation and write code that accesses it directly and this is partly what this chapter is all about. Even if you don't need to extend what the library or SDK implements, it is a good idea to know how things work.

In this chapter we take a look at how the ESP32 presents its hardware for you to use and how to access it via either basic software or via the ESP32 IDF SDK – hence this chapter is very ESP32specific.

Registers

Some processors have special ways of connecting devices, but the ESP32's processor uses the more common memory-mapping approach. In this, each external device is represented by a set of memory locations or "registers" that control it. Each bit in the register controls some aspect of the way the device behaves. Groups of bits also can be interpreted as short integers which set operating values or modes.

How do you access a register? Simply by storing the values in it or by assigning its value to a variable. This is nothing new in C. The big difference is that you now have to refer not to a memory location provided by the system, but to a fixed address provided by the documentation. You still use a pointer, but one that is initialized by a constant or literal.

The only difficult part is in working out the address you need to use and the value that sets or resets the bits you need to modify. For example, if you look in the documentation for the ESP32 you will find that the GPIO registers start at address 0x3FF44000. However, if you look up the starting address for the ESP32 S3, you will find that they start at 0x60004000. You cannot assume that all versions of the ESP32 have the same memory map, but you can assume that the registers mostly work in the same way. The registers are defined by the offset from their starting address or an absolute address.

For the ESP32, the start of the table of GPIO registers is:

Name	Description	Address	Access
GPIO_OUT_REG	GPIO 0-31 output register	0x3FF44004	R/W
GPIO_OUT_W1TS_REG	GPIO 0-31 output register_W1TS	0x3FF44008	WO
GPIO_OUT_W1TC_REG	GPIO 0-31 output register_W1TC	0x3FF4400C	WO

This gives an offset of 0x4, 0x8 and 0xC for each register. This is also true for the ESP32 S3, but the offsets are relative to 0x60004000 giving addresses of 0x60004004, 0x60004008 and 0x6000400C respectively.

The three registers control the GPIOs in output mode. How the GPIO line gets into output mode is a matter of using other registers described later in the table, but if we assume that the GPIO line is fully configured in output mode then these three registers control the state of GPIO0 to GPIO31. There are three similar registers for GPIO32 to GPIO39.

The big problem in making use of this information is that the "Description" part of the table is cryptic and often incomplete. You almost have to know what sorts of things the register is used for before it makes any sense. The first register is simple – if you write a 1 to bit n then GPIOn will be set active, usually high voltage, and if you write a 0 to bit n then the line is deactivated, usually low voltage. The other two registers are slightly more difficult to understand due to the use of W1TS and W1TC – which stand for Write One To Set and Write One To Clear. Once you know this, it is obvious that the first register is a bit-set register and the second a bit-clear register. That is, if you write a 1 to bit n using the W1TS register then GPIOn will be activated, but if you write it using the W1TC register, GPIOn will be deactivated.

You might wonder why we need three registers to control the GPIO lines? It is true that you don't need anything beyond the first, but the other two make things easier. By writing a bit pattern to GPIO_OUT_REG you set or reset all of the GPIO lines depending on whether there is a 1 or a 0 at bit n. If you only want to change a subset of lines, then you have to read the current state of the lines, notice whether GPIO_OUT_REG has read or write access, and then modify just the bits corresponding to the lines you want to change. This isn't difficult, but you can avoid having to do this by using GPIO_OUT_W1TS_REG with a bit pattern that sets just the lines that correspond to a 1 or GPIO_OUT_W1TC_REG which resets the same lines.

This becomes easier to understand after an example.

Blinky Revisited

Now we can re-write Blinky again, but this time using direct access to the GPIO registers.

```
uint32_t* GPIObase = (uint32_t*)0x60004000;  //EP32 S3
//uint32_t* GPIObase = (uint32_t*)0x3FF44000; //ESP32
uint32_t* GPIOSet = GPIObase + 8 / 4;
uint32_t* GPIOClear = GPIObase + 0xC / 4;
uint32_t mask = 1 << 2;
void setup() {
  pinMode(2, OUTPUT);
}
void loop() {
  *GPIOSet = mask;
  delay(1000);
  *GPIOClear = mask;
  delay(1000);
}
```

This program uses the standard Arduino function to set the GPIO line to output. If you think that this is cheating, it is an exercise in setting the line correctly using the GPIO control register.

The GPIOBase address has to be set correctly for the processor we are running the program on. Notice that as we are using pointers to uint32_t, pointer arithmetic works in multiples of 4. Hence, to move the address on by 4, we just add 1 and, in general, to set an offset of x we add x/4.

To toggle GPIO2 we make use of the set and clear registers and a mask that has bit 2 set to 1. Notice that 1<<n is a bit pattern with bit n set to 1. Alternatively you could use:

```
mask = 0x02
```

Once we have the mask, the loop simply stores it in the set and clear register alternately. Notice that as only bit 2 is a 1 this only changes the state of GPIO2.

This raises the question of how fast is this direct manipulation of the GPIO line's state?

Changing the loop to read:

```
    while (true) {
        *GPIOSet = mask;
        *GPIOClear = mask;
    }
```

reveals that the fastest pulses are 60ns high, i.e. 8.3MHz, and 190ns low. This is about eight times faster than using the library functions and more than 30 times faster than using MicroPython.

GPIO_REG.h

The need to adjust addresses depending on which version of the ESP32 is being used is a nuisance, but it can be avoided. The header file gpio_reg.h, which is part of the ESP IDF, contains definitions for many of the hardware registers adjusted for the device in use. For example:

```
#define GPIO_OUT_W1TS_REG
#define GPIO_OUT_W1TC_REG
```

gives the correct address for the registers, accounting for the target device. This allows you to write code that works on any device. For example, the Blinky program can be written:

```
#include "soc/gpio_reg.h"
uint32_t mask = 1 << 2;

void setup() {
  pinMode(2, OUTPUT);
}

void loop() {
  *(int32_t*)GPIO_OUT_W1TS_REG = mask;
  delay(1000);
  *(int32_t*)GPIO_OUT_W1TC_REG = mask;
  delay(1000);
}
```

This should work on any model of ESP32 without changes, but it would have to be recompiled with an appropriate target set. The only downside of this approach is that gpio_reg.h is still under development and hence may change.

Example 1 - Simultaneous Setting of GPIO Lines

Both the Arduino library and the ESP IDF SDK only provide functions to change single GPIO lines at a time, but it is very easy to create functions that set multiple lines at a time. A set function simply writes the mask to the GPIO_OUT_W1TS_REG register:

```
void gpio_setgroup(uint32_t mask) {
    *(int32_t*)GPIO_OUT_W1TS_REG = mask;
}
```

A clear function is just as easy and writes to the GPIO_OUT_W1TC_REG register:

```
void gpio_cleargroup(uint32_t mask) {
    *(int32_t*)GPIO_OUT_W1TC_REG = mask;
}
```

As before, only the set bits in the mask are affected.

318

While these two functions operate on single GPIO lines, you often want to select a set of bits and set or clear them in one operation, for example, when you want to change two or more GPIO lines in phase, i.e. all high or all low, you can use:

```
gpio_setgroup(0x3)
gpio_cleargroup(0x3)
```

This operates on the bottom two bits and so toggles GPIO0 and GPIO1, with both turning on and off at exactly the same time.

Now consider how to set GPIO0 high when GPIO1 is low. What we need is a function that will set any group of GPIO lines to 0 or 1 at the same time:

```
void gpio_value_mask(int32_t value, int32_t mask) {
    *(int32_t*)GPIO_OUT_REG  = (*(int32_t*)GPIO_OUT_REG & ~mask) |
                                              (value & mask);
}
```

The mask gives the GPIO lines that need to be changed, i.e. it determines the group and the value gives the state they are to be set to. For example, if mask is 0111 and value is 0100 and the low four bits of the register are 1010 then reg & ~mask is 1000, value & mask is 0100 and finally reg | value is 1100. You can see that bits 0 to 3 have been set to 100 and bit 4 has been unchanged.

The trick to working out how to do this is to construct one mask to set the bits that need to be set and another to unset the bits that need to be unset. If a bit is to be set, it needs a 1 in the mask and a 1 in the data and the mask to set bits is:

```
setmask = mask & data
```

If a bit is to be unset it needs a 1 in the mask and 0 in the data, so the mask to reset bits is:

```
resetmask = mask & ~data
```

Applying both to the value gives the required result:

```
(value | setmask) & ~(resetmask) =
                    (value | (mask & data)) & ~(mask & ~ data)
```

which, after simplification, is:

```
value & ~mask | mask & data
```

Using this it is easy to create a function to do the job.

As demonstrated in Chapter 4, the gpio_value_mask function can be used to set GPIO lines simultaneously:

```
#include "soc/gpio_reg.h"

uint32_t mask = (1 << 2) | (1 << 4);
uint32_t value1 = (1 << 2);
uint32_t value2 = (1 << 4);

void gpio_value_mask(int32_t value, int32_t mask) {
  *(int32_t*)GPIO_OUT_REG = (*(int32_t*)GPIO_OUT_REG & ~mask) |
(value & mask);
}

void setup() {
  pinMode(2, OUTPUT);
  pinMode(4, OUTPUT);
}

void loop() {
  gpio_value_mask(value1, mask);
  gpio_value_mask(value2, mask);
}
```

As we are changing the same pins each time, we only need a single mask. The value, however, changes each time. If you run this program you will see an almost perfect pair of out-of-phase 6μs pulses

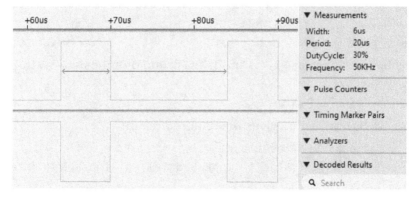

Example II – PWM LEDC Rollover

In Chapter 4 it was explained that the LEDC PWM generator uses a timer rollover event to determine when the next pulse is about to be generated. This could be useful in many situations. However, at the time of writing, the SDK doesn't provide any functions to access the timer count or set up an interrupt for overflow. This is another case where working directly with the

320

hardware is your only choice. In this case the hardware differs between the ESP32 and the ESP32 S3 and there is no header file to smooth out the differences, which go beyond a simple change in base address.

The reason for this is that the ESP32 has fast and slow PWM generation whereas the ESP32 S3 has only the slow PWM. Apart from this the hardware works in the same way and the register configuration is very similar if you allow for the fact that half of the registers are missing in the EPS32 S3 due to there being only one PWM block.

The timer counter register is read-only and located at:

	ESP32 Counter	ESP32 S3 Counter
Low-speed timer 0	0x3FF59164	0x600190A4
Low-speed timer 1	0x3FF5916C	0x600190AC
Low-speed timer 2	0x3FF59174	0x600190B4
Low-speed timer 3	0x3FF5917C	0x600190BC

You can see that the addresses agree in the final hex value, but this isn't particularly easy to express as base address plus offset.

Once we know the address we can easily read the register using a function:

```
int32_t gettimercount(int timer) {
    int32_t *base=(int32_t*)0x600190A4; //ESP32 3S
    //int32_t *base=(int32_t*)0x3FF59164 ; //ESP32
    return *(base+timer*2);
}
```

This works, as long as you set the base variable correctly for the current target. In a production case you would most likely define a macro to implement conditional compilation. The problem with using gettimercount is that you cannot rely on getting an exact value. For example, if you wanted to do something at the rollover point then in principle you need to test for the count to be zero:

```
if(gettimercount(0)==0) do something
```

The problem is that the rollover could be missed if you sample at the wrong time. A better idea is to test for something close to zero:

```
if(gettimercount(0)<10) do something
```

Now you are guaranteed to detect rollover if you sample within 10 clock pules of it. However, we have a new problem. If you sample too fast you could trigger the action more than once at each rollover.

A better solution is to use the rollover interrupt. This is supported in hardware, but not by the API. You could write a function that triggered an interrupt and use an interrupt handler to perform the action, but it is often easier and safer to simply use the interrupt as an event recorder.

LEDC_INT_RAW_REG has status bits that are set even if the interrupt in question isn't enabled. So you could read this register and check the relevant interrupt bit to discover if a rollover has just occurred with a lower danger of missing it and, as long as you reset the interrupt, no danger of acting on it more than once. The relevant addresses are:

	ESP32	ESP32 S3
LEDC_INT_RAW_REG	0x3FF59180	0x600190C0
LEDC_INT_CLR_REG	0x3FF5918C	0x600190CC

Using this information we can write a simple function that returns true if a rollover has just occurred:

```
bool isrollover(int timer) {
    int32_t *base=(int32_t*)0x600190C0; //ESP32 3S
  //int32_t *base=(int32_t*)0x3FF59180; //ESP32
    bool value = *((int32_t*)base) & 1<<timer;
    *((int32_t*)base+3) = 1<<timer;
    return value;
}
```

As an example of how this might be used, consider the sine wave generator developed in Chapter 8. In principle what we wanted to do was update the duty cycle following each rollover. The best that we could do without a function like isrollover is to choose an update frequency that matched the PWM frequency. Using isrollover we can ensure that the update occurs after each rollover. The modified main program is:

```
bool isrollover(int timer) {
    int32_t *base=(int32_t*)0x600190C0; //ESP32 S3
  //int32_t *base=(int32_t*)0x3FF59180; //ESP32
    bool value = *((int32_t*)base) & 1<<timer;
    *((int32_t*)base+3) = 1<<timer;
    return value;
}
uint8_t wave[256];
void setup() {
  ledcAttach(2, 150000, 8);
  for (int i = 0; i < 256; i++) {
    wave[i] = (uint8_t)((128.0 +
          sinf((float)i * 2.0 * 3.14159 / 255.0) * 128.0));
  }
}
```

```
void loop() {
  for (int i = 0; i < 256; i++) {
    analogWrite(2, wave[i]);
    while (!isrollover(0)) {};
  }
}
```

This works but the Arduino library wastes some time and the result has a small number of spurious pulses.

The Arduino Nano ESP32 doesn't support the LEDC library.

Keeping Time With the RTC

The ESP32 has a built-in Real Time Clock, RTC which, while not having a battery backup, can be kept accurate using SNTP (Simple Network Time Protocol) to retrieve the time from the Internet. There are Arduino libraries for SNTP, but it is easier to use the NTP client supplied as part of the ESP IDF. This allows you to look up the time from an NTP (Network Time Protocol) server and then you can use it to set the RTC.

```
#include "esp_netif_sntp.h"
esp_sntp_config_t config=
                ESP_NETIF_SNTP_DEFAULT_CONFIG("pool.ntp.org");
esp_netif_sntp_init(&config);
if (esp_netif_sntp_sync_wait(pdMS_TO_TICKS(10000)) != ESP_OK) {
    printf("Failed to update system time within 10s timeout");
}
```

The Arduino Nano ESP32 doesn't install the SNTP header.

The host that you set should be one of the many NTP pool servers. A pool server has a list of time servers that it issues in response to a DNS request so as to spread the load. For example, if you query pool.ntp.org or time.nist.gov then a different SNTP server is returned each time on a round robin basis so that the load is spread between the servers in the pool.

The RTC works with the standard Posix C time and date functions defined in sys/time.h. This is included as part of the standard Arduino environment so you don't need the header.

```
gettimeofday(ptv, ptz);
settimeofday(ptv,ptz);
```

where ptv is a pointer to a struct timeval:

```
struct timeval {
  time_t      tv_sec;     /* seconds */
  suseconds_t tv_usec;    /* microseconds */
}
```

and ptz is a pointer to a struct timezone which is deprecated and should be set to NULL.

You can convert the number of seconds into a more useful form using:

```
struct timeval t;
gettimeofday(&t, NULL);
struct tm *tm= gmtime(&(t.tv_sec));
printf("date = %d\n", tm->tm_wday);
```

The struct tm has the following fields:

- tm_sec   Seconds [0, 59]
- tm_min   Minutes [0, 59]
- tm_hour   Hour [0, 23]
- tm_mday   Day of the month [1, 31]
- tm_mon   Month [0, 11] (January = 0)
- tm_year   Year minus 1900
- tm_wday   Day of the week [0, 6] (Sunday = 0)
- tm_yday   Day of the year [0, 365] (Jan/01 = 0)
- tm_isdst   Daylight savings flag

In principle you can set the time zone using:

```
setenv("TZ", "UTC+1", 1);
tzset();
```

where the offset can be positive, i.e. moving to the West, or negative, i.e. moving to the East. For example:

```
struct timeval t;
gettimeofday(&t, NULL);
setenv("TZ", "UTC-1", 1);
tzset();
struct tm* tm = localtime(&(t.tv_sec));
printf("hour = %d\n", tm->tm_hour);
printf("min = %d\n", tm->tm_min);
```

moves East as UTC-1 adds one hour to the UTC time.

The function mktime(&tm) returns a time_t value giving the number of seconds since the epoch, the beginning of the Unix time standard and the reference point from which time is measured in most computer systems.

If you need a data/time string then strftime is the function you need to use:

```
 strftime(string, max, format, tm)
```

where string is a C string with space for max characters, format is a string that specifies how the struct tm should be formatted. The possible range of format specifiers is too large to list here, but a common one is the RFC2822-date format:

```
    struct tm* tm = localtime(&(t.tv_sec));
    char date[100];
    strftime(date,100,"%a, %d %b %Y %T",tm);
    printf("date = %s\n", date);
```

which displays:

```
date = Tue, 20 Aug 2024 17:46:37
```

Commonly encountered low-level functions include:

- ◆ `time()`
  Returns number of seconds since 00:00, Jan 1 1970 UTC, i.e the epoch
- ◆ `clock()`
  Returns number of seconds since the program started
- ◆ `difftime(t1,t2)`
  Returns the difference between two `time_t` values as a double without overflow

Other functions are supported, but they are considered obsolete.

There is also a low-power memory associated with the RTC which can be used to store data while the processor is in deep sleep mode, see the next section.

Putting all this together to set the RTC using SNTP:

```
#include "esp_netif_sntp.h"
#include <WiFi.h>
int wifiConnect(char* ssid, char* password) {
  int status = WiFi.begin(ssid, password);
  while (status != WL_CONNECTED) {
    switch (status) {
      case WL_NO_SSID_AVAIL:
        Serial.printf("No AP with name %s can be found", ssid);
        return status;
      case WL_CONNECT_FAILED:
        Serial.printf("Connection failed");
        return status;
      case WL_CONNECTION_LOST:
        Serial.printf("Connection lost possible security problem");
        return status;
    }
    delay(100);
    status = WiFi.status();
  }
  return status;
}
void setup() {
  Serial.begin(9600);delay(2000); Serial.begin(9600);
  Serial.println();
  int status = wifiConnect("ssid", "password");
  Serial.println(status);
    esp_sntp_config_t config =
        ESP_NETIF_SNTP_DEFAULT_CONFIG("pool.ntp.org");
    esp_netif_sntp_init(&config);
    if (esp_netif_sntp_sync_wait(pdMS_TO_TICKS(10000)) != ESP_OK)
    {
        printf("Failed to update system time within 10s timeout");
    }
```

```
    struct timeval t;
    gettimeofday(&t, NULL);
    setenv("TZ", "UTC-1", 1);
    tzset();
    struct tm *tm = localtime(&(t.tv_sec));
    printf("hour = %d\n", tm->tm_hour);
    printf("min = %d\n", tm->tm_min);
    char date[100];
    strftime(date, 100, "%a, %d %b %Y %T", tm);
    printf("date = %s\n", date);
}

void loop() {
}
```

Sleep

An important feature of the ESP32 is that it has a low-power sleep mode which makes it suitable for battery operation. This is a big subject and can become very complicated, but no look at the ESP32 would be complete without an insight into its power-saving modes. The main problem is that there is no support for sleep mode in the Core Arduino library and there is only partial support in the ESP32 implementation. However, the ESP IDF has full support and is very easy to use.

The ESP32 has a complete low-power system based on the RTC. When the machine is put into sleep mode the processors and all of the power-hungry peripherals are off and only the RTC is running. That is, the RTC is the core of the reduced power system of the ESP32 and many of its features are prefixed with "RTC".

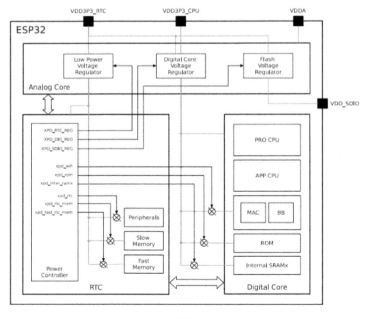

There are five standard functions which put the ESP32 to sleep:

- `esp_light_sleep_start()`
- `esp_deep_sleep_start()`
- `esp_deep_sleep_try_to_start()`
- `esp_deep_sleep(wakeuptime)`
- `esp_deep_sleep_try(wakeuptime)`

where *wakeuptime* is the maximum number of microseconds the machine will sleep for. That is, if it isn't woken up by some other event, it will wake up after *wakeuptime*μs. The `try` versions of the functions will return if the wake up condition is already satisfied. The other functions initiate sleep indefinitely.

You can select what systems are powered down using:

`esp_sleep_pd_config(domain, option)`

where *domain* is one of:

- `ESP_PD_DOMAIN_RTC_PERIPH`
  Peripherals including RTC IO, sensors and ULP co-processor
- `ESP_PD_DOMAIN_RTC_SLOW_MEM`
  RTC slow memory
- `ESP_PD_DOMAIN_RTC_FAST_MEM`
  RTC fast memory
- `ESP_PD_DOMAIN_XTAL`
  Crystal oscillator
- `ESP_PD_DOMAIN_RC_FAST`
  Internal Fast oscillator
- `ESP_PD_DOMAIN_VDDSDIO`
  Power supply voltage rail
- `ESP_PD_DOMAIN_MODEM`
  WiFi, Bluetooth

and *option* is one of:

- `ESP_PD_OPTION_OFF`   Power down in sleep mode
- `ESP_PD_OPTION_ON`   Keep on during sleep mode
- `ESP_PD_OPTION_AUTO`   Keep on if needed by a wake-up option

There are several wake-up functions but the simplest is:

`esp_sleep_enable_timer_wakeup(wakeuptime)`

which will wake from light or deep sleep after *wakeuptime*μs.

The difference between deep and light sleep is that in `deepsleep` the contents of main memory is lost and this has a big effect on the way programs behave.

In lightsleep the radio is switched off but the CPU is in standby. Power consumption in lightsleep is around $800\mu A$ and it takes around 1ms to wake up.

In deepsleep the CPU is powered down and all state information is lost. Power consumption can be anywhere between $10\mu A$ and $150\mu A$ depending on what other peripherals are in use and the time to wake up is around 1ms. These figures should be compared to the 250mA to 800mA that the device uses while active and using its radio.

There are also more ad-hoc ways of saving power by reducing the CPU clock rate and shutting down peripherals. These can reduce power, but they also reduce performance and need to be carefully tuned.

You can use the light-sleep mode to pause a program. The state of the program is preserved as the memory is preserved during light sleep. This means that you can use lightsleep to pause polling loops etc. Deep-sleep mode, on the other hand, does not preserve main memory, which means that when it ends the machine essentially reboots. Two examples will make the difference clear.

First lightsleep can be used to pause a polling loop:

```
void setup() {
  Serial.begin(9600);
  Serial.println();
}

void loop() {
  esp_sleep_enable_timer_wakeup(1000000);
  for (int i = 0; i < 10; i++) {
    Serial.printf("starting sleep %d \n", i);
    Serial.flush();
    esp_light_sleep_start();
    Serial.printf("back from sleep %d \n", i);
  }
}
```

If you run this program, notice esp_sleep.h is automatically included. You will see the for loop pause while the machine is in light-sleep mode for one second. The for loop continues after the sleep without loss of data. In this sense lightsleep works in the same way as the much used sleep function, but it switches off the radio hardware during the sleep period.

This doesn't work on the Arduino Nano ESP32 because of a problem restarting the USB Serial object.

deepsleep doesn't restart your program like lightsleep. Instead it causes the system to be reloaded and hence your program to be run just as if the machine had been just turned on.

For example:

```
void setup() {
  Serial.begin(9600);
  Serial.println();
}

void loop() {
  esp_sleep_enable_timer_wakeup(1000000);
  for (int i = 0; i < 10; i++) {
    Serial.printf("starting sleep %d \n", i);
    Serial.flush();
    esp_deep_sleep_start();
    Serial.printf("back from sleep %d \n", i);
  }
}
```

If you run this you will see starting sleep 0 and then the system goes into deep sleep for 1 second After 1 second the ESP32 restarts and you will see a message that the machine is starting and you will see starting sleep 0 again. The for loop never gets beyond the first printf because the machine is restarted each time.

If all of the data is lost after a deep sleep, how can this be useful? In most cases you need to keep some state data when the program restarts. The RTC has a 2KB memory which is maintained during deep sleep. You can store data in it using either RTC_IRAM_ATTR for read/write data or RTC_RODATA_ATTR for read-only data. The RTC supports fast and slow memory, each with advantages and disadvantages. In this simple instance we can let the system choose where to store the data.

To keep the state between deep sleeps you have to save it in the RTC memory before entering deep sleep mode and you have to restore it when the program starts. This sounds easy, but it is surprisingly difficult. The reason is that you are effectively having to restore the entire state of the program after a complete restart.

For example, how can you restore the state of the simple for loop given as a light sleep example? It seems that the only state is the value of the loop index i and this should be stored in RTC memory, but this doesn't take account of the fact that restarting the program will reinitialize it to 0.

You might think that simply avoiding initializing it is the answer:

```
static RTC_DATA_ATTR int i = 0;
void app_main(void)
{
    esp_sleep_enable_timer_wakeup(1000000);
    for (; i < 10; i++) {
        printf("starting sleep %d \n", i);
        fflush(stdout);
        esp_deep_sleep_start();
        printf("back from sleep %d \n", i);
        fflush(stdout);
    }
}
```

If you try this you will discover that it is still stuck on a value of 0. The reason is obviously that the for loop doesn't increment the index until the loop reaches the end and hence the index is still 0 when the deep sleep starts and hence when the program restarts.

It is clear that we have to increment the index before going into deep sleep:

```
static RTC_DATA_ATTR int i=0;

void loop() {
  esp_sleep_enable_timer_wakeup(1000000);
  for (i++; i < 10; i++) {
    Serial.printf("starting sleep %d \n", i);
    Serial.flush();
    esp_deep_sleep_start();
    Serial.printf("back from sleep %d \n", i);
  }
}
```

Now the for loop increments the index at the start and we do see starting sleep 1, to starting sleep 9 but we never see back from sleep. The reason is again obvious – the program goes into deep sleep before the second message is displayed and it resumes at the start of the for loop and so never reaches the second half of the loop.

It is very difficult to restart a for loop when a program is restarted without the use of features that are non-standard C. The only option is to build the program so that it can save its state and restart correctly. In practice, what this means is that deep sleep is really only easy to use when a program implements a task that completes before the deep sleep state is entered. When the machine wakes up the program gets to run again from the beginning with the exception of any state data that has been stored in the RTC memory.

Notice that this also means that you have to restore the hardware state as well as the software state. In particular, there is the problem of what to do about WiFi. You need to check that there is a WiFi connection and restore it if there isn't one.

There is also the ability to run a function, the deep sleep wake stub, before the main program starts. This can be used to decide if it is worth running the main program or to make preparations for running. In most cases this isn't necessary.

Implementing a good deep sleep program is difficult because in principle you need an extended exception handling facility that will restore, not only the program's state, but the hardware's state. Such a facility doesn't exist.

Wake Using ULP

We have already seen that the ESP32 can wake after a set time, but there are also other events that can wake it up before this time is up. You can set the touch inputs to wake the device or some of the GPIO lines and a third way of waking up the ESP32 is to use the ULP (Ultra Low Power) processor. This is a very simple processor that uses very little power and can be programmed to use peripherals such as the I2C, SPI or any GPIO line while the main processor is sleeping. It can also wake the processor when a condition is satisfied. The ULP processor provides a way to monitor and collect data while the main processor is sleeping and this is very useful. Deep sleep consumes $10\mu A$ without the ULP processor. Adding the ULP typically requires an additional $100\mu A$. Unfortunately it has to be programmed using a simple assembler rather than C and its use is beyond the scope of this book.

Wake Using EXT0 and EXT1

There are two external wake-up signals, EXT0 and EXT1. The only difference between them is that EXT0 will wake the device based on the state of a single GPIO line whereas EXT1 can monitor multiple GPIO lines:

```
esp_sleep_enable_ext0_wakeup(gpio_num, level)
esp_sleep_enable_ext1_wakeup_io(io_mask, level_mode)
```

There are corresponding disable functions.

The first will wake up the processor when the GPIO line transitions to the specified level. The second does the same thing, but you can specify a set of GPIO lines via the io_mask and a set of levels via the bits in level_mode, one for each GPIO line.

The GPIO lines that you can use vary according the model of ESP32:

Model	GPIO
ESP32	0, 2, 4, 12-15, 25-27, 32-39
ESP32-S2	0-21
ESP32-S3	0-21
ESP32-C6	0-7
ESP32-H2	7-14

This works with `deepsleep` or `lightsleep`.

For example:

```
esp_sleep_enable_ext0_wakeup(2, 1);
for (int i=0; i < 10; i++) {
    printf("starting sleep %d \n", i);
    fflush(stdout);
    esp_light_sleep_start();
    printf("back from sleep %d \n", i);
    fflush(stdout);
}
```

This pauses the `for` loop in a light sleep state until GPIO2 goes high.

This is simple enough, but there are some subtle points. The GPIO lines that wake up the device from sleep are part of the RTC low-power domain. These RTC GPIO lines are separate from the standard GPIO lines and are used to conserve power while in sleep mode. Not all of the standard GPIO lines have RTC GPIO equivalents. What this means is that you can only use GPIO lines that are listed in connection with deep sleep as these are the only ones duplicated as RTC GPIO hardware and hence the only ones connected to the RTC.

When entering a deep sleep state any pullup/down resistors are maintained. This can result in wasted power so setting `pull` to `None` just before entering sleep is a good idea. In general, RTC GPIO-capable pins retain their state. However, non-RTC GPIO lines are disconnected and to keep their state you need to use the `hold` parameter in the `Pin` constructor. However, notice that setting `hold` to `True` also stops any change in configuration being applied until `hold` is set to `False`. You can also set all of the non-RTC GPIO lines to hold using:

`esp32.gpio_deep_sleep_hold(True)`

Wake Using TouchPads

You can also use any of the TouchPads, see Chapter 12, to wake the ESP32:

```
esp_sleep_enable_touchpad_wakeup(void)
```

If any of the touch inputs exceed the set threshold they are considered "touched" and the device wakes up.

You can find out which pad caused the wake up using:

```
pad = esp_sleep_get_touchpad_wakeup_status()
```

The system can also wake up on events from the WiFi, Bluetooth and UART and you can find out what woke the system using:

```
esp_sleep_get_wakeup_cause
```

which returns one of:

- `ESP_SLEEP_WAKEUP_UNDEFINED`☺
- `ESP_SLEEP_WAKEUP_EXT0`
- `ESP_SLEEP_WAKEUP_EXT1`
- `ESP_SLEEP_WAKEUP_TIMER`
- `ESP_SLEEP_WAKEUP_TOUCHPAD`
- `ESP_SLEEP_WAKEUP_ULP`
- `ESP_SLEEP_WAKEUP_GPIO`
- `ESP_SLEEP_WAKEUP_UART`
- `ESP_SLEEP_WAKEUP_WIFI`
- `ESP_SLEEP_WAKEUP_COCPU`
- `ESP_SLEEP_WAKEUP_COCPU_TRAP_TRIG`
- `ESP_SLEEP_WAKEUP_BT`

Digging Deeper

There is much more to explore about the ESP32 hardware, but you now should have the confidence to read the datasheet to find out how the registers control things. The biggest difficulty is finding the register that contains the bits that reflect the status of, or that control, whatever it is you are interested in. Once you have found this out, the only remaining problem is in working out how to set or clear the bits you need to work with without changing other bits.

It also has to be said that hardware documentation at this level is often incomplete due to assumptions the writer makes about what you should already know. In such a circumstance your best approach is the experimental method. Work out the simplest program you can think of to verify that you understand what the hardware does. And if you are wrong always check the addresses and bits you are changing before concluding that things work differently from the documentation.

Summary

- All of the ESP32's peripherals, including the GPIO lines, are controlled by registers. These are special memory locations that you write and read to configure and use the hardware.

- Exactly where the registers are positioned in the address space is usually given in the documentation as a base address used for all of the similar registers and an offset that has to be added to get the address of a particular register.

- With knowledge of how things work, you can add functions that are missing from the Arduino library or the ESP-IDF.

- You can also use features of peripherals that are not supported, such as changing GPIO lines at the same time or detecting when the PWM timer wraps.

- There is a Real Time Clock, RTC, that you can set using SNTP.

- If you want to use the ESP32 with a battery source then you need to work with power-saving modes.

- Low-power modes are implemented as part of the RTC. Some GPIO lines have low-power counterparts the RTC GPIO.

- Light sleep is easy to work with because it saves the current state of the system and you can restart your program from where it entered light sleep.

- Deep sleep saves more power, but the CPU is switched off and the system loses track of its state. The entire system is restarted when it wakes up and your program has to restore its state.

- The system can be woken up either by a set time, a change in RTC GPIO lines or a touch input.

Chapter 18

FreeRTOS For Task Management

So far we have been able to mostly ignore the fact that the ESP32 uses a simple operating system to implement a degree of parallel processing in the dual-core ESP32 models. If you have access to two cores then it is possible to run two programs at the same time, which is true parallelism. Even if the ESP32 module you are using has only a single core it is still possible to run multiple tasks, but only one task runs at any given moment. If you start from first principles then managing a program that is made up of multiple tasks is difficult. This is where the Free Real Time Operating System, FreeRTOS, comes into the picture. It provides a standard way of creating and managing tasks and determining which core runs any given task.

You may be surprised that we have left this topic until the very end. The reason is that, for most of the time, you can ignore the issues of running multiple tasks and using more than one core. The default situation is that one core is used for applications and the other manages the WiFi. This is very computation intensive and, if data isn't to be lost, needs attention in real time. As a result, from the application programmer's point of view, the dual-core ESP32 looks a lot like a single-core machine with a separate processor dedicated to running the WiFi. An application runs on the APP_CPU and any interrupt handlers or other asynchronous code that could potentially be run on another core, is run on the same core. In this sense you can mostly ignore the second core and just be pleased that it provides you with WiFi without disturbing the running of your own program.

Add to this the fact that the Arduino library not only tries to ignore any suggestion of multi-tasking, it tries to cover it up for the sake of simplicity. It only just supports interrupts in the form of event handlers and doesn't provide any support for more general asynchronous approach. As already stated, the ESP32, even when running the Arduino library, uses FreeRTOS which manages the two cores and provides ways of running and managing multiple tasks. The Arduino library modifies the way a program is initially run, using setup and loop, but after this it more or less leaves FreeRTOS alone to work unmodified.

When you are trying to find out how the basic hardware of the ESP32 works, it is best to keep things as simple as possible and ignore the possibility of using tasks, apart from the need to implement interrupt handlers. Later you can expand things to include multiple tasks and even to using more than one core. Notice that, while this might be a more powerful way to construct applications, it is more complex and hence more difficult to get right and much more difficult to debug. Of course, it also makes your programs specific to devices that use FreeRTOS and to a lesser extent to the ESP32.

What is FreeRTOS?

FreeRTOS is an open source project to make a realtime operating system available on a wide range of processors. The basic FreeRTOS is a single-core operating system aimed at making running multiple tasks easier. The version of FreeRTOS used by the ESP32 is ESP-IDF FreeRTOS and this has been extended to work with two cores to utilize Symmetric Multi-Processing (SMP), a technique where multiple processors work together to execute tasks simultaneously. This is the version of FreeRTOS that is available as a component in ESP-IDF and the one currently used in all ESP32 programs.

As well as FreeRTOS and ESP-IDF FreeRTOS there is also Amazon SMP FreeRTOS, which has been extended to support as many cores as you need i.e. N-core SMP. At the time of writing this is being ported to ESP-IDF, but its status is experimental and so best avoided until it becomes stable.

The bottom line is that you should use ESP-IDF FreeRTOS unless there is a good reason to experiment. The good news is that the basic operation and API of all FreeRTOS versions is more or less identical and you should find moving between them easy. It is worth learning ESP-IDF FreeRTOS because the skill generalizes. From this point on the use of FreeRTOS should be taken to mean ESP-IDF FreeRTOS.

There is a further complication in that the Arduino library makes use of a pre-compiled version of FreeRTOS, which makes it difficult to modify how it works. If you are using the ESP32 IDF then there is a tool which makes configuring FreeRTOS easy, but this doesn't work for the Arduino system. In most cases you don't need to reconfigure FreeRTOS because it has been configured to work in most conditions. However, it isn't necessarily tuned to give the best performance for your particular application.

Scheduling and Tasks

FreeRTOS works in terms of tasks. A task is a function that can be run as if it was a "main" program in its own right. That is, a task is like a function call, but it doesn't block its creator until it has finished. Tasks never return and are generally written as infinite loops. Tasks can be destroyed via FreeRTOS. Creating a FreeRTOS program is all about creating and managing tasks.

The basic FreeRTOS call to create a task is:

```
xTaskCreate(pTaskFunction, pName, StackDepth, pParameters,
                                    Priority, pTaskHandle)
```

Its parameters are:

- ◆ pTaskFunction   Function to run as the task
- ◆ pName   Name used to identify the task to the programmer
- ◆ StackDepth   Stack size in bytes
- ◆ pParameters   Pointer to parameters to be passed to the task
- ◆ Priority   Scheduling priority of the task
- ◆ pTaskHandle   Pointer to a task handle for managing the task

The function looks like an interrupt handler, for example:

```
void TaskFunction(void *arg)
```

The stack size should be set to be large enough to store all of the local variables that are created by the task or by any functions it calls. You can find out how close you are to running out of stack memory using uxTaskGetStackHighWaterMark, which reports the smallest free stack space since the task started running.

The memory needed for the task is allocated by FreeRTOS. If you want to control this then you can use xTaskCreateStatic() and supply pointers to memory to be used by FreeRTOS. In most situations you don't need to do this.

If there are two cores then the created task will run on either core and can even swap which core it is running on. In the jargon, the task is said to have no core affinity. Usually we do want to assign a core affinity to a task as we generally want it to run on the Application CPU, known as APP_CPU or CPU1 and not interfere with the working of WiFi/Bluetooth on the Protocol CPU, PRO_CPU or CPU0. To assign a task to a particular core we can use:

```
xTaskCreatePinnedToCore( pTaskFunction, pcName,
        StackDepth,pParameters,Priority, pTaskHandle, CoreID)
```

which is the same as xTaskCreate, but with an extra CoreID parameter which is 0 for CPU 0 or 1 for CPU 1.

A task can be in one of four states: Running, Ready (to run), Blocked or Suspended. The difference between Blocked and Suspended is that a task that is Blocked is waiting on something that the system can supply, such as the time being up for a task that has called vTaskDelay. The system can change the status of a task from Blocked to Running on its own. A task can change its state to Suspended by calling vTaskDelay and also becomes Suspended by another task calling vTaskSuspend in which case it can only be returned to the Ready state by another task calling vTaskResume.

On a single-core machine there can be only one Running task rather than two on a dual-core machine. Tasks are stored in a list which the scheduler has access to. The system is configured so that every portTICK_PERIOD_MS milliseconds there is a timer interrupt that runs the scheduler. This causes the currently running task to change state to Ready and the scheduler examines the list of Ready tasks and runs the one with the highest priority. If there are multiple tasks with the same priority then they each get their turn to run in a round robin fashion.

This is a very simple scheduler, but there are a few things to notice. The first is that a task doesn't have any choice about giving up control if the system selects another task to run. That is, FreeRTOS is a priority-based preemptive scheduler. Also notice that if there are tasks that are ready to run with a higher priority, then lower-priority tasks don't get a look in.

So how do lower-priority tasks ever get to run? The answer is that tasks of any priority are not always in a Ready state. If a task is waiting for input, then it will be Blocked and hence not ready to run. If a task has suspended itself using a vTaskDelay(t / portTICK_PERIOD_MS) then it is not ready to run until the time is up. Currently portTICK_PERIOD_MS is set to 1ms. If it has been suspended by itself or another task then it will not be ready to run until another task causes it to resume. For all these reasons, it may well be that there are no tasks of a given priority in the Ready state. In this case the scheduler looks for the highest-priority task that is ready to run.

To summarize:

- Every task has a fixed priority assigned when it is created.
- The scheduler gets to run whenever the current task leaves the running state, either because it is suspended or is blocked. If this doesn't happened for portTICK_PERIOD_MS milliseconds, then the running task is interrupted and the scheduler runs.
- When the scheduler runs, it first examines all tasks suspended for a time and if that time is up they are marked as Ready.
- The scheduler then looks for the task in the Ready state with the highest priority. If there is more than one then the tasks are run in turn, i.e. in round robin fashion.

This is a very simple scheduling algorithm and it has the advantage that you can mostly work out what is going to happen. However, the picture is slightly complicated by the fact that tasks can have core affinities. If two high-priority tasks both want to run on the same core, then one of them will run and the other will have to wait while a lower-priority task runs on the other core. Similarly, round robin selection among tasks of equal priority has also to take account of the tasks' core affinities.

The Standard Tasks

Working with the scheduling algorithm would be easy if there were only the tasks you created in the system. There are, however, five standard tasks that the system starts before your program is loaded:

Task Name	Description	Affinity	Priority
Idle Task (IDLEx)	An idle task (IDLEx) is created for (and pinned to) each Core x The idle task also resets the watchdog timer	Core 0	0
FreeRTOS Timer Task (Tmr Svc)	FreeRTOS will create the Timer Task if any FreeTOS Timer APIs are called	Core 0	CONFIG_FREERTOS _TIMER_TASK_ PRIORITY
Main Task (main)	Task that simply calls setup and loop	CONFIG_ESP_ MAIN_TASK_ AFFINITY	1
IPC Tasks (ipcx)	IPC tasks are used to implement the Inter-processor Call (IPC) feature	Core x	24
ESP Timer Task (esp_timer)	ESP-IDF creates the ESP Timer Task used to process ESP Timer callbacks	Core 0	22

These tasks aren't running all of the time, but the priorities that you assign to tasks that you create can stop them running at all.

You may have been wondering why all Arduino programs start with setup and loop and not the usual C/C++ main? The reason is that FreeRTOS is the first program to start and it usually lets you start your "main" task using vTaskStartScheduler(). In this sense there is no "main" program under FreeRTOS, just tasks. ESP-IDF FreeRTOS does things slightly differently and, in turn, so does the Arduino library.

FreeRTOS starts the application running by calling app_main(void) from the main task, which it starts automatically. The idea is that app_main then creates any additional tasks your app may require and returns when it is finished. The Arduino version of app_main starts a task called loopTask at priority 1. This calls your setup function and then starts an infinite loop that calls your loop function. In other words, loopTask is equivalent to:

```
void loopTask(void *pvParameters) {
 setup();
for (;;) {
    loop();
    }
}
```

Notice that this implies that both setup and loop run at Priority 1, which allows all of the standard tasks to run with the exception of IDLEx, the idle task.

A First Example

Creating a task is easy. It is how tasks behave when running together that is harder. As a simple example, consider running two tasks on the same core at the same priority. The first task sets a GPIO line high and the second sets it low. This allows you to use a logic analyzer to see when each task is running:

```
void task1(void* arg) {
   for (;;) {
     digitalWrite(2, 1);
   }
}
void task2(void* arg) {
   for (;;) {
     digitalWrite(2, 0);
   }
}

void setup() {
   Serial.begin(9600);
   Serial.println();
   pinMode(2, OUTPUT);

   vTaskSuspendAll();
   TaskHandle_t th1;
   xTaskCreatePinnedToCore(task1, "task1", 2048, NULL, 1, &th1, 1);
   TaskHandle_t th2;
   xTaskCreatePinnedToCore(task2, "task2", 2048, NULL, 1, &th2, 1);
   xTaskResumeAll();
}

void loop() {
}
```

You can see that both tasks are run on CPU 1 at Priority 1. If you try this out you will see:

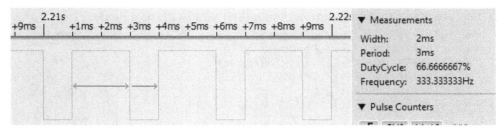

As there are two tasks with the same priority you may expect each to run for half of the time, but it is clear that this isn't the case. task1 appears to run for two time slots but task2 runs for only one. The reason for this apparent anomaly is that at Priority 0 there are three tasks – the two we created and the loopTask. So what happens is that task1 starts running for one time slot. Then the loopTask task gets to run and this leaves the GPIO line high, even though task1 is suspended. Then loopTask is preempted at the end of the time slot and task2 starts running.

If you change the priority of the tasks to 2 then you do see the tasks running for an equal time as promised, but now the loopTask doesn't get to run at all. The watchdog timer is still refreshed as the idle task is still running on Core 0.

You might be wondering why all tasks are suspended and then resumed as the new tasks are being created. The reason for this is that the Arduino implementation of the task create functions includes a yield which allows the operating system to select another task to run. If the first task created has a higher priority than loopTask then it is suspended and never gets a chance to run again unless the higher priority task yields. What this means is that the second task never gets created. To avoid this we have to suspend all tasks while creating new tasks of a higher priority. This is not a problem in the ESP IDF implementation of FreeRTOS.

Managing Tasks

There are some simple functions that allow you to manage tasks:

- vTaskSuspend(TaskToSuspend)
- vTaskResume(TaskToResume)
- xTaskResumeFromISR(TaskToResume)
- vTaskDelete(TaskToDelete)
- vTaskSuspendAll()
- xTaskResumeAll()

where all of the parameters are task handles. A task that is suspended remains suspended until another task resumes it. Notice that you need a special function to resume a task from an interrupt handler. The SuspendAll function stops all tasks except for the one that called it, but leaves interrupt handlers free to operate.

Tasks run forever unless they are deleted. Deleting a task safely is subject to a range of conditions. Basically, make sure that a task that is about to be deleted has freed all of its allocated memory and resources such as spinlocks. The internally-used memory is freed by the idle task when it next runs. You can also delete a suspended task from another task. A task can self-delete, assuming it has cleaned up its resources using:

vTaskDelete(Null)

There are several functions that will get or set information about tasks:

- uxTaskPriorityGet(TaskHandle)
- uxTaskPriorityGetFromISR(TaskHandle)
- vTaskPrioritySet(TaskHandle,NewPriority)
- eTaskState eTaskGetState(TaskHandle)
- string = pcTaskGetName(TaskHandle)
- TaskHandle = xTaskGetHandle(pcNameToQuery)
- TaskHandle = xTaskGetCurrentTaskHandle()
- TaskHandle = xTaskGetIdleTaskHandle()
- uxTaskGetStackHighWaterMark(TaskHandle)
- uxTaskGetStackHighWaterMark2(TaskHandle)

To discover how generous our allocation of a 2kByte stack is, try:

```
TaskHandle_t th1;
xTaskCreatePinnedToCore(task1, "task1", 2048, NULL, 1, &th1, 1);
delay(10);

int s=uxTaskGetStackHighWaterMark(th1);
Serial.printf("%d\n",s);
```

This prints 1240, which means that at most 808 bytes are used by the stack, suggesting it could be made smaller.

There are some functions concerned with tasks and time:

- `ticks = xTaskGetTickCount()`
- `ticks = xTaskGetTickCountFromISR()`
- `vTaskDelay(TicksToDelay)`
- `xTaskDelayUntil(pPreviousWakeTime, TimeIncrement)`
- `xTaskAbortDelay(TaskHandle)`

The delay function makes use of `vTaskDelay` to introduce delays into programs. It simply puts the task into a Blocked state and the operating system changes it back to Ready when the time is up. The `TaskDelayUntil` function is similar to `delay_until` given in Chapter 4. The big difference is that all times are in terms of ticks. The task is resumed when the tick count gets to:

`pPreviousWakeTime + TimeIncrement.`

So, to generate an initial delay of n time slots you would use:

```
TickType_t xLastWakeTime = xTaskGetTickCount ();
xTaskDelayUntil( &xLastWakeTime, n );
```

The clever part is that `xTaskDelayUntil` stores the current tick count, when it is called, in `xLastWakeTime`, which means the next time you call it you get a delay of n time slots, irrespective of exactly when the next call occurs. In other words, a set of `xTaskDelayUntil` calls will result in the task being woken up again after n time slots, irrespective of how long it runs before calling the function again.

There are some functions that are helpful if you are trying to debug tasks and they are described in the documentation.

Race Conditions

There is a fundamental problem with tasks and asynchronous/parallel programming in general. The problem is that tasks share the same memory space and indeed the two cores share the same memory space. This is convenient in one sense as it makes communication between tasks very easy, but it also makes it dangerous. The problem is that an operation that one task is performing can be interrupted by another task performing an operation of its own. As long as the tasks are using different areas of memory, there is no problem. If they are working with the same area of memory then things can be less safe. We have already encountered the problem in Chapter 7 in connection with interrupt service routines, but it is worth exploring further.

The most basic race condition is sometimes called "tearing". If a memory access is not "atomic", i.e. it can be split by another operation, then you may not retrieve a sensible value. For example, suppose memory reads are atomic in byte access and you want to read two bytes. If the memory location is

0xFFFF and task 1 starts to read it then the first byte it gets is 0xFF. If task 2 now writes 0x0000 to the memory location and task 1 reads the second byte it now has 0xFF00, which is not the original value and not the value written by task 2. It is as if the final value is the result of tearing up the original and new value and putting them together.

Tearing does not occur with 32-bit or less access as memory is always accessed in 32-bit chunks as an atomic operation. However, you might expect tearing to occur with a 64-bit integer as two 32-bit accesses are required. Tearing does occur, but it can be difficult to capture it in action.

For example:

```
uint64_t flag1 = 0;
uint64_t flag2 = 0;

void task1(void* arg) {
    for (;;) {
        flag1 = 0xFFFFFFFFFFFFFFFF;
        flag2 = 0xFFFFFFFFFFFFFFFF;
        if (flag1 != flag2) {
            Serial.printf("task 1 %llX   %llX\n", flag1, flag2);
        }
    }
}
void task2(void* arg) {
    for (;;) {
        flag1 = 0x0;
        flag2 = 0x0;
        if (flag1 != flag2) {
            Serial.printf("task 2 %llX   %llX\n", flag1, flag1);

        }
    }
}

void setup() {
  Serial.begin(9600);
  Serial.println();
  vTaskSuspendAll();
  TaskHandle_t th1;
  xTaskCreatePinnedToCore(task1, "task1", 2048, NULL, 1, &th1, 1);
  TaskHandle_t th2;
  xTaskCreatePinnedToCore(task2, "task2", 2048, NULL, 1, &th2, 1);
  xTaskResumeAll();
}

void loop() {
}
```

If you run this program using the usual compiler configuration then you will see no errors. The debug option rearranges the code so that a race condition is unlikely to happen. To set the compiler optimizations you need to edit the file platform.txt to change the lines:

```
# EXPERIMENTAL feature: optimization flags
#  - this is alpha and may be subject to change without notice
compiler.optimization_flags=-Os
compiler.optimization_flags.release=-Os
compiler.optimization_flags.debug=-Og -g3
```

to read:

```
# EXPERIMENTAL feature: optimization flags
#  - this is alpha and may be subject to change without notice
compiler.optimization_flags=-O0
compiler.optimization_flags.release=-O0
compiler.optimization_flags.debug=-Og -g3
```

If you set the compiler to no optimization and restart the IDE, you will see errors like:

```
task 2 FFFFFFFF    FFFFFFFF
task 2 FFFFFFFF00000000    FFFFFFFF00000000
task 1 FFFFFFFF00000000    FFFFFFFFFFFFFFFF
task 2 FFFFFFFFFFFFFFFF    FFFFFFFFFFFFFFFF
```

You can see that we have values that should not occur and sometimes are identical which means the if statement shouldn't have evaluated to true. The only interpretation is that the values are being changed in the middle of the comparison by the other thread. In addition, updates to the values are sometimes complete when the printf displays their values, in which case they are identical, but wrong in the context of the task doing the printing. Or the update is incomplete and we see torn values with all ones in one half of the value and all zeros in the other. Notice that this behavior disappears if you compile the program with optimizations selected.

If we permit a simultaneous read, update, write of a shared resource then we have a natural race hazard. For example, if task 1 is adding one to a memory location, it does so by retrieving the value, adding one and storing the result back in the location. The problem occurs if, for example, Task 1 is interrupted after reading the location and before it has stored the result back. The operating system can start Task 2, which could add one to the same location. Of course, as Task 1 hasn't saved the result of adding one back in the location both tasks increment the same initial value and when both complete the addition the location has only been incremented by one, not by two as it should have been. The problem is even worse if Task 1 and Task 2 are running on different cores. Then Task 1 doesn't even have to be interrupted by the operating system as Task 2 can access that same location any time it likes with the same result. If both cores try to access the same memory location at the same time then the hardware serializes the access and one core accesses before the other.

To illustrate the idea of a race condition:

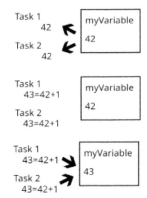

This is clearly a problem because if both tasks had added one to 42 the answer should be 44.

This is a race condition in which the value stored in the memory location depends on which task gets to write it first. The order of access matters to the outcome. Such problems are very difficult to debug because they occur erratically depending on timing and this makes them look like some sort of hardware problem. A race condition can make a repeated calculation give a different result each time. As the bug depends on timing, it can be difficult to reproduce reliably and it is usually the case that the problem vanishes when the program is run in a debugger due to the slower execution rate.

So shared variables are dangerous, but not all shared variables are as dangerous. The reason is that some operations are "atomic" and cannot be divided into separate steps and interrupted by another task. For example, a machine-level memory access is atomic as the operating system cannot be interrupted in the middle of a memory access.

It can be difficult to work out exactly what operations are atomic as it depends, not only on the processor, but on the compiler as well. For example, if you write x++ is this atomic and is it different from writing x=x+1? It depends on whether or not the processor has an atomic increment operator. If not, both involve retrieving a memory location into a register, incrementing the register and storing the result back into the memory location and this is clearly not atomic unless extra steps are taken to make it atomic.

As an example of how simple things can go wrong the following program creates two tasks that increment an in-common 64-bit variable. The reason for using a 64-bit variable is that the ESP32 uses a 32-bit processor and this means that accessing a 64-bit value requires two memory accesses which is clearly not atomic:

```
int64_t count = 0;

void task1(void* arg) {
    for (int i = 0;i < 0xFFFFF; i++) {
        count = count + 1;
    }
    for (;;) {
    }
}
void task2(void* arg) {
    for (int i = 0;i < 0xFFFFF; i++) {
        count = count + 1;
    }
    for (;;) {
    }
}

void setup() {
  Serial.begin(9600);
  Serial.println();
  vTaskSuspendAll();
  TaskHandle_t th1;
  xTaskCreatePinnedToCore(task1, "task1", 2048, NULL, 1, &th1, 1);
  TaskHandle_t th2;
  xTaskCreatePinnedToCore(task2, "task2", 2048, NULL, 0, &th2, 0);
  xTaskResumeAll();
  delay(4000);
  Serial.printf("%llX\n", count);
}

void loop() {
}
```

The delay is included to give ample time for both tasks to complete. If you run this program with optimization turned off you will discover that you don't get the same answer twice. Typically, you might see:

```
1493E1
17DEFD
14A630
182307
```

and so on. If you re-run the program, but with the tasks on the same core, then you get some repeated results due to the more deterministic nature of the way the tasks are run.

It can be confusing to find a deterministic program apparently producing different results each time it is run and it does feel as though a hardware problem should be responsible – but it is 100% code.

If you replace the 64-bit counter with a 32-bit counter then, with the default compiler settings, you don't see any race conditions. However, if you split the increment into two statements:

```
temp = count + 1;
count = temp;
```

and compile without optimization, you do get a race condition. If you compile with optimization the use of the `temp` variable is removed and you don't get a race condition.

You can see from all of this that working out what is safe and what is not is very difficult and a small change in the way an algorithm is expressed or a change to the compiler's optimization level can result in a race hazard where there was none.

Locks

The solution to race hazards is to use locks to restrict access to a resource to a single task at a time. If a task needs to read, update and write a shared resource, then the resource should be locked from before the read to after the write. In the case of there only being a single core then we could ensure that access to a shared resource was exclusive to the task by simply turning off interrupts. If there are no interrupts, then the task cannot be interrupted! However, as there are two cores, this isn't enough as another task could try to access the same resource at the same time.

To cope with managing two cores we have to add a spinlock to the mix by way of modified critical region functions:

```
taskENTER_CRITICAL(pspinlock)
taskEXIT_CRITICAL(pspinlock)
```

where `pspinlock` is a `portMUX_TYPE` spinlock allocated statically or dynamically. There are also `ISR` versions of the `ENTER` and `EXIT` routines.

If CPU 0 locks a resource with a spinlock then interrupts are disabled. When CPU 1 tries to access the same resource it has to lock the same spinlock, but as CPU 0 already has it locked, it has to wait in a tight loop until it is free. Notice that there is nothing stopping CPU 1 accessing the resource without trying to lock it. This is a purely cooperative locking scheme. Also notice that while waiting on a lock the core in question does no useful work. For this reason, critical sections should be kept as short as possible and certainly should not call any long-running blocking functions.

To protect the counting program from race conditions you could replace the two tasks with:

```
static portMUX_TYPE my_spinlock = portMUX_INITIALIZER_UNLOCKED;
void task1(void* arg) {
    for (int i = 0;i < 0xFFFFF; i++) {
        taskENTER_CRITICAL(&my_spinlock);
        count = count + 1;
        taskEXIT_CRITICAL(&my_spinlock);
    }
    for (;;) {
    }
}
void task2(void* arg) {
    for (int i = 0;i < 0xFFFFF; i++) {
        taskENTER_CRITICAL(&my_spinlock);
        count = count + 1;
        taskEXIT_CRITICAL(&my_spinlock);
    }
    for (;;) {
    }
}
```

With these changes we get the correct result, 1F FFFE, repeatedly.

The cost of using locks is both the potential wasted time when the locked-out core simply waits, and the overhead in locking and unlocking access to a shared resource. Even so, locking is usually the only way to make a program reliable.

Queues

Tasks can communicate with each other via shared memory as long as they make use of locks to avoid race conditions. The situation is more complicated if a task is producing lots of data that is intended to be processed by other tasks. This is the producer-consumer dilemma and, in general, there can be multiple producer tasks and multiple consumer tasks. The generally accepted solution to this problem is to use a shared queue of some sort. A queue is simply a data structure that can accept data to be stored until it is read. Queues differ in where they allow you to add data, at the front or back of the queue, and where they allow you to read data, again the front or back of the queue.

There are a number of different shared buffers provided by FreeRTOS and by the ESP-IDF extension, but the simplest and most useful is xQueue, which technically is closer to being a deque as you can add new items at the front or the back, but only remove items from the front. Notice that this means it is safe from race conditions by design and no further locking is needed.

To create an xQueue you can either allocate the memory statically or on the heap:

```
xQueueCreate(NumberOfItems, ItemSize)
xQueueCreateStatic(NumberOfItems, ItemSize,
                            pQueueStorage, pQueueBuffer)
```

Both return QueueHandle to be used in subsequent functions. In the case of Create the queue is created on the heap. If you want to create it in static storage you need to pass pointers to two blocks of memory:

```
StaticQueue_t QueueStorage;
uint8_t QueueBuffer[ NumberOfItems * ItemSize ];
```

You can also delete an xQueue:

```
vQueueDelete(QueueHandle)
```

Once you have an xQueue you can add items to it and retrieve items:

```
xQueueSendToFront(QueueHandle, pItem, TicksToWait)
xQueueSendToBack(QueueHandle, pItemTo, TicksToWait)
```

and there are FromISR versions of these functions. If TicksToWait is 0 then the functions return at once, even if the queue is full. Otherwise the functions wait for the specified time see if the queue has space. All items are stored and retrieved by value. If you want to work with references, you have to explicitly store a pointer. Notice that if you add items to the back of the queue you have a FIFO (First In First Out) queue and if you add items to the front of the queue you have a LIFO (Last In First Out) queue also known as a stack.

There are two functions that can be used to retrieve items:

```
xQueueReceive(QueueHandle, pBuffer, TicksToWait)
xQueuePeek(QueueHandle, pBuffer, TicksToWait)
```

The difference is that Receive removes the item from the queue and Peek doesn't. Also notice that both functions will block until TicksToWait times out. This means that the task is in a pending state and no processor time is wasted waiting for input. If you want to wait on multiple queues then use a queueset which blocks until one of the queues in the set has data ready to read.

There are two functions that tell you about the state of the queue:

```
number=uxQueueSpacesAvailable(QueueHandle)
number= uxQueueMessagesWaiting(QueueHandle)
```

As an xQueue is safe from race conditions, there is even an advantage to be had to sharing one in place of a single variable that you would have to protect with a critical section.

To make this easier there is:

```
xQueueOverwrite(QueueHandle, pItem)
```

which will overwrite the current item at the head of the queue. Notice that it does not protect you against a read, modify, write race condition.

As a very simple example, consider having one task, task1, that writes data to the queue and a second task, task2, that reads it:

```
QueueHandle_t q;
int64_t count = 0;

void task1(void* arg) {
    for (;;) {
        xQueueSendToBack(q, &count, 2);
        count++;
        vTaskDelay(1);
    }
}
void task2(void* arg) {
    int64_t data;
    for (;;) {
        xQueueReceive(q, &data, 20);
        Serial.printf("%llX %d\n", data,uxQueueSpacesAvailable(q));
    }
}

void setup() {
  Serial.begin(9600);
  Serial.println();
  q = xQueueCreate(100, sizeof(int64_t));
  vTaskSuspendAll();
  TaskHandle_t th1;
  xTaskCreatePinnedToCore(task1, "task1", 2048, NULL, 1, &th1, 1);
  TaskHandle_t th2;
  xTaskCreatePinnedToCore(task2, "task2", 4048, NULL, 1, &th2, 1);
  xTaskResumeAll();
 }
void loop() {
}
```

If you run the program you will see that the reading task, task2, keeps up with task1, the writing task, and the queue is always empty after the read. This is how it has to be in that, if the rate of writing were faster than the rate of reading, then the queue would fill up and overflow.

A queue isn't magic and cannot increase the throughput of a system. All it can do is smooth out the flow to make the average write rate equal the average read rate. That is, a queue only works if the average read and write rates are the same and the burst rate is less than the size of the queue.

Watchdog Timer

One piece of hardware that we haven't yet considered is the watchdog timer. This is a very simple idea and once you have encountered it there are few problems in using it. A standard problem for any IoT device is how to cope with a system crash – caused by software or hardware. Clearly you need to protect your system from crashes as much as possible, but despite precautions bad things still happen.

What should your system do if it crashes?

The usual, but not universal, answer is that it should restart and try to pick up where it left off. This is what a watchdog timer is all about. It has to be a very reliable piece of hardware, preferably implemented separately from the main system and, if possible, powered separately. In practice, most processors have a watchdog timer built in, which makes them easy to implement, but not as robust as you might like. The watchdog timer simply counts down at a steady rate and when it reaches zero it applies a hardware reset signal to the main processor. The application software sets the countdown time and before this interval is up it resets the timer. Resetting the timer is an "I'm alive and well" signal that stops the system from being restarted. If the application has crashed then the timer will not be reset and the system will restart.

There are at least three watchdog timers, the S3 for example has an additional watchdog.

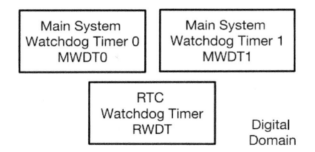

The RWDT and MWDT1 watchdog timers are used during the boot process to recover from errors and the MWDT1 is used as an interrupt watchdog to make sure that interrupt routines do not take too long to complete.

The MWDT0 watchdog is used to implement the Task watchdog, which is the one that mostly concerns us. This is used by default to detect any task that runs for too long by monitoring the idle task, but you can configure it to monitor any tasks or disable it entirely. The default behavior is to print a warning and backtrace and then continue running the app. The Arduino library looks after the Task watchdog so in normal use you should never see it triggered but you can make use of it for your own monitoring tasks. It is reset by the idle task which runs on Core 0 at Priority 0. As long as you do not block Core 0 with a high priority task that doesn't release the core at regular intervals, the watchdog should be well fed.

You can configure the watchdog timer at run time:

- ◆ `esp_task_wdt_init(pconfig)`
- ◆ `esp_task_wdt_reconfigure(pconfig)`
- ◆ `esp_task_wdt_deinit()`

where `pconfig` is a pointer to `esp_task_wdt_config_t`, a struct with three fields:

- ◆ `timeout_ms`   Timeout in milliseconds
- ◆ `idle_core_mask`   Bitmask of the core idle task to monitor
- ◆ `trigger_panic`   If `true` causes a panic

The `reconfigure` function will only work if the watchdog has been initialized and the `deinit` function also unsubscribes any tasks or users.

For an overall test that your program is running testing the idle task is usually sufficient, but you can also monitor individual tasks:

- ◆ `esp_task_wdt_add(task_handle)`
- ◆ `esp_task_wdt_delete(task_handle)`
- ◆ `esp_task_wdt_reset()`

Each task added must call the reset function within the watchdog's timeout period. Any one task not doing this triggers the timeout.

An alternative way of managing timeouts at a finer level than tasks is to add users:

- ◆ `esp_task_wdt_add_user(puser_name, puser_handle)`
- ◆ `esp_task_wdt_delete_user(user_handle)`
- ◆ `esp_task_wdt_reset_user(user_handle)`

The `add_user` function returns a user handle which has to be used to delete or reset the user. If any user fails to reset the watchdog in the required time then a timeout occurs. Currently the Arduino Nano ESP32 does not support watchdog users.

You can customize what happens with a user timeout by defining the:

`esp_task_wdt_isr_user_handler()`

You are limited to what you can do in the handler as it is an interrupt handler. As a simple example consider the following program:

```
#include "esp_task_wdt.h"

esp_task_wdt_user_handle_t uhandle;
void setup() {
  Serial.begin(9600);
  Serial.println();
  esp_task_wdt_add_user("TestWD", &uhandle);
}

void loop() {
  esp_task_wdt_reset_user(uhandle);
  delay(10);
}
```

It registers a user TestWD with the watchdog and then enters an infinite loop which pauses for 10 milliseconds and resets the watchdog for the registered user. When you run the program nothing much happens! This is because it resets the watchdog timer for the registered user and the 10 millisecond delay allows RTOS to gain control and so the event watchdog for the CPU is reset. If you remove the call:

```
esp_task_wdt_reset_user(uhandle);
```

then you will see an error message on the monitor every 5 seconds:

```
0x4200a2a7: task_wdt_timeout_handling at …
```

Implementing watchdog handling is very similar to working with deep sleep states in that you really need to restart the task or user action that caused the timeout. This also generally involves some sort of exception handling and perhaps even restoring hardware to a previous state, which is always difficult.

It is worth knowing that C has an exception handling mechanism in the form of the longjmp function. To know more about it, see Dive 17 of **Deep C Dives: Adventures in C**, ISBN: 978-1871962215.

FreeRTOS Considered

There are many features of FreeRTOS still to explore. If you know about asynchronous programming you will be able to find the standard locks – mutex and semaphore. There are also additional features such as event groups and direct task events, message, stream and ring buffers and so on. This chapter has introduced the basics of creating and managing tasks and allowing them to communicate. In most cases this is all you need as complex asynchronous architectures are best avoided in IoT applications.

Tasks are, in general, a useful extra, but they are dangerous and can be overused. There is a commonly encountered design methodology which creates a task for every action in the program – a task to read each sensor, a task to process the data from each sensor, a task to react to the data and a task to control each actuator. This design allows a loosely-coupled set of tasks to function as an application and sometimes it works – but it relies on the available processors having lots of spare processing power. The idea is that if a task needs attention a core should be free to run it in a very short time. This implies that the cores are engaged in running the idle task most of the time. If this is not the case then a pending task will have to wait until a core is free.

Things are even more complicated when there are multiple cores and tasks with a range of priorities. It is usual to assign I/O tasks high priorities so that they can run as soon as they are in a Ready state. Notice, however, that as the time slot on an ESP32 is typically 1ms or more, even urgent tasks have to wait this long and interrupt service routines have a much shorter latency, typically 10μs.

As long as there is a lot of spare processing power, an asynchronous design is simple and mostly works. However, any system that uses events is subject to the occasional exceptional condition due to the variability in the external world. So, a queue that has been happily receiving data without overflowing can be overrun by a rarely encountered conjunction of data sources. Similarly, a sensor that has taken 1ms to service can suddenly slow to a halt and refuse to supply data for 20ms due to noise and so on.

In an asynchronous system it is difficult to provide guarantees of service time, even in a lightly loaded system.

Sometimes this doesn't matter as the user will simply wait an unnoticeably longer time for the system to respond. In other, mission-critical situations, it is crucial that service times are within a known interval. In such cases, a polling loop hosted by a single task is the best approach.

Summary

- FreeRTOS is an open source project to make a realtime operating system available on a wide range of processors.
- The version of FreeRTOS used by the ESP32 is ESP-IDF FreeRTOS and this has been extended to work with two cores to utilize Symmetric Multi-Processing (SMP).
- FreeRTOS works in terms of tasks. A task is a function that can be run as if it was a "main" program in its own right. Tasks never return and are generally written as infinite loops.
- All Arduino programs start with `setup` and `loop` and not the usual C/C++ `main`
- Each task has a priority and tasks get to run on a processor according to their priority.
- At each tick the scheduler stops the current task and selects the task with the highest priority to run next from the available tasks.
- Tasks with equal priority take equal turns to run.
- As well as the custom tasks a program creates, there are some standard tasks created by the system.
- A range of functions allow you to control how tasks are run.
- The problem with multi-tasking is the danger of creating race conditions where the outcome of a computation depends on the order in which tasks are run.
- To avoid race conditions you have to use locks to restrict access to shared resources.
- An alternative to using locks is to use safe data structures such as xQueue to allow tasks to interact and pass data to each other.

Index

Programming The ESP32 In C Using The Espressif IDF
ISBN: 978-1871962918

C is the ideal choice of language to program the ESP32, ensuring that your programs are fast and efficient, and here it is used with the Espressif IoT Development Framework, ESP-IDF and VS Code, a combination which makes it simple to get started and provides a wealth of functions not found elsewhere.

The purpose of this book is to reveal what you can do with the ESP32's GPIO lines together with widely used sensors, servos and motors and ADCs. After covering the GPIO, outputs and inputs, events and interrupts, it gives you hands-on experience of PWM (Pulse Width Modulation), PWM for Motor control, the SPI bus, the I2C bus and the 1-Wire bus, the UARTs and of course WiFi. To round out, it covers direct access to the hardware, adding an SD Card reader, sleep states to save power, the RTC, RMT and touch sensors. It also devotes a chapter to FreeRTOS which takes us into the realm of asynchronous processing.

Programming the ESP32 in MicroPython
ISBN: 978-1871962826

Although MicroPython is slower than C, most of the time this doesn't matter and it is much easier to use. It is based on Python 3 and is fully object-oriented.

Another good thing about MicroPython on the ESP32 is that it is very easy to get started. After a simple installation procedure you have a working MicroPython machine which you can program almost at once using the Thonny IDE or PyCharm which has more extensive syntax checking and input prompting.

The purpose of the book is to reveal what you can do with the ESP's GPIO lines together with widely used sensors, servos and motors and ADCs. After covering the GPIO, outputs and inputs, events and interrupts, it gives you hands-on experience of PWM (Pulse Width Modulation), the SPI bus, the I2C bus and the 1-Wire bus. We also cover direct access to the hardware, adding an SD Card reader, sleep states to save power, the RTC, RMT and touch sensors, not to mention how to use WiFi.

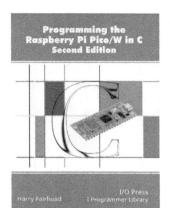

Programming The Raspberry Pi Pico/W In C, 2nd Edition

ISBN: 978-1871962796

This book explains the many reasons for wanting to use C with the Pico, not least of which is the fact that it is much faster. This makes it ideal for serious experimentation and delving into parts of the hardware that are otherwise inaccessible. Using C is the way to get the maximum from the Pico and to really understand how it works.

Master the Raspberry Pi Pico

ISBN: 978-1871962819

There is far too much to the Pico to cover in a single book and this follow-on volume takes your Pico C programming to the next level. Chapters are devoted to more advanced PIO programming, using the second core and many of the more advanced hardware features such as DMA, watchdog timer and saving power. For the Pico W it covers TLS/HTTPS connections, access point mode, other protocols and using FreeRTOS.

Programming the Raspberry Pi Pico/W in MicroPython, Second Edition

ISBN: 978-1871962802

MicroPython is a good choice of language to program the Pico. It isn't the fastest way, but in most cases it is fast enough to interface with the Pico's hardware and its big advantage is that it is easy to use.

The purpose of the book is to reveal what you can do with the Pico's GPIO lines together with widely used sensors, servos and motors and ADCs. One of the key advantages of the Pico is its PIO (Programmable I/O) and while this is an advanced feature, it is introduced in this book. After finding out how the PIO works, we apply it to writing a PIO program for the DHT22 and the 1-Wire bus.

Raspberry Pi IoT In C, 3rd Edition
ISBN: 978-1871962840

This book takes a practical approach to understanding electronic circuits and datasheets and translating this to code, specifically using the C programming language. The main reason for choosing C is speed, a crucial factor when you are writing programs to communicate with the outside world. If you are familiar with another programming language, C shouldn't be hard to pick up. This third edition has been brought up-to-date and focuses mainly on the Pi 4, Pi5 and the Pi Zero.

Raspberry Pi IoT in C With Linux Drivers, 2nd Edition
ISBN: 978-1871962857

This second edition has been updated and expanded to cover the Raspberry Pi 5 and the Raspberry Pi Zero W/2W. There are Linux drivers for many off-the-shelf IoT devices and they provide a very easy-to-use, high-level way of working. The big problem is that there is very little documentation to help you get started. This book explains the principles so that you can tackle new devices.

Micro:bit IoT In C, 2nd Edition
ISBN: 978-1871962673

The second edition of this book covers V2, the revised version of the micro:bit. The other important change is that it now uses the highly popular VS Code for offline development and let's you get started the easy way by providing downloadable templates for both V1 and V2 of the micro:bit.
The micro:bit lacks WiFi connectivity but using a low-cost device we enable a connection to the Internet via its serial port which allows it to become a server. The book rounds out with a new chapter on the micro:bit's radio and the V2's sound capabilities

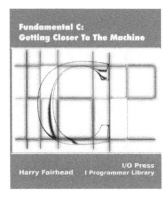

Fundamental C: Getting Closer To The Machine
ISBN: 978-1871962604

For beginners, the book covers installing an IDE and GCC before writing a Hello World program and then presents the fundamental building blocks of any program - variables, assignment and expressions, flow of control using conditionals and loops.

When programming in C you need to think about the way data is represented, and this book emphasizes the idea of modifying how a bit pattern is treated using type punning and unions and tackles the topic of undefined behavior, which is ignored in many books on C.

Applying C For The IoT With Linux
ISBN: 978-1871962611

If you are using C to write low-level code using small Single Board Computers (SBCs) that run Linux, or if you do any coding in C that interacts with the hardware, this book brings together low-level, hardware-oriented and often hardware-specific information.

It starts by looking at how programs work with user-mode Linux. When working with hardware, arithmetic cannot be ignored, so separate chapters are devoted to integer, fixed-point and floating-point arithmetic. It goes on to the pseudo file system, memory-mapped files and sockets as a general-purpose way of communicating over networks and similar infrastructure. It continues by looking at multitasking, locking, using mutex and condition variables, and scheduling. It rounds out with a short look at how to mix assembler with C.

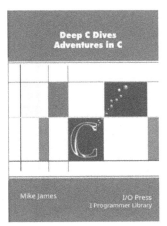

Deep C Dives: Adventures in C
ISBN: 978-1871962888

This book provides in-depth exploration of the essence of C, identifying the strengths of its distinctive traits. This reveals that C has a very special place among the programming languages of today as a powerful and versatile option for low-level programming, something that is often overlooked in books written by programmers who would really rather be using a higher-level language. To emphasize the way in which chapters of this book focus on specific topics, they are referred to as "dives", something that also implies a deep examination of the subject.

www.ingramcontent.com/pod-product-compliance
Lightning Source LLC
LaVergne TN
LVHW062303060326
832902LV00013B/2024